EXTRAVAGANCES

Habits of Being

Extravagances

CRISTINA GIORCELLI AND

PAULA RABINOWITZ *editors*

HABITS OF BEING 4

UNIVERSITY OF MINNESOTA PRESS

MINNEAPOLIS · LONDON

The publication of this book was supported by an Imagine Fund grant for the Arts, Design, and Humanities, an annual award from the University of Minnesota's Provost Office.

Excerpts from *Omeros* by Derek Walcott copyright 1990 by Derek Walcott. Reprinted by permission of Farrar, Straus and Giroux, LLC.

Published by the University of Minnesota Press
111 Third Avenue South, Suite 290
Minneapolis, MN 55401–2520
http://www.upress.umn.edu

Library of Congress Cataloging-in-Publication Data
    Extravagances / Cristina Giorcelli and Paula Rabinowitz, editors.
    (Habits of being ; 4)
    Includes bibliographical references and index.
    ISBN 978-0-8166-9728-1 (hc)— ISBN 978-0-8166-9729-8 (pb)
    1. Clothing and dress—History. 2. Dress accessories—History. 3. Fashion—
History. 4. Clothing and dress in literature. 5. Fashion in literature. 6. Wealth in
literature. I. Giorcelli, Cristina. II. Rabinowitz, Paula. III. Abito e identità.
TT504.E95 2015
646'.3—dc2   2015016661

Printed in the United States of America on acid-free paper

The University of Minnesota is an equal-opportunity educator and employer.

20 19 18 17 16 15   10 9 8 7 6 5 4 3 2 1

To Anne Hollander (1930–2014), generous friend and memorable contributor

Contents

Preface and Acknowledgments

This four-volume English-language series extracts more than forty of the best essays included in the ongoing editions *Abito e Identità: Ricerche di storia letteraria e culturale*, edited by Cristina Giorcelli and published since 1995 by Edizioni Associate (volumes 1–3) and Ila Palma Press (volumes 4–12) of Rome, Italy. *Habits of Being* augments these Italian-published essays with newly commissioned ones and with examples of work by contemporary artists who explore the interface between text and textile. The result of almost two decades of research by international teams of scholars from Algeria, France, Hungary, Italy, and the United States, the series focuses on the multiple forms and meanings attached to various articles of clothing in literature, film, performance, art, and other cultural arenas as well as on the social, economic, and semiotic connotations of clothing. Bringing together the work of literary and film critics, art and fashion historians, semioticians, sociologists, historians, and ethnographers, as well as psychoanalysts, artists, and fashion designers, these books offer an English-speaking audience a rare glimpse of the important studies being published in Italy, that most modish of nations.

Moving among thematic, chronological, and aesthetic concerns, *Habits of Being* tracks clothing (and especially accessories) around four cardinal points—top, bottom, inside, outside—to allude to the complex implications of power, meaning, and sensibility associated with, for example, the head (of state as much as of body) or the foot, interiority or exposure. Each book addresses a complex of ideas encased within a set of terms that at times appears contradictory. The first volume, *Accessorizing the Body*, reconsiders the cliché that clothes represent a "second skin" by showing how the body itself became an accessory within various political and artistic movements of the twentieth century. Volume 2, *Exchanging Clothes*, focuses on the transnational circulation and exchange of apparel and its appropriations across time and space to consider how depictions of clothing in classic texts (for instance, Homer's epics) might migrate into understandings of how items of clothing actually mutate within the secondary economy of used-clothing stores. Volume 3, *Fashioning the Nineteenth Century*, is more traditional, organized by period (the nineteenth century) and place (Europe and the United States) to explore a crucial era within the consolidation and spread of Western culture, when dress signified class and other distinctions through excess and detail, even as mass production turned clothing into an available commodity. This fourth and final volume, *Extravagances*, interrogates connections between ornamentation and the quotidian, considering how aspects of apparel decorate everyday lives as men button their coats and women slip bracelets on their wrists. Traveling from head to ankle, from North America to the Southern Cone and across the Atlantic to West Africa, the essays provide a catalog of details—a red scarf, plaited hair, a pulled thread—that unravels the subtle signals of clothing.

Each book in *Habits of Being* addresses social and economic processes involving dress as well as psychic and ontological aspects of identity. For instance, "circulation" references global exchange of commodities or a pair of shoes walking the streets; "movement" stresses the fluidity of meaning—political, sexual, historical—attached to articles of clothing when worn in various contexts; "detail" focuses on accessorizing the body and the role of clothing in the construction of social formations; "intimacies" exposes how what appears outside is a complex of social meanings extending deep inside to the interior of the body and its psychic formations; and "value" addresses economic disparities coded within dress and examines how replication and individuation differentiate affect. These are fluid categories that leak one into another, because any attention to clothing and its representation necessitates awareness of what is seen and what is remembered for and by whom for what purpose activating which desires.

As an ongoing research project, the subjects covered in *Habits of Being* range from boarding-school attire to Futurist vestments, from lesbian pulp to Henry James, from used-clothing stores to analysts' couches, from Spanish Fascist promotion of appropriate female dress to Hungarian Jewish tailors embroidering the yellow star. The mix of essays offers a compelling argument for the inherent interdisciplinarity of fashion studies. Looking at how dress is represented in a work of fiction necessarily opens into a discussion of class, of social procedures, of psychic dimensions, of the texture of language itself—after all, *text* and *textile* share the same Latin root *texere*, to weave. Considering materials (literally, the stuff out of which stuff is made) requires a discourse that brushes economics up against aesthetics. That so many scholars (experts in the history of Italian education, in the history of East European socialism, in the ethnography of Algerian wedding practices, to name a few) can unite through attention to items of clothing speaks to the transhistorical and cross-cultural ubiquity of clothing. It is a basic human need. Yet the vast differences and arcane meanings attached to any particular fashion trend or item of dress vary and change across classes, genders, time, and space. These vital embellishments appear utterly unnecessary. Such is the contradiction we all face daily.

Fashion studies extends from the ethnographic approach of Joanne Eicher (whose work appears in this volume) to the art historical readings of Anne Hollander (who contributed to volume 2), from literary critic Marjorie Garber's inventive readings of transvestism to Germano Celant's exhibition of Giorgio Armani's couture at the Guggenheim Museum in 2000, which has inspired many other such shows since then. This fluidity has attracted many distinguished scholars to our project. Most considered clothing for the first time in their careers. Yet, once analyzed, the subject captivated them so deeply that they willingly extended their research to create original meditations on the materials covering bodies both real and imagined. By no means exhaustive, these essays offer a range of styles, from rigorously archival to deeply textual, on objects and the affects they induce in their wearers and in those who observe them, describe them, desire them, and perhaps also shop for them.

As literary critics, much of our focus is on the ways in which literature relies on and participates in the construction of bodily presence through narrative or lyrical obsession with dress and habit. Because dress is at once tactile and visual (and often aural as well, as the crinkly sound of a crinoline or the swish of satin attests), the art of creating literary effects of touch and sight (and sound), especially when they are so intimately associated with character, offers tour de force examples of a writer's skill in conveying affect through description. More obviously, film, photography, and visual culture present opportunities to foreground clothing, tracking its changing sensations over time. Film, especially from Hollywood's Golden Era, worked hand in glove with the fashion industry, displaying the latest styles or costuming actresses in period clothing again and again to convey a world of opulence and ease seemingly accessible to all. Dress codes, whether in the form of school uniforms or corporate and government protocols, enforce, by contrast, a sense of clothing as a restrictive binding controlling one's ability to express individuality. Clothing both opens up and clamps down the body and its myriad identities. Even the same article of clothing can be at once freeing and restrictive—an empty sign full of meaning.

The essays in *Habits of Being* are concerned with how subjectivity and identity, intimately tied to processes of incorporation, projection, and desire, are evoked by an item of apparel. Before scholars engage the subject, each book commences with an essay by a woman psychoanalyst. Given the complexity of the problematic of clothes, it seemed essential to open with a reflection that ponders their meaning in relation to identity from the point of view of her school—Freudian, Lacanian, Jungian. In every case, her evocative, even innovative, elaboration on the sparse shreds that the various masters have incidentally jotted down calls for new ways of thinking about the habits of being. For instance, Freud noted Dora's *schmuckasten* but could never fathom what she meant when she asserted her right to own, and show off, such a fashionable item; sometimes a cigar is just a cigar, but a purse is never just a purse. In every book we have also included a conversation with or a statement by a noted fashion designer; these views by masters of fashion whose hands-on expertise and attention to detail augment the psychoanalytic and philosophical considerations of the analysts. Then we open the arena to scholars. Each book also features a woman artist who appropriates traditional Western assumptions that weaving and sewing are aspects of women's work to create stunning visual links between text and textile. Like careful shoppers, we have been selective in our choices. They remind us that all clothing is at once conceptual (someone designed each piece) and material (someone made it). Made for use yet extravagant, quotidian yet unique—what else is culture?

Attention to the mechanisms by which clothing and its representation affect psychic and social structures underlies most of the essays, no matter how diverse their approaches. Representations of clothing, like the items themselves, can take on a fetishistic quality. Identity is perhaps little more than a matter of habit, of what is put on every day to construct one's being. A habit of being. Clothed in the world and in the imagination.

This book is the result of deep commitments of our many contributors; we are grateful for their collaboration, enthusiasms, and insights. We thank our research assistant, Laura Brennan, for help on this volume. Support for the project has come from the Dipartimento di Studi Euro-Americani of the Università degli Studi di Roma Tre; the Department of English, the Samuel Russell Chair in the Humanities of the College of Liberal Arts, and the Imagine Fund of the University of Minnesota; and a Rockefeller residency in Bellagio, Italy. Our editor at the University of Minnesota Press, Douglas Armato, has been devoted to this effort from the beginning, and editor Danielle Kasprzak, as well as Nancy Sauro and Laura Westlund, helped guide us and trusted us to follow them throughout the process of turning an Italian series into an American one. Our reviewers (Caroline Evans, Cynthia Kuhn, and an anonymous reader) gave us cogent and encouraging suggestions that helped make this a stronger work.

The essays by Mariapia Bobbioni, Amanda Salvioni, and M. Giulia Fabi were published in Italian in *Abito e Identità: Ricerche di storia letteriaria e culturale* 12 (2012). Camilla Cattarulla's essay first appeared in Italian in *Abito e Identità* 5 (2004); Paola Colaiacomo's essay appeared in Italian in *Abito e Identità* 10 (2010), as did versions of Cristina Giorcelli's and Paula Rabinowitz's essays, both published in English. The poem by Maria Damon and Adeena Karasick first appeared in *Open Letter: A Canadian Journal of Writing and Theory* (Fall 2012). Versions of the essays by Margherita di Fazio and Maria Anita Stefanelli were first published in Italian in *Abito e Identità* 11 (2011). Cristina Giorcelli's interview with Guillermo Mariotto appeared in Italian in *Abito e Identità* 7 (2007). Portions of Charlotte Nekola's essay first appeared in "The Flowers of Evil and the Lilac Sea: Why Bad Women Wear Flowers," *Abito e Identità* 6 (2006). We are grateful to the original publishers, especially Editrice Ila Palma, for granting permission to publish these works in English.

Clothing, Dress, Fashion: An Arcade

The woman shall not wear that which pertaineth unto a man,
neither shall a man put on a woman's garment:
for all that do so are abominable unto the LORD thy God.

DEUTERONOMY 22:5

You got there first: beautiful
and the clothes

SAPPHO

You must needs have dresses embroidered with gold;
you like to do your perfumed hair in countless different ways;
you must have sparkling rings upon your fingers.
You adorn your necks with pearls brought from the East,
pearls so big that your ears can scarcely bear the weight of them.

OVID, *The Art of Beauty*

Know, first, who you are, and then adorn yourself accordingly.

EPICTETUS

A complete description of people's costumes is apt to be tedious, but as in stories the first thing that is said about the characters is invariably *what they wore,* I shall once in a way attempt such description.

LADY MURASAKI, *The Tale of Genji*

Apparel may well be a part of majesty.

THOMAS ELYOT, *The Governor*

But seest thou not, I say, what a deformed thief this fashion is?

WILLIAM SHAKESPEARE, *Much Ado about Nothing*

Clothing is the sign that separates men from animals.

JEAN-ANTOINE CONDORCET, *Sketch for an Historical Picture of the Progress of the Human Mind*

Those who make their dress a principal part of themselves will, in general, become of no more value than their dress.

WILLIAM HAZLITT, "On the Clerical Character"

Man was an animal compounded of two dresses, the natural and celestial suit, which were the body and the soul; that the soul was the outward, and the body the inward clothing.... By all which it is manifest that the outward dress must needs be the soul.

JONATHAN SWIFT, "A Tale of a Tub"

The first spiritual want of a barbarous man is Decoration.

THOMAS CARLYLE, *Sartor Resartus*

What shall we call our "self"? Where does it begin? Where does it end? It overflows into everything that belongs to us—and then it flows back again. I know a large part of myself is in the clothes I choose to wear. I've a great respect for *things!* . . . these things are all expressive.

HENRY JAMES, *Portrait of a Lady*

It was dressed entirely in black, and of the very finest cloth;
it had patent leather boots, and a hat that could be folded together,
so that it was bare crown and brim; not to speak
of what we already know it had—seals, gold neck-chain, and diamond rings;
yes, the shadow was well-dressed, and it was just that which made it quite a man.

HANS CHRISTIAN ANDERSEN, "The Shadow"

Fashion is what one wears oneself. What is unfashionable is what other people wear.

OSCAR WILDE, "An Ideal Husband"

The History of the Glove! Why, it is the history of the world.

OCTAVE UZANNE, *L'Ombrelle—Le Gant—Le Manchon*

Fashion includes a peculiar attraction of limitation, the attraction of a simultaneous beginning and end, the charm of novelty coupled to that of transitoriness.

GEORG SIMMEL, "The Philosophy of Fashion"

The clothes are the background, the frame, if you like: they don't make success, but they are part of it.

EDITH WHARTON, *The House of Mirth*

The human animal shows in its clothing as conspicuously as in many other ways, the peculiar power of extraphysical expression.

CHARLOTTE PERKINS GILMAN, "The Dress of Women"

A blue coat is guided away, guided and
guided away, that is the particular color that is used
for that length and not any width not even more
than a shadow.

GERTRUDE STEIN, "A Blue Coat"

The clothes . . . seem to exist, not so much in the author's mind, as in the emotional
penumbra of the characters themselves.

WILLA CATHER, "The Novel Démeublé"

I made my song a coat
Covered with embroideries
Out of old mythologies
From heel to throat;
But the fools caught it,
Wore it in the world's eyes
As though they'd wrought it.
Song, let them take it,
For there's more enterprise
In walking naked

WILLIAM BUTLER YEATS, "A Coat"

What a strange power there is in clothing!

ISAAC BASHEVIS SINGER, "Yentl the Yeshiva Boy"

There is much to support the view that it is clothes that wear us and not we them.

VIRGINIA WOOLF, *Orlando*

The eternal is in any case far more the ruffle on a dress than some idea.

WALTER BENJAMIN, *The Arcades Project*

Let there be fashion, down with art.

MAX ERNST, *Let There Be Fashion, Down with Art*

Fashion is art's permanent confession that it is not what it claims to be.

THEODOR ADORNO, *Aesthetic Theory*

"Nuncle, you're looking wonderful this evening. Black suits you perfectly. But what are you looking at? Are you courting death?"

GIUSEPPE TOMASI DI LAMPEDUSA, *The Leopard*

If there's one thing I know, it's how to wear the proper clothing.

GRACE KELLY to **JIMMY STEWART** in *Rear Window*

The male subject, like the female subject, has no visual status apart from dress and/or adornment.

KAJA SILVERMAN, "Fragments of a Discourse on Fashion"

"The fragrance of gardenias is a drama played out somewhere between jasmine and tuberose," while the smell of a narcissus "hovers between the fragrance of roses, white flowers, and horse droppings."

JEAN-CLAUDE ELLENA, *The Diary of a Nose*

Dress is a sculpture in movement.

VIVIANE AUBRY, *Costumes II*

As a playful and gratuitous representation and a factitious sign, fashionable dress has broken all ties with the past; it draws the essence of its prestige from the ephemeral, scintillating, fascinating present.

GILLES LIPOVETSKY, *The Empire of Fashion: Modern Democracy*

The mirror is the place where we discover that we have an image and, at the same time, that this image can be separate from us, that our *species* or *imago* does not belong to us.

GIORGIO AGAMBEN, *Profanations*

A contemporary metropolis is that social site where individuals present and represent themselves first of all through the form and style of appearances.

ROBERTO GRANDI, "Fashion and the Ambiguous Representation of the Other"

A person without clothes is a person without language.

WEST AFRICAN PROVERB, quoted in **ANNE MCCLINTOCK**, *Imperial Leather*

The real opposition is not between soul and body, but between life and garment.

MARIO PERNIOLA, *Sex Appeal of the Inorganic*

I enter the garment. It is as if I were going into the water. I enter the dress as I enter the water which envelops me and, without effacing me, hides me transparently.

HÉLÈNE CIXOUS, "Sonia Rykiel in Translation"

Clothes like lovers, or, better, instead of lovers.

SEAN BLAZER, *Merchants of Fashion*

To write on clothing implies trying to consider garments no longer . . . as secondary elements, as accessories, but as primary, founding elements that determine individual behaviors as well as social structures.

FRÉDÉRIC MONNEYRON, *The Essential Frivolity: On Clothing and Fashion*

Fashion is the foundation of dress. Style is imparted to it by the wearer, and the accessories are its expression.

CARRIE A. HALL, *From Hoopskirts to Nudity*

Marie Antoinette sold her soul, and eventually the crown of her husband's realm, to her milliner, Rose Bertin.

COLIN MCDOWELL, *Hats, Status, and Glamour*

For clothing, its style is its essence.

ANNE HOLLANDER, *Seeing through Clothes*

Among primates, only humans regularly use adornment.

VALERIE STEELE, "Appearance and Identity"

Adornment *is* the woman, she exists veiled; only thus can she represent lack, be what is wanted.

STEPHEN HEATH, "Joan Riviere and the Masquerade"

Dress is the way in which individuals learn to live in their bodies and feel at home in them.

JOANNE ENTWISTLE, *The Fashioned Body*

Perfume . . . is our own shadow. It is a luxurious mirage, our transparency, a majestic choreography, a kind of inner palace, an architecture of exquisite crystal.

SERGE LUTENS, "My Perfumes"

Clothes are inevitable. They are nothing less than the furniture of the mind made visible.

JAMES LAVER, *Style in Costume*

I think my clothes allow someone to be truly an individual.

VIVIENNE WESTWOOD, in "A Conversation with Vivienne Westwood" by Tara Sutton

I never thought people would want to wear clothes with monkeys and bananas on them. It gave me great insight into people, into how willing people are to put themselves out there. Fashion is an incredible tool for understanding people, for understanding the world.

MIUCCIA PRADA, in *Schiaparelli and Prada: Impossible Conversations*

If we think to distance ourselves from current fashion by finding another fashion from which to fashion ourselves, chances are it will be the one that current fashion predicted we'd pick.

MARK STRAND, "A Poet's Alphabet"

WORN OUT OF BOUNDS

Paula Rabinowitz

In his parable about the power of both clothing and literature to liberate mind and body, *Balzac and the Little Chinese Seamstress,* Dai Sijie tells the story of two young men, both sons of medical professionals disgraced during the Cultural Revolution, who are sent down to rural Sichuan from their home in its capitol Chengdu to work in the mines. The two are seen as oddities by the villagers among whom they live and work. One plays a violin and both are expert *benzi,* film explainers, who enchant the villagers with their renditions of the plots of various films from North Korea. The novel turns on two interlinked events: their meeting with the Little Seamstress who works with her tailor father, and the discovery of a suitcase belonging to another sent-down worker, son of a poet and writer, that contains a stash of books, translations of French novels. Balzac captivates the three young people. His words seduce. The narrator is so entranced by *Ursule Mirouët* he decides to copy a passage of the slim volume onto the inside of the worn-out sheepskin coat he is given as a gift by a villager for warmth. He etches a passage where Ursule somnabulates directly onto the animal skin like a tattoo to be worn close to his own.

Writing on the skin of an old mountain sheep was not easy: the surface was rough and creased and, in order to squeeze as much text as possible into the available space, I had to use a minute script. . . . By the time I had covered the entire inside of the jacket, including the sleeves, my fingers were aching so badly it felt as if the bones were broken. At last I dozed off.[1]

This erotically charged effort finds its parallel in the slip of cloth Luo pulls from his jacket to show his friend, the narrator, that

was torn from a shirt that had undoubtedly belonged to the Little Seamstress—it had a patch sewn on by hand. Inside were some dried leaves. They all had the same pretty shape. Like butterfly wings, in shades ranging from deep orange to brown streaked with pale gold, but all of them were stained black with blood. (59)

His roommate and the Little Seamstress had made love standing by a gingko tree, and she had fashioned this talisman as a token of her lost virginity. Already lovers, Luo wears the jacket one day to a rendezvous with her, transferring the text from one body to another, and then it is passed to her and she spends the afternoon reading the passage as he later recounts:

When she'd finished reading she sat there quite still, open-mouthed. Your coat was resting on the flat of her hands, the way a sacred object lies in the palms of the pious. . . . She ended up putting your wretched coat on (which looked very good on her, I must say). She said having Balzac's words next to her skin made her feel good, and also more intelligent. (62)

This encounter of skin, cloth, and text recurs throughout the novel, as the tailor comes to stay in the men's room during his yearly visit to the village, and the narrator recounts the entire plot of *The Count of Monte Cristo* over nine nights, resulting in "a discreet influence" by Dumas as the tailor sewed "fluttering bell-bottoms" with "a five-pointed anchor" that "became the most popular decorative feature in female fashion on Phoenix mountain" with women "embroider[ing] tiny anchors on buttons with gold thread" (127). The design of the lilies on Mercedes's corset was kept from the tailor—this was a secret only for the Little Seamstress.

Eventually, the Little Seamstress becomes pregnant, and the narrator manages to get her an illegal abortion from a doctor in town who knew his father by bribing him with the famous Fu Lei translation of *Ursule Mirouët* that he had already written onto his sheepskin. In the end, the seamstress uses her talents to make "herself a brassiere. She had been inspired by something in *Madame Bovary*" (178). Then she refashions a Mao coat she had made for the narrator into a "nifty jacket," bobs her hair, acquires a pair of white sneakers, and sneaks off in them, after her "Balzacian re-education," to live alone in the city (180). Dai's story, based loosely on his own reeducation, connects what is worn to where one goes. Through text and the labor of writing, through textiles and the labor of sewing, clothing and narration and desire veer in surprising ways.

The intertwined stories of the four young people and one's suitcase full of translated French novels from another century, all banned during the insane fervor of the Cultural Revolution, sends each on "divergent" paths: Four Eyes escapes reeducation thanks to the suitcase's treasures—he pays off Luo and the narrator with books after they trek to the mountaintop, "roving beyond limits," to collect authentic peasant songs for a new journal; the Little Seamstress and Luo dive into "flagrantly excessive" sex in the rustic stream and forest inspired by the erotic implications of French romance; she uses her skills at sewing to reimagine a new "discrepant" life of urban sophistication; the narrator "strays out of bounds" to arrange her abortion by trading on its wares.[2] All this takes place as each goes about dressed in everyday wear—of workers and peasants, stitched from discarded remnants of others' clothing. Text and textile interwoven into an extravagant elegy. This enchanted novel, set in the People's Republic of China in 1973, captures the ephemeral, yet material, power of fashion and dress. A bright white sneaker, an embroidered button, and an inscribed sheepskin coat present emblems of possibilities for their wearers.

This final volume in the series *Habits of Being* considers how the mundane everyday act of wearing clothes (a redundancy as the word "wear" comes from the Old English referring to "clothe") often strays out of bounds—*extra vagates* (from the Latin, to wander off the usual path)—as the wearer, which the *Oxford English Dictionary* tells us is the one who can "carry or bear on one's body or some member of it, for covering, warmth, or ornament," veers from the practical (covering, warmth) to "be decked out," extravagantly ornamented.[3] In various ways, the essays in this volume consider how wearing an object—a crown, a flower, an earring, a button, even a length of material—strays beyond the bounds of the body on which it is placed into the "discrepant" territory of "flagrantly excessive." Public signs of love, money, honor, prestige, desire, and power displayed extravagantly.

As in previous volumes, *Extravagances* commences with two meditations on habits of being; both consider how an identity can be made or unmade through clothing's history. Gattinoni designer Guillermo Mariotto reveals the sources of his wildly reimagined history of garments by explaining how the "gesture" of an accessory—altering buttons or pockets, as he does on his marvelous tributes to Saint Teresa or Queen Elizabeth I included here—can retrieve the past for an avant-garde contemporary look. Psychoanalyst Mariapia Bobbioni reverses the consideration of history's pull on identity by investigating how traumatic moments when a mother might alter her daughter's look—through dyeing her hair, or destroying a favored cap (thus messing with their heads)—can ramify throughout their lives rendering psychic damage that may be signaled by the adult woman's choice of dress and demeanor.

The works by scholars (historians, literary and film critics, ethnographers) and artists (photographers, weavers and embroiderers, sculptors, poets) take up the worn threads of these forays into history, psyche, and aesthetics in surprising and profound ways. The volume's essays consider the gestures of objects as they move down the body from a king's crowned head to a *tapada*'s exposed ankle in two directions—back and forth across the Atlantic from England to the Americas to Africa and down the hemisphere from the United States to the Southern Cone. These rich essays address how wearing something—"carry or bear on one's body or some member of it"—even something as mundane as a button, can open extravagant interpretations and understandings of behavior, desire, and art. When the habits of being get close scrutiny, they appear anything but habitual. As Joanne Eicher concludes, subtlety can be spectacular.

We begin with Paola Colaiacomo's elegant meditation on William Shakespeare's history plays, which focus on the transference between rulers of the signifier of royalty and the realm—wearing the crown. Chronologically, this meditation comes first, heading back, so to speak, to early modern Britain but pulling us into the twentieth century when Edward abdicated the throne and so his crown to marry an American woman, Wallis Simpson, and further into our own moment to consider what it means to wear something as she dissects the branding strategy of the Japanese clothing empire Uniqlo. Her evocative attention to the fine distinctions implied by the crown itself and its resting place, the head, and the changes these meanings acquire over time and across dynasties, shows how Shakespeare's uncanny phrasing astutely marked value and power as it was lodged, or dislodged, by accession, jealousy, and war. So when painter Beatrijs Lauwaert shaves her head and paints its baldness displaying a crown, she is consciously evoking the history of European royalty and woman's objectification, as she replaces a woman's crowning glory—her long hair—with a paper cut-out diadem (to use a favorite word of Emily Dickinson).

From pate to ears: Cristina Giorcelli explains, in her case study of American literary allusions to earrings, that these miniature objects, usually matched pairs, but often in literature found singularly, crystallize the intimate link between pain (piercing the lobe) and arousal, as the earring and its hole move the vagina and clitoris to the top of the body to be discreetly observed. The earring can feminize or masculinize, as its hoop or pendant shape also evokes the phallus (see the accompanying images of Shakespeare and Athena), and it is precisely this ambivalence, this doubling, that has put the earring into literary circulation. There, but just barely. This subtle presence is continued down the front of the body in the seemingly insignificant button, as Margherita di Fazio explains in her comprehensive survey of the place of the button in European literature. Buttons can speak about wealth—as in a jewel-encrusted Marie Antoinette example—or about poverty, as lowly objects salvaged from a worker's shirt for reuse accumulate in a sewing box. Buttons must be sewn on by hand; they require time and concentration to place them properly. Often invisible, their absence calls attention—as Alexander Pushkin's missing button does. And unbuttoning opens more than one's coat. Perhaps the sexiest scene in any movie occurs when Daniel Day Lewis slowly unbuttons Michele Pfeiffer's glove in Martin Scorsese's film of Edith Wharton's *Age of Innocence*.

Charlotte Nekola returns to the head, just above the ear, and the chest and shoulder of the bad women in films noirs to explore how wearing a flower, instead of a crown, speaks of death and deception despite the evocation of innocence that the bloom also poses. Marcel Proust may have found his beloved "within a budding grove," but in the American 1940s and 1950s a woman who wore a corsage was cursed, and her *fleurs du mal* spread danger to those intimately connected to her. Finding evidence in fashion spreads, pulp fiction, and B-movies for this curse, she posits that wartime made flowers unbearable extravagances so extreme as to verge on being unpatriotic. Flowers are excessive on the can-do suit of the working woman. This excess was precisely what drew Elsa Schiaparelli to fashion her "convulsive gloves" designed to show off the extremes of couture as surrealist objects of horrible beauty. But they also served to showcase, as Victoria Pass argues, how women had been constructed as wild beasts by surrealism, and in taking the metaphor literally, constructing gloves out of skin, she, along with her collaborator Meret Oppenheim, stripped bare assumptions about art, fashion, and femininity. These gloves push the limits of taste and practicality out of bounds; they collapse street and museum as a woman's hand serves as a display case.

Maria Anita Stefanelli focuses attention on the wrist and arms of Derek Walcott's complex Caribbean Island Helen, maid and waitress, by attending to the history of, on the one hand, the invented "native" dress—a costume really—she wears at work in a restaurant, exposing shoulders and arms for tourists, and, on the other hand, the yellow dress Helen gets as a hand-me-down from Maud for whom she keeps house. But more important, Stefanelli focuses attention on the bracelet Helen tries on before a mirror and her boss Plunkett while cleaning his wife's dresser. This borrowed/stolen bangle connects Helen and Maud to a history of British colonial rule over different islands—the West Indies and Ireland—linking slave manacle to Celtic torque to a "bracelet of white cowries from a narrow wrist."[4] So the bracelet, like the string of islands running through the Caribbean or the lacy shorelines of its beaches, encircles the Western hemisphere with Africa binding them to Britain's history of slavery and imperialism. Moreover, this exchange of frock and bracelet, voluntary or not, serves to forge a poetic lineage from Homer through William Butler Yeats to Walcott.

Appropriating emblems of past cultures, indigenous or European or African, was crucial for the self-fashioning of two modernist women artists—Frida Kahlo (whose attire inspired a Schiaparelli gown) and Georgia O'Keeffe—whose canvases, bodies, and houses functioned as apparel wrapping them in various guises that proclaimed their identities. The total picture presented by coordinating looks—in their works on canvas, in home decorating, and on the surfaces of their bodies—domesticated extravagance. Each artist was at once a housekeeper known for wearing workable styles (even Kahlo's elaborately staged *Mexicanidad* were based on the basic rebozo, huipil, and skirts of Mayan women) and a New Woman expressing a wild abandon as model, painter, lover, and wife. They saw how self-presentation—through clothing, hairstyle, decor, and above all signature aesthetics—was essential for a woman to blast her way into the modern art world. Staging dress and home decor to foreground identity, or its disintegration, was central to the construction of a New African-American Woman, too, as M. Giulia Fabi argues in her complex intertextual reading of clothing and color in W. E. B. Du Bois's underexamined novel, *The Quest of the Silver Fleece,* and Nella Larsen's *Quicksand.* Each book moves back and forth between the South and North as the protagonists succumb to or resist the violence, both physical and psychic, perpetrated on black women by racial and gender suspicions borne from slavery and its Jim Crow legacy.

This movement South continues the analyses by Camilla Cattarulla and Amanda Salvioni and the haunting photographs of Tarrah Krajnak, who returns to the orphanage where she lived as a child to document the aging nuns who cared for her before her adoption. These ghostlike renderings of the folds of the nuns' habits, as they hold a rosary or stand before a television, provide a child's-eye vision of her place in a disjointed world held together by familiar touchstones—white polyester or wrinkled and veined hands. These women still inhabit the Lima of the artist's birth. Their habits may be rememberings of the veils shrouding the colonial-era *tapadas,* who not only used shawls and veils, according to Cattarulla, as vehicles for modesty but subversively claimed the anonymity these coverings offered women (and men) to roam Lima's streets between the sixteenth and nineteenth centuries. The *tapadas* expose how repression paradoxically can serve as a means for women's empowerment: being invisible emboldened women to look. Extravagantly taking to the streets, defying traditional Catholic ideas about womanhood, the *tapadas* forged a space where their circulation allowed for deceit, desire, and a morsel of freedom by wearing their veils to the utmost. The more they covered themselves with elaborate drapery, the less they were seen but the more they saw.

Being seen in the colors of one's party during the nineteenth century could mean death in Buenos Aires. According to Amanda Salvioni, literature and art—not to mention fashion and accessories—dissected the color-coded politics fueled by Argentina's civil war. One might literally be caught dead wearing sky blue in the wrong company, so a complex system of attaching red—the color of the dictatorial governor Juan Manuel Rosas's party—served to inoculate the more cosmopolitan resisters from military or partisan violence. These color contortions offered satirists a means to critique government policies, on the one hand, but they also identified who should be considered a true patriot, on the other.

Joanne Eicher dissects the subtle and spectacular dress of Kalabari men and women in the Niger delta, returning across the Atlantic to the origin of clothing, Africa. As she explains, West Africa was a port of entry for goods from the British Empire—hence the importance of madras cloth—and a notorious site of the slave trade. These various historical traces can be seen in the variety of clothing and accessories adorning Kalabari men, women, and children during everyday life and especially for ceremonial events— such as funerals. One facet of Kalabari style—the careful extraction of a cloth's threads— points to the extravagant methods people use to create distinctions. The material's subtle differences in design signify clan and family affiliations or economic pastimes. Being threadbare is not a sign of being worn out.

Threadbare rags—*shmatas* in Yiddish—are also reclaimed in the wildly witty "intertextile" poem "Shmata," by Maria Damon and Adeena Karasick. Together these two collaborating poet/artists have fashioned a visual and textual meditation on the words and materials that have created Jewish (women's) identities in the Diaspora. A riff, a rap, a rag, a wrap, an exuberant feast of language that steps far out of bounds yet revels in the remnants of speech and stuff that might be balled up in the back of anyone's closet— like that of this granddaughter of a rag seller who has not only her own *shmatas* but her mother's and aunt's cluttering hers.

Aided by Balzac's texts, a bra and a pair of white sneakers put on during the Cultural Revolution sent a young girl to seek a new life far from her village. To wear, to be clothed, the essays in this volume suggest, is something so mundane as to be unremarked; yet when something is worn and made unique through its contact with skin, hair, sweat, through the small touches that turn mass-produced wear into one's own piece, it moves out of bounds, extravagantly, and with it habits change.

NOTES

1. Dai Sijie, *Balzac and the Little Chinese Seamstress,* trans. Ina Rilke (New York: Anchor Books, 2002), 58. Further references in text.

2. Each of the quoted words comes from the definition of extravagance and its variants: "extravagant, *adj.* and *n.*," OED Online, June 2013, http://www.oed.com/view/Entry/67142?p=emailAmh GRF/V4xfZ.&d=67142.

3. "wear, *v.1*," OED Online, June 2013, http://www.oed.com/view/Entry/226606?p=emailAm A79w1XndJi.&d=226606.

4. Derek Walcott, *Omeros* (London: Faber and Faber, 1990), 313.

1

WHEN WOMEN SPEAK . . .
THEIR CLOTHES TALK

Mariapia Bobbioni

Against the backdrop of modern life, a troubled humanity displays the loss of desire and a pursuit of pleasure that masks a delusion of omnipotence. The responsibility for this situation lies partly in fashion and the way mass media manipulate it to identify the female through the body and its clothing. We are presented with a dual vision of woman as the media and the market desire her to be. On the one hand, the female imagination comes to accept the ideal represented by models, actresses, or other figures of the star system; on the other, the ordinary woman living in her own body, one often far from the ideal, questions and analyzes these images.

This dichotomy contrasts a female figure created in shopwindows and show business—a figure fixed in hollow perfection, whose beauty must be absolute and as far as possible from any intimation of transience or loss. This figure, the ideal of a certain intangibility, is linked with this luxury, as if to deny that our civilization is going through a period of great upheaval (unemployment, disease, sustainability, war, etc.). The ordinary woman, in fact, would rather choose her own style by refashioning her dress and clothing on her own terms.

The often unconscious decision to wear a certain material or color is significant for subjective reasons. Cristina Campo observed: "In ancient times dress was a symbol or a combination of symbols; one could tell at a glance what fate it carried, or rather by what fate it was carried."[1] To speak of the fate of a subject hints at one's own story, in Sigmund Freud's interpretation. Psychoanalysis reveals elements of this story through a gesture, the choice of a new dress, a sudden change of hairstyle: extending thought to the body and dress, the subject allows him/herself to be constantly *in formation*. In this sense, we can talk about the ethics of aesthetics. Jacques Lacan, in a conversation with Eugénie Lemoine Luccioni, observed that a child is not born naked, for it emerges from the placenta, a wrapping, an environment we all know very well; and if, as Lemoine Luccioni maintains, for the female especially, objects are a kind of consolatory prosthesis to compensate for a lack, then it makes sense to stress the importance of things, because they are timeless and slow down our inevitable progress toward death.

Stefan Zweig unveils the ethics of aesthetics in his description of a private encounter with Rainer Maria Rilke:

> All that was vulgar was unbearable to him, and although he lived in restricted circumstances, his clothes always gave evidence of care, cleanliness, and good taste. At the same time, they showed thought and poetic imagination; they were a masterpiece of unpretension, always with an unobtrusive personal touch, such as perhaps a thin silver bracelet around his wrist. For his aesthetic sense of perfection and symmetry entered into the most intimate and most personal details. Once I watched him in his rooms prior to his departure—he declined my help as superfluous—as he was packing his trunk. It was like a mosaic work, each individual piece gently put into the carefully reserved space; I would have felt it to be an outrage to disturb this flowerlike arrangement by a helping hand.[2]

The history of woman acquires a new dimension when observed through her clothes and her naked body. The transformation of the female figure is written in the modifications in style that mirror changes in social and cultural fields. Fashion is a mentality that emphasizes the ethical element in aesthetics. It discerns what the subject does not know herself, a desire that is difficult to define. Fashion speaks of the subject's unconscious, of her imaginary representations, of her need to qualify herself symbolically. Lemoine Luccioni's *La Robe* gathers material on the psychoanalysis of clothing by listening to many women's accounts during their psychotherapy.[3] The dress as object—in the mother-daughter relationship and against the background of pre-oedipal and oedipal scenarios—can leave a strong impression on the formation of the female subject, and consequently of her sexuality.

To begin to understand these metaphorical and visceral references to dress, one might turn to Roland Barthes's rereading of Ferdinand de Saussure, glossing Nikolai Trubetskoy, in which he compares the distinction between *langue* and *parole* to that between clothing and dress, where, like *langue*, "clothing would be an institutional system," while as *parole*, dress would be an individualized expression within it.[4] *Langue*, as an institution, is independent of the individual; it is a set of rules within which the individual places his/her *parole*, which is an individual act. Barthes compares the former to clothing, the social phenomenon that is the object of historical and sociological research, an institutional reality surrounding the individual within which each subject organizes a space; *parole*, like dress, is a manifestation of an individual reality, the act of dressing oneself.

Pushing the analogy further, one might connect the mother to *langue* and clothing, and the child to *parole* and dress. In a lovely image, Donald Winnicott sees the mother as the child's window onto the world.[5] The mother figure—her voice, the smell of her skin, the softness of the clothes she wears—represents herself but also the world, an epoch, an environment, a history, a culture. She allows the child to define itself *because* of her look; in the future, the mother's face will enable the child to look for it in other, unknown faces. This becomes the means to discover new ones, as Emanuel Lévinas maintains.[6]

The mother, through *langue*, through this window to the world, to language, clothing, and style that exist outside, enables the child to develop, to speak, to enact its *parole*. In the mirror phase, as described by Lacan, the child begins to recognize and to define itself, to understand something about its body and, consequently, its clothing.[7] A child of four can already discuss how to match the colors of its clothes; the child performs a verbal act that leaves a sign on its body and that, in part, reflects back a sense of satisfaction in relation to an ideal of itself, thus opening the possibility of its symbolic positioning. In the mother-daughter relationship, in which, according to Lacan, a kind of "kidnapping" takes place, the dress-object becomes a vehicle of great intensity, sometimes a means of survival.

Françoise Dolto tells the story of a mother who was hospitalized when her infant daughter was only five days old. The baby was left with her father, who tended her lovingly, but she refused the bottle or any other means of feeding. The pediatrician suggested that the worried father should consult Dolto, who made a precious and precocious suggestion that saved the child: "Go to the hospital and take the nightdress your wife is wearing, so that it is full of her smell; wrap the bottle in it and then offer it to the child."[8] The child accepted the bottle without hesitation. The subject's primary narcissism, Dolto notes, which permits the survival of the body, is rooted in the first repetitive sensuous relations that accompany the mother's psychic dimension—breathing, feeding and the satisfaction of desire, smell, touch, and hearing. The image of the body becomes a safety net binding the child to the mother. During the mirror stage, from six to eighteen months old, a process of identification, a transformation in the subject when viewing an image, occurs because initially the subject is unknown to itself and the reflected image appears meaningless unless the mother or another familiar person is seen beside it. Only she can reunite the image of the subject's body to its ideal—of its body, of its self; only through the correlation with the other can the subject recognize and redefine its own image.

The child learns about itself through the other. In this subjective articulation the mother charges the child with a strong sexual significance because, as Freud notes, the mother "regards him/her with feelings that are derived from her own sexual life: she strokes, kisses, rocks the child and quite clearly treats him/her as a substitute for a complete sexual object."[9] After the pre-oedipal and oedipal experiences, which the mother herself has lived through, this sexual dimension is transmitted. Where will the mother unconsciously place her daughter? In what bodily, aesthetic image will she position her? Which clothes will reveal a ghost of homosexuality or an excess of castration or of phallic imposition? Because dress extends the body, dress also discloses a bulimic or an anorexic body.

A psychoanalytic session allows a male patient to reach that point in which what Lacan calls "the cipher of his mortal destiny" is revealed to him in the "Thou art that," but "It is not in our mere powers as practitioners to bring him to that point where the real journey begins."[10] Of course, this would be true for female patients, too. It is a question of recalling and retelling one's story through which, in verbalization, the subject moves somewhere else, aware of its ghost and often liberating a word that becomes new in a fluid language, the language of the subject's desire.

FLAXEN HAIR, A MASK OF THE SELF

A mother could not refrain from bleaching her nine-year-old daughter's hair flaxen blonde and continued this modification into her adolescence, at which point, in desperation, the girl rebelled. The signifier in this story is the golden-haired doll, who is manipulated, a doll deprived of voice and the right to speak, incapable of expression, of either imposing on or opposing another. Forced into a mask, the girl paraded as her mother's ghost who desired her to be blonde and beautiful, perfect, top of her class, untouchable, designed to be displayed in a glass case. Under this sacrificial logic, the girl built herself a mask so as not to see the world or be seen by it, expressing no emotions, existing for the sole purpose of becoming her mother's desire. Where was her own desire? For a long time, this mode of presenting herself became her way of relating to others. She behaved like a character in Marie Hermanson's novel *Musselstranden* who, visiting a small shop, makes a discovery:

On one wall hung a row of masks. They were all animal heads. She took one from the wall and tried it on in front of the mirror. It was a fox's head. When she met her own gaze peering out of the oblique holes in the mask, she felt such a wave of happiness that it took her breath away. She turned and looked around the shop, at the other customers and the young man at the counter. She felt completely different. Her fear had vanished.[11]

These feelings are similar to those of the young woman: the image that her mother had imposed on her and that she had refused so powerfully in adolescence, she later carefully reconstituted for herself in adulthood, actually proud and happy to be doing so. Because the head and its hair represent majesty, the seat of thought and knowledge, it became the crown through which her nightmarish hairstyle triumphed over her body, practically disfiguring it. The remembrance and reenactment of that ritual resolved the entire structure of the victim-executioner pattern that had left no space for a femininity other than the mechanical logic of a project—the perfect accomplishment of duties at work, the careful planning of an emotional life. She was alternately on top or underneath, as if maneuvered by a puppet master in a kind of ecstatic modality, a curious style defined as a cold and indifferent "happiness."

THE HAT WITH A TAIL

Why on earth would a mother cut the tail off a magnificent marmot fur hat, which the little girl loved precisely because of its tail? In ancient China, the pigtail was a phallic prerogative of the Manchu lords and invaders. The pigtail, as phallus, substitutes for the missing penis and so did the tail of this magnificent hat. What was the mother envious of? What was it that she could not tolerate? Not having worked through her own castration meant that her daughter's attempt at compensation through her choice of such consoling headgear was doubly serious. The castration of a castration: a mother does not accept her own and berates her daughter. Before the daughter's recounting, this episode was reflected in her life through a fierce intolerance of any relationship with men. As such a response caused bitter tears, she judged her encounters with men to be inadequate because these men were beneath her—to be depreciated just as she herself did not feel adequately appreciated. Obviously, it was not the literal cutting of the tail that created this devastating scenario for the child; as always, it was an act traversing a terrain whose imaginative identifications are exhaustingly complex. A mother who is structurally castrating—because she refuses to accept the transmission of the father's discourse to the daughter—runs the risk of weakening the child's emotional equilibrium in a morbid love-hate bond with herself, in which the male figure is disembodied, disfigured.

AN IMPOSITION: THE BOW TIE

The little girl tugged at its elastic, wanted to pull it off, found it unbearable. This was the story she told, once even bringing a photograph: pretty, in shorts, blouse, cardigan with a badge, and the inevitable bow tie. The child could not bear the coercion, the short hair, nor "that thing" that could only be masturbated and nothing else. "Who wanted to be a boy?" she said one day. This sentence began to explain many of her other forms of behavior that produced sexual blocks and the awkward way she moved her body and wore her clothes. Her mother had never experienced sexual pleasure with her husband, the little girl's father. In later years, when the patient had grown up, her mother was constantly demanding attention and favors as if she were a widow, as if the only possible husband and man of any worth were her daughter, the child on whom an empty body had been imposed over the real one by her mother's desire. It was a body the child had never recognized as her own; it displayed the discomfort of a subject who does not feel at home in her own shoes. Yet that unease opened the door to very valuable work to recover the "lost habit," the one she wanted when she tried to reject the hateful bow tie.

*

A case study reveals the tragic aspect of human stories as the subject reports absence, frustration, and contradiction. Clothes are a sign of these dimensions. A subject who is in psychoanalysis is not easily satisfied by media manipulation and by delusions of omnipotence, but is instead someone trying to understand how to think and know and live. Yet, if fashion is considered as a signifier, a subject intent on discovering her transformation and consequently glimpsing her true subjectivity may find pleasure in recovering the past, in taking up different periods and styles, perhaps by wearing one of her grandmother's blouses or a brooch her aunt pinned to her lapel. Fashion then becomes a sort of female inheritance written on the body.

Modern scenarios offer a system that aims to produce an effect of *bêtise*, of stupidity. The average woman becomes imprisoned in the narcissistic fantasies of eternal youth: the female figure on the magazine cover translated into a woman who *must* seduce. The consequences may be a rigidly intolerant aesthetic delusion that bespeaks the impossibility of accepting limits, the wish to wallow in omnipotence so as to apparently remain aloof from the tragic aspects of life. The modern female subject, the one presented by mass media and found in many areas of our social structure, seems to be locked in a small autistic notion of well-being and translated into a general idea of eternal beauty, in which a whole and incorruptible body triumphs, possibly, even over death. Pain *must not* exist; it can only be presented as the setting for a market of emotions, as the public exhibition of a private fiction. By denying its tragic aspect, life is denied, and also the true history of the subject is denied.

Thus the claims of the body must be ignored: if a symptom appears, we are required to eliminate it, not to interpret it. Society does not tolerate a pause; to stop and think is a waste of time. "The Superego does not contrast the Id, it flanks it. The ego is not a third entity any longer, the mediator between the two, but as body-ego it becomes the site of pleasure. Existence, living, is justified by having a body, and the idea is to give the body pleasure."[12]

Dress, "a thing" we all must reckon with every morning when we wake up and put on clothes, becomes a masquerade, rather than serving to protect or adorn oneself. As Lemoine Luccioni notes:

> When the length of fringe is exaggerated, longer than the dress itself, then the Baroque appearance of the dress can be rightly defined a symptom. . . . The irruption of the unconscious, rather than barring the subject, drowns him/her in the fantastic. Even sexual restrictions are denied. Men as well as women are covered in lace and feathers. The imagination absorbs the symbolic.[13]

The media are gigantic containers for a circus of the imagination in which the female subject is no longer one relating to other subjects, but one who comforts herself by becoming an object in a game that may be perverse if governed by omnipotence and immortality. As Paul Virilio says, "Past, present and future contract in the omnipresent instant. . . . Event-based history . . . disappears in the acceleration of a now untimely reality."[14] Becoming a clone, being ageless, does not help the subject to retrieve a self. The uniqueness of words, however, offers a vehicle for the continuing formation of the subject. This is the privilege of those who believe, with Lacan, that the end of an analysis leaves little more than the core of an apple. Still, we work hard to achieve this slight result through the constant and humble labor of understanding.

NOTES

1. Cristina Campo, *Gli imperdonabili* (Milan: Adelphi, 1987), 116 (my translation).

2. Stefan Zweig, *The World of Yesterday* (New York: Viking Press, 1943), 142–43.

3. Eugénie Lemoine Luccioni, *La Robe: Essai Psychanalitique sur le vêtement* (Paris: Seuil, 1981).

4. Roland Barthes, *The Language of Fashion*, ed. Anthony Stafford and Michael Carter (Oxford: Berg, 2006), 27. See also Roland Barthes, *The Fashion System*, trans. Matthew Ward and Richard Howard (New York: Hill and Wang, 1983).

5. See Donald Winnicott, "Mirror-role of Mother and Family in Child Development," in *Playing and Reality* (New York: Routledge, 2005), 149–59.

6. "Even when I shall have linked the Other to myself with the conjunction 'and,' the Other continues to face me, to reveal himself in his face." Emanuel Lévinas, *Totality and Infinity* (Dordrecht: Kluwer Academic, 1991), 80–81.

7. See Jacques Lacan, "The Mirror Stage as Formative of the Function of the *I* as Revealed in Psychoanalytic Experience" [1949], in *Ecrits*, trans. Alan Sheridan (Abingdon: Routledge, 2007), 1–8.

8. Françoise Dolto, *L'image incosciente du corps* (Paris: Editions du Seuil, 1984), 67 (my translation).

9. Sigmund Freud, *Three Essays on the Theory of Sexuality* [1905], in *The Standard Edition of the Complete Psychological Works of Sigmund Freud*, trans. and ed. James Strachey (London: Hogarth Press, 1953), 7:223.

10. Lacan, "Mirror Stage as Formative," 8.

11. Marie Hermanson, *La Spiaggia*, trans. C. Giorgetti-Cima (Parma: Guanda, 2002), 73 (my translation).

12. Giovanni Lo Castro, "Il corpo supporto di scritture," in *La psicoanalisi e il corpo* (Naples: Ellissi, 2002), 143 (my translation).

13. Lemoine Luccioni, *La Robe*, 51 (my translation).

14. Paul Virilio, *Futurism of the Incident: Stop-Eject* (Cambridge, Mass.: Polity Press, 2010), 71–72.

2

AN ACCESSORY IS A GESTURE
IN CONVERSATION WITH CRISTINA GIORCELLI

Guillermo Mariotto

In French—the language of fashion par excellence—the word *maître* can be used to refer to an artist or a fashion designer. This is very similar to the way the word *maestro* is used in Italian, but *maître* in French can also mean the captain of a ship. This is a particularly appropriate appellation for Guillermo Mariotto, who since the mid-1990s has bravely and successfully steered his elegant ship, the Maison Gattinoni, through the turbulent, alluring seas of fashion.

Born in Caracas of Venetian stock on his father's side and Venezuelan on his mother's, Mariotto has knowingly combined these two inheritances, clearly making the most of both traditions. There is his Italian love of art, adventure, and elegance and his fascination with the mystery, rhythm, and color of his Venezuelan forebears.

Having studied industrial design at the Institute of Arts and Crafts at Berkeley (and could there be any doubt regarding this choice of subject, having seen the structures of his clothes?), Mariotto immigrated to Italy early in the 1980s. At first, he was interested in furniture and interior design (for Interlinea) and then, thanks to Principessa Anna Massimo, he made his mark in the world of fashion with Basile and Titta Rossi. In 1988, a meeting took place that changed the course of his professional life overnight (his personal life instead has always had strong, solid foundations). This change put an end to his accomplished sculptures in wood (furniture), an end to the well-crafted architectural spaces (interiors), and an end to the second-line collections of young, imaginative designers. In their place came the highly fashioned, solid, yet ethereal, opulent, fairytale-like clothes of the Maison Gattinoni. That fateful meeting was with Raniero, the son of the founder of the Maison, Fernanda Gattinoni. Since the premature death of Raniero, the Italian and international fashion world now reverses Mariotto as the creative director of Gattinoni; he has become that new, distinct *maître* of high fashion who is sought after and lauded throughout Western Europe, the Middle East, and Russia. Now the Americas, his birthplace, will also have the chance to appreciate his talents.

Intelligent, curious, and sharp, with a natural flair for the symbolic, Mariotto has found in Rome—the city of the Baroque—a focal point and source of inspiration. He visits the museums and galleries and studies the painters of the past, above all of the fifteenth and sixteenth centuries, from Sandro Botticelli and Leonardo da Vinci to Michelangelo and Titian. He scrutinizes their canvases, poring over the magnificent costumes, the elaborate embroidery, and the iridescent arabesque patterns on their precious fabrics. He captures the delicate balance of splendor and understatement.

However, Mariotto would not be so quintessentially Latin American if he did not have a darker, tragic side, and this explains his attraction to the paintings of the Flemish school. He loves Hieronymus Bosch with his horrible deformations and viscid repugnant bodies, those terrifying hallucinations that are nonetheless redeemed and rendered irresistible by the incisive lines, the dreamlike space, the formal energy, and the colors: brilliant, transparent, and opalescent, yet possessing a certain warmth.

Painting, however, is not all that inspires Mariotto. Perhaps his temperament explains his strong feeling for music and also for movement. All music—from Mozart and Tchaikovsky to samba and the Beatles. His skirts, blouses, trousers, and capes float and flow and seem to follow their own inner rhythm, dictated by the type of fabric, sustained by the cut, and coordinated by the motion of the body, moving to *their* particular music.

Indeed, music is at the very root of his creativity. It is therefore no coincidence that Mariotto designed the costumes for the centennial production of *Madame Butterfly* (conducted by Placido Domingo) at the Torre del Lago Puccini Festival in 2004. Another undertaking was designing the costumes for a musical based on the life of Padre Pio, *Actor Dei*, staged by a group of emerging performers in May 2007. The costumes of the leading characters—from those of the saint and the friars to that of the woman possessed by devils—bring Mariotto's multifaceted cultural awareness to the theatrical space and, above all, help create the characters themselves.

According to Mariotto, "accessories are gestures." I interpret this as meaning that, like gestures, accessories have significance and, like gestures, they accompany the movement of the body through space, adding a three-dimensional quality to intentions, even to those that are most secret. What is more calculated and wanton, he asks himself, than the so-called ballet flat? At first sight, its low-slung design seems to proclaim innocence and virginity, but with the tips of the toes so knowingly half hidden (and thus half revealed), the ballet flat can entice as successfully as the most experienced seductress in stilettos.

I ask him to show me the accessories for the magnificent clothes that he dedicated to great women of the past in his 2006 Fall–Winter collection, women deemed great because they changed the history of the world through what they did, through their personalities, their farsightedness, their skill at seduction, or their adverse destinies. They had courage, intelligence, wisdom, and beauty in abundance, also an inclination and desire for self-sacrifice, mysticism, and, at times, even cruelty. To name but a few, there are Theodelinda, queen of the Lombards; Lucrezia Borgia; Joanna I of Naples; Maria Theresa of Austria; Charlotte Corday; Queen Christina of Sweden; Charlotte, empress of Mexico; and Anita Garibaldi. I have the impression from what he says—and how he says it—that Mariotto is a fashion designer who truly admires (strong) women. He not only provides the clothes; Mariotto wants there to be more women with similar qualities and abilities in an age when, even though women are not fully valued, in many instances they are no longer held back either. He admits that months of historical and pictorial re-

FIGURE 2.1 Gattinoni, "Queen Elizabeth I," Fall–Winter 2006 Collection. Courtesy of Gattinoni Couture.

search were necessary before a vivid image of each woman emerged. This entailed capturing the meaning of those lives with the language of today, that is, with the fabrics, visual significance, and flavor of the moment; it entailed creating the clothes that these women would be wearing *now* in order to display their stature, be it intellectual, moral, professional, or religious.

Going through the collection, Mariotto tries to satisfy my request to explain how he chose the appropriate accessories for each of the women. I finally realize that he perceives accessories *differently* from the way they are generally perceived. They are not complements, supplements, or external embellishments to clothing. They are not additions, albeit important ones, to clothes, but intrinsic features that make the clothes what they are. In fact, the details that comprise these finishing touches are the sine qua non of not just the *outer* but also the *inner* significance of the clothes. Thanks to his finely tuned sensitivity, they encapsulate the unique—and historical—identity of each woman.

For Elizabeth I he designed a richly austere overcoat. Classic in form (recalling Mary Quant, some have commented), it is made of black cashmere stitched with black chiffon diamond shapes to create a brocade effect. At the points where the diamonds touch, a large white pearl shines encircled by rose petals (the flower on the Tudor coat of arms). The severity and commanding nature of the Virgin Queen are conveyed in full. For Empress Theodora, he created a see-through mauve blouse, splendidly embroidered with various colored stones (recalling the Ravenna mosaics), that is worn over see-through black georgette trousers. The transparency and the style of the pants, beneath such jewel-encrusted imperial splendor, allude to Theodora's past as a courtesan, belly dancer, and circus mime performer.

For Teresa of Avila (who was from a family of silk merchants), there is a black cashmere overcoat, inlaid with chiffon and georgette strips in a geometric pattern of squares and rectangles, short parallel lines, and (appropriately enough) crosses, all studded with diamonds. These geometric forms strongly recall the saint's unswervingly abstract, ascetic life, which is further highlighted by a large brooch with a diamond at the center from which golden rays shine, giving the impression of a monstrance. This brooch, worn directly *over* the heart, would be a traditional accessory if it were not that it makes visible and material what cannot be seen. For Isabella of Castile, who according to legend declared that she would not change her clothes until the Moors had left Spain, an outfit in pale gray (a conscious rejection of white). It is an ethereal, organdy-and-lace creation, strewn with glass crystals and tiny rings that recall Isabella's clear intelligence and staunch loyalty to her husband. For Queen Victoria, whose reign was crowned with various achievements, there is a magnificent white dress with an imposing train covered in pearls and roses of tulle and chiffon, given that she loved—and loved growing—flowers. We could continue, as twenty-four great women are reinterpreted in this manner.

I watch Mariotto as he becomes enthusiastic, his eyes shining as he talks. A tenuous but fitting analogy is the romantic, picturesque description that Washington Irving gave of Vasco Nuñez de Balboa, one of the conquistadors of the New World.[1] Arriving in present-day Panama and Colombia by way of the Caribbean, he was convinced that there was a sea further west. He had his large ship taken apart, and his crew carried the pieces through the jungle, the swamps, and the sinking sands of a country infested with snakes and poisonous plants. Finally, after terrible adventures and appalling exhaustion, after deceit, massacre, and many deaths, Balboa reached the west coast. There he set eyes on that vast expanse of water hitherto unknown to Europeans that would later be called the Pacific Ocean. After kneeling down and thanking God for arriving at his destination and

FIGURE 2.2

Gattinoni, "Santa Teresa d'Avila," Fall–Winter 2006 Collection. Courtesy of Gattinoni Couture.

FIGURE 2.3 Gattinoni, "Santa Teresa d'Avila," Fall–Winter 2006 Collection. Courtesy of Gattinoni Couture.

being the first European to witness such beauty, Balboa had his ship reassembled and ecstatically sailed the new ocean. Wildly courageous, totally focused, and driven by the force of imagination and myth (rather than a simple appetite for gold and glory), this errant knight of adventure must have left a trace in the tastes and sentiments of the indigenous peoples and their descendants. It is fitting to compare this past *maître* of epic conquest with the *maître* of such an elegant and visionary present.

NOTE

1. Washington Irving, "Vasco Nuñez de Balboa: Discoverer of the Pacific Ocean," in *Voyages and Discoveries of the Companions of Columbus* (Philadelphia: Carey and Lea, 1831), 147–276.

3

WEARING A CROWN

Paola Colaiacomo

"Speak thou for me, and tell them what I did," Richard starts out in the third and last part (but the first to be written) of the trilogy dedicated by a young William Shakespeare to Henry VI.[1] The person so charged is the Duke of Somerset, or rather his head, nonchalantly kicked across the floor as Richard enters the throne room at Westminster. Waiting for him is his ferocious father, Richard of York, who has occupied the palace. Richard Jr. was not even duke of Gloucester at that point; for this, he must wait until later in the play (*3H6*, 2.6.103). The following year (1591) Shakespeare was to give him a play of his own, the glitzy and somber *Richard III*. For the moment, "Dicky" (*3H6*, 1.4.76) has to bide his time as the most sensitive element in the cast.[2]

In Shakespeare, the first scene sets the dominant theme of the play; in the third *Henry VI*, this is the savage contest for the crown. What sets Richard apart from the other representatives of the two houses fighting for the kingdom—York and Lancaster—is the fetishistic relationship between head and crown that has him in its thrall: a searing passion for the object itself, extreme to the point of self-destruction, such as few ever experience. Ultimate suffering as extreme life-sport known, perhaps, to the collector or the artist, whose immersion in the object can, however, be cathartic and peace-imposing.

Since childhood the Flemish artist Beatrjis Lauwaert had wanted to shave off her long and beautiful copper locks; one day, well into adulthood, she plucked up the courage. The first thing to emerge from her bald pate was a self-portrait with crown. In her own words:

Self portrait (oil on canvas), 1989. Our son Maarten, who was 12, cut off my long hair and shaved my head, in our little garden in Ghent. It was early summer. It was a dream of mine: I had wanted to do it since childhood. In 1989 I finally found the courage.

This self portrait expresses how I felt afterwards, with no hair: naked, pure, and strong, in peace and harmony with myself and the world: closer to the universe, with its stars, moon, planets, and sun.

. . . It has the colours, dignity, and silence of an icon. The crown isn't of gold but of painted paper.

We don't know why, in the painting, the crown has been installed on the exposed and sensitized part of the skin, almost as if it were the organic result of the mute desire of childhood now satisfied by the self portrait, with no need of words. The ritual significance of the exchange—not hair but crown; not gold but painted paper—is established in a public performance a few years on:

A few years later, in 1995, when Maarten was 18, we repeated the experiment, but in Antwerp, in the exhibition hall of the postgraduate academy, in the form of a ritual and public performance. There was a recording of the sea and seven white garments. We filmed it both as a documentary and an independent work of art.[3]

CROSS AND CROWN

Bodily apex in which "the animal organs are contained," according to Robert Burton's Galenic physiology, the head houses the noble organ of the brain, projected toward the

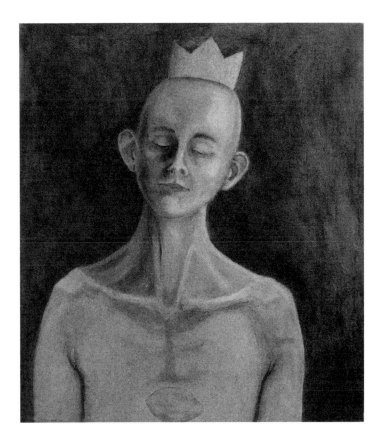

FIGURE 3.1 Beatrjis Lauwaert, *Self-Portrait*, 1989. Oil on canvas,
74 × 65 cm. Courtesy of the artist.

outside world via the eyeballs.[4] But when the mental functions have to be assigned to
some part of the anatomy, the age of Shakespeare is undecided as to head or heart: "Tell
me, where is fancy bred, / Or in the heart, or in the head?" runs the first line of the song
that perhaps nudges Bassanio toward his correct choice of the lead casket, as has often
been noted, guided by the head/lead rhyme.[5]

Taking Burton as our guide, it is intriguing to imagine that Richard Jr.'s "fancy" in that first scene is equally influenced by the "head." Imagine Richard's skull fired by the vital animality of his inner organs and pitched toward the artificial fastigium represented by the crown, opening the way to the ultimate self-refinement: the head's quasi-metamorphosis into the splendor of gold and stones. Two elements, both hard though in different ways, the one organic, the other inorganic, would then unite on his head, a concrescence crowning an unfashionable body, irreducible to proper proportion.[6]

The gesture of decapitation has established sufficient physical intimacy between conqueror and conquered to allow Richard to take up the head of his adversary and make it the macabre mouthpiece of his desire. From within the physical magnetism pulling him toward the crown, Richard orders the scuffed ball of Somerset's head to "speak": but even supposing it could tell its adventures, the rhetorical circle would still close around the crown alone, since everything he has done and will do, from palace intrigue to deeds of war, will continue to recognize no other galvanizing tension, like the play itself, which can be read as an authentic Passion play of the crown. Yet before the advent of the beatific "golden time" (3H6, 3.2.127) that can be measured for Richard only by possession of the crown, many times will death have to send its signals, with its time-honored ally, gold. In *The Merchant of Venice*, the King of Morocco haughtily throws open the gold casket and pulls out a "death's head": "O hell! What have we here? / A carrion Death, within whose empty eye / There is a written scroll!" (*MV*, 2.7.62–64). What awaits Richard, more indirectly, is a disguised head and cross: the head is that of the king he wishes to be, but the cross on the other side of the coin is the all too transparent memento of a momentarily suspended death sentence. Crown and cross are but a short space apart, as it were.

The baroque cross-crown dualism resurfaces in the twentieth century in the degraded regality of the dukes of Windsor. Wallis and Edward—WE, in their chosen livery—registered the stations of their passion on a bracelet of platinum and diamonds from which, like so many trinkets, hung the "king's crosses."[7] On the significant events of their relationship—illnesses, dangers averted, birthdays, etc.—one or the other of them would add a cross, so that this particular jewel, among the many the couple owned, acquired the value of a written code, a diary that was both public and secret, worn on Wallis's wrist on all official occasions, not least their wedding day. Of the various jeweled crosses on the bracelet, two were probably more precious than the others. The first is a cross of baguette diamonds, engraved "The King's Cross God Bless WE 1.3.36." Edward was already king at that date, although still uncrowned (as he was to remain), and could still legitimately hope that Wallis would be at his side for his coronation. "Do you really think that I would be crowned without Wallis at my side?" he had commented to his childhood friend Bernard Rickatson-Hatt, editor-in-chief of Reuters and the duchess's future biographer.[9] The second is a cross of rubies, sapphires, and emeralds added by Wallis, reading: "Our Marriage Cross Wallis 3 VI 37." The date is that of their wedding, which took place six months after the abdication. It would have been of questionable taste to overshadow the official coronation of the new king, George VI, Elizabeth II's father, by the "scandalous" event splashed across every newspaper. By this point all hope of reigning together had disappeared. The marriage cross was the last for WE: with the crown behind them forever, there was no reason to go looking for any others.

NATURAL LAW

If sovereign power is condensed for Richard in the crown-object, for all other contenders it lies in the constituent law. Warwick, "setter-up and plucker-down of kings" (3H6, 2.3.37), circumscribes the claims of York Sr. within the terms of the feudal pact—literally *physio-cratic*—between the king and the land of the kingdom. "I'll plant Plantagenet, root him up who dares. / Resolve thee, Richard; claim the English crown" (3H6, 1.1.48–49). Obediently, he moves to the throne and sits down.

At the basis of the idea itself of "reign," there is a foundational act of appropriation of the land, a communal good, by one man: an ancient, timeless act of violence that power has not only condoned but legitimized across centuries. Warwick touches a nerve in the physiology of sovereignty when he expresses the looked-for enthronement of "Plantagenet" (viz. the duke of York), which he is ready to defend with arms, in terms of husbandry of the soil: the rooting of a tree. His words evince traces of a right that is even older than that artificially established with the kingdom: the right of all men to freely partake of the fruits of the earth they themselves have tilled. A natural right, neither divine nor absolute like that of kings, but human, fleeting, and mortal; or if divine, in the sense of "willed by the gods," like the metamorphosis of the nymph Daphne into a tree, a backsliding, from human to vegetable, with the accompanying loss of the motor faculties—the condition to which Warwick would reduce Plantagenet once he has rooted him to the throne. He, for his part, is heraldically committed to his fate as a Plantagenet. He is already a *plante genêt*, the nickname of their ancestors the Angevins who, legend goes, wore it in their hats: a sprig of broom.

EXPERIMENTAL SHAKESPEARE

Here, in the scene of the occupied "bloody Parliament" (*3H6*, 1.1.39), the physical integrity of the crown is defended by Edward—the future Edward IV—and, above all, the young "Dicky," both supporters of war as final solution. Doggedly they spur their father to action, urging him to "tear the crown from the usurper's head . . . set it on your head" (*3H6*, 1.1.114–15). There is no question for them of legal quibbles or dynastic niceties: the crown may be taken by force but not "entailed," stolen but not mutilated. As a legal term, "entail" (*3H6*, 1.1.194) boasts the strong etymological root of cutting, from the French "taille." Even the cutting down to size of a garment is a diminution of the body's singularity in presupposing its adapting to a given standard. With a fixity of purpose all the more extraordinary given his awareness of the remoteness of the crown—"many lives stand between me and home" (*3H6*, 2.2.173)—Richard strives for the possession of the crown, which to him is "home." It is this "home," and no other, that is to bear his personal seal though the head may come away too as the crown is "pluck[ed]" down and rehoused.

This experimental Shakespeare seems less interested in the symbolism than the metatheatrical possibilities of the crown-object. The fusion is clear, though a margin of separability is also left open. The plays to follow—for example, *Lear*—explore the opposite aspect of the problem, but for now the thing seems to maintain some of its arcane and archaic power. This magical power of the thing—an embarrassment in the age of Francis Bacon, yet undeniable—still resounds in the head-crown attraction explored here through Richard the character who, of all those present, is the most charged and dense with futurity.

Periodically, whenever the title is expected to pass from Lancaster to York, the symbol is depleted and tends to revert to the original "thingness" of its referent. "Crown," with all its charged semantics, is then likely to revert to "diadem." "Now, perjur'd Henry, wilt thou kneel for grace / And set thy diadem upon my head?" (*3H6*, 2.2.81–82) is the provocative question of the challenger, Edward, the duke of York's eldest son and presumed heir to the throne. The very impracticability of the gesture Edward requests here is sufficient to communicate at what distance from the materiality of the object he is speaking. The scene of a king who kneels and voluntarily transfers the crown to another head would have met instant censure.

In the whole court, only Richard dares treat the crown as a tangible object of desire: "and fearless minds climb soonest unto crowns" (*3H6*, 4.7.62). His craving for the crown from moment to moment takes on the urgency of physiological necessity, or imperious demand for a precious talisman by a queen-cum-witch whom none can gainsay. In the long monologue of act 3, scene 2 (lines 124–95), the crown is a promised land, a golden age, a dream, a "home." More precisely, it is the necessary tool of a cruel eros, à la Sade, crushing enjoyment out of the image of his skull constricted—"round impaled" (171)— within the golden circle. His "mis-shaped trunk" becomes, in anticipation, a mere support for the head and its "glorious crown" (170–71), obliterating any bodily deformity.

But in its turn this inanimate crown, accessory in the perverse erotic game, imposes its own timing and rhythm, which are those of deferment, on the animate, anatomical crown of the head. Fetishistically, the object triumphs through the pleasure-pain of delayed enjoyment. The pleasure procured by this bodily humiliation is such as to justify the most savage crime and the most treacherous deceit. In the imagination, evil's latitude knows no restriction, embracing both antiquity and the contemporary: in scenting victory Richard becomes Ulysses and Proteus, Sinon and "the murderous Machiavel" whom he will "set . . . to school" (193). If such vicarious feats are possible, his present ambition is completely plausible: "Can I do this, and cannot get a crown?" (195). A crown: even at moments of the highest dramatic and emotional tension, Dicky is nothing if not self-ironic.

INDIAN STONES

"But, if thou be a king, where is thy crown?" Henry of Lancaster's keeper asks him while he is prisoner in a forest near the Scottish border. "My crown is in my heart, not on my head; / Not decked with diamonds and Indian stones, / Nor to be seen," is the swift and simple reply (3H6, 3.1.62–64). This meditation-out-loud of Henry's has, with its image of the secret, crowned heart, much of the post-Tridentine Catholic adoration of the Sacred Heart.[9] Or, alternately, of the blasphemous kitsch of David La Chapelle. Henry's interiorized crown of contentment is a considerable psychological distance from the object burning with inner light and pointing Richard the way out of the dark wood of desires and nightmares that trap him like a cornered beast and crush the breath from him:

And yet I know not how to get the crown,
For many lives stand between me and home:
And I—like one lost in a thorny wood,
That rends the thorns and is rent by the thorns,
Seeking a way and straying from the way,

Not knowing how to find the open air,

But toiling desperately to find it out—

Torment myself to catch the English crown. (*3H6*, 3.2.172–79)

In appearance, nothing could be farther from Richard's worldly wish to "catch the crown" than Henry's adoration of the invisible crown within the heart. Yet, almost as if the splendor of gold and gems were an obligatory topos and territory for a monarch, Henry, though weak and defeated, now enters this territory and moves within it with inbred ease.

One is struck by the realistic detail in his description of the exquisite workmanship of diamonds and precious stones in the purely imaginary crown he disavows. From the invisible depths of the kingly sacred heart the "Indian stones" project us to contemporary Elizabethan reality and the commercial fever of the late sixteenth century, when the British crown began to sponsor companies operating in India, outposts of future dominions. As such the lines would have produced a sort of cultural short-circuit in the original listeners. Between the different pressures of remote conquests and close-at-hand difficulties, there stood, as guarantor of continuity, a crown: a secret crown of diamonds and Indian stones, buried in the king's heart. But a crown clamors to be seen and exhibited.

TIME AND CROWN

The image of the "crown in the heart" is in line with Richard II's famous meditations on the crown in the eponymous play, written in 1595 when the third part of *Henry VI* was being performed nightly on London stages. The crown is one of the two mystic bodies he possesses: the one grief-laden, the other joyful. I am here using the image of the two bodies not so much in Ernst Kantorowicz's sense—in connection with medieval legal theories on sovereignty—but in that of Walter Pater.[10] What Shakespeare's kings share, according to Pater, is a streak of "common humanity thrown onto greatness ... refined for regal usage, like all other ordinary things, by Shakespeare's infallible eloquence."[11]

The sorrowful body represents Richard's common humanity. Obliged to resign the crown, the king is still unable to remove its associated cares and griefs. When Boling-broke scoffs at him, "I thought you had been willing to resign," he promptly adjusts the other's aim: "My crown I am, but still my griefs are mine" (R2, 4.1.190–91). Even if the crown is renounced, the cares of the crown will stay with him: "The cares I give, I have, though given away, / They 'tend the crown, yet still with me they stay" (198–99). Much of the royal body's grief is over time wasted: time, crown, and grief forming the clay from which that body is molded. At the limit of the theater of the absurd, Richard is made time's "numbering clock." And just as he has "wasted time," now it is time's turn to waste him, the king (R2, 5.5.42–50).

But the joyful body knows nothing of this introspection. Regally as spectacle, this body places itself before the "hollow crown" (R2, 3.2.160), as before a stage on which Dario Fo's *Mistero Buffo* of Fame and Death, or—with due Fame-Fashion slippage—of Fashion and Death, as in Giacomo Leopardi's *Dialogue,* are played out.[12] The movement is from a time that comes about in the Beyond History of future life where fame lives perpetually in the shade of faith in Immortality, to a time where no division between hereafter and "herebefore" obtains: the time, that is, of Fashion, where everything must be "Now." In both positions, however—the introspective one of the clock-king who counts his wasted hours on earth, and the extroverted one of the king who becomes a tardy spectator of his own *vanitas*—"the sense of 'divine right' in kings is found to act not so much as a secret of power over others, as of infatuation to themselves."[13]

CURRENCY AND CROWN

The element of "infatuation" brings us back to the character "Richard" and to a region of historical and dramaturgical creativity suspended between *Henry VI, Part Three,* and *Richard III.* In this region, passion for the "golden crown" translates as a materialization of the crown-object: not yet allegorized into the stage or the "deep well" of tears it will be for Richard II in the eponymous play (*R2*, 4.1.184–90), the crown is brought back, in purely materialist terms, to its raw material—gold—either minted as money or worked as a jewel, in both cases acting as trigger to bodily self-contemplation and sensual ecstasy.

In the third *Henry VI*, Richard's cynical materialism fuses the distance between crown and "gay ornaments" (*3H6*, 3.2.149). Unable to procure the one, he will have the others, so as to find his "heaven in a lady's lap" (148). And if the fulfillment of this libertine vow is for the moment "more unlikely / Than to accomplish twenty golden crowns" (151–52), in his own play the successful courtship of Lady Anne will instantly translate into the idea of the looking glass with the desire to "entertain a score or two of tailors / To study fashions to adorn my body" (*R3*, 1.2.256–57). The awareness of his own deformity as an all but unsurmountable bar to sexual satisfaction facilitates the shift toward the crown/coin linkage:

> I'll make my heaven in a lady's lap,
> And deck my body in gay ornaments
> And witch sweet ladies with my words and looks.
> O miserable thought! And more unlikely
> Than to accomplish twenty golden crowns. (*3H6*, 3.2.148–52)

If the twenty golden crowns are neither regal adornments nor jewels, they are at least as many coins: or all these things at the same time.

Wealth adorned by the goldsmith's art, which turns it into a cult object; jewel and gay ornament for the body; hard coin buying beauty and the illusion of immortality: at the moment, the crown is all these things for Richard, and if the time is not yet ripe to wear it, the decisive move has been made, because it is he who succeeds in attracting the crown within the force field of a worldly energy denied to Henry, *roi fainéant* if ever there was one.[14] What has begun is the secular metamorphosis of the crown. From talisman, theological jewel, and ceremonial symbol of a potentially immaterial sovereignty, the crown is now reduced to regality miniaturized, albeit still precious, in the charms on a bracelet;

rerouted toward the lay status of a jewel; made to aspire to the zero degree of the infinitely reproducible object, transporting it to the borderless kingdoms of the souvenir, where it will be translated into a series of postproduced self-quotations.[15]

If a king has two bodies, a crown has many, many more.

POETIC ILLUSION

And, father, do but think
How sweet a thing it is to wear a crown,
Within whose circuit is Elysium
And all that poets feign of bliss and joy. (*3H6*, 1.2.28–31)

For once Richard cajoles his father into the position of taking the crown by force. His father, for his part, is unaware that the rub of his son's suave words lies in that "wear": at a moment that is so decisive for his faction, Richard has reduced the possession of the crown—however legally won or otherwise—to the mundane act of wearing it. Richard describes the act of kingship, once victoriously acquired, as a simple wearing of the crown, adding the detail that what is worn with the regal diadem will be the magnificent fictions of poetry. This has nothing to do with the realpolitik of the war for the succession: Richard's "wearing" of the crown has the irresistible force of poetic illusion.

"And, in truth, the really kingly speeches which Shakespeare assigns to him," notes Pater of Henry V in his play, "as to other kings weak enough in all but speech, are but a kind of flowers, worn for, and effective only as personal embellishment."[16] Richard, who will later be king, is already sufficiently protean—as he himself comments: "I can add colours to the chameleon, / Change shapes with Proteus for advantages" (*3H6*, 3.2.191–92)—to take on the vaguely feminine touch of the Henry who precedes him historically, but textually postdates him in the Shakespearean canon. When his father decides to follow the urging of his sons, renege, and snatch the kingdom prematurely—"Richard, enough. I will be king or die" (*3H6*, 1.2.35)—Richard rushes forward, as his father describes, crying: "A crown, or else a glorious tomb!" (*3H6*, 1.4.16). The concrete precision contains perturbing echoes of the twice-repeated cry of his swan-song in *Richard III*: "A horse! A horse! My kingdom for a horse!" (*R3*, 5.4.7 and 13).

Here, however, it is the old York who has reached his last scene. He is soon to be taken prisoner and decapitated by order, if not by the hand, of the terrifying Queen Margaret who, besides being Henry's wife, is the only character to appear in every play of the tetralogy: "Off with his head and set it on York gates, / So York may overlook the town of York" (*3H6*, 1.4.179–80). The head-chopping queen is the direct ancestor of the one who, three hundred years later, Alice will meet on a croquet lawn. In Lewis Carroll's rewriting of the War of the Roses in board-game format, overzealous gardeners are hastily painting red the roses of a white bush planted by mistake, before the King and Queen discover their mistake and have their heads. In the game version, heads fly off in a second, and just as quickly return to their place: "Off with her head! Off—" orders the Queen of Hearts who, with the King, has strolled out of the pack of cards they both belong to and can't bear to have Alice contradict her. The order remains unfinished: the enfant terrible shuts her up instantly with a well-aimed: "Nonsense!"[17]

PAPER CROWN

No one, however, can silence Queen Margaret—"She-wolf of France, but worse than wolves of France" (*3H6*, 1.4.111)—when, before dealing the final blow, she mocks the duke of York by arousing what she believes to be his erogenous zone, his head, with a paper crown. Yet the physical outrage is quite unable to pierce the carapace of pain that has closed round him when he hears her boast of the torture inflicted on his dying son, his youngest child, by herself and her lover Clifford, to whom, in a far-off time, on separating from him, she had given her heart forever and who had sworn to keep it like "A jewel, locked into the wofull'st cask / That ever did contain a thing of worth."[18]

A festive paper crown is certainly not able to wound York more mortally than having to wipe his eyes with a cloth soaked in the blood of the adolescent Rutland. But the queen's cruelty now backfires. The mock-coronation of him who had haughtily, sacrilegiously declared himself king and is now less than nothing changes on her lips into a blasphemous parody of the Passion:

York cannot speak unless he wears a crown.
A crown for York! And, lords, bow low to him.
Hold you his hands while I do set it on.
[*Puts a paper crown on his head.*]
Ay, marry, sir, now looks he like a king! (*3H6,* 1.4.93–96)

Some ten lines later, head and crown will be off. "Off with the crown and with the crown his head" (*3H6,* 1.4.107). This is all the more inappropriate for the daughter of the man who "bears the type of King of Naples, / Of both the Sicils and Jerusalem" (*3H6,* 1.4.121–22), but the outrage of the paper crown is so bloody, possibly more extreme than the murder itself, as to go beyond the confines of this play and reverberate in that of Richard, where—now considerably closer to the crown of gold—he continues to throw it in her face. The pain and bereavement that has been her lot all derive, he insists, from "The curse my noble father laid on thee / When thou didst crown his war-like brows with paper" (*R3,* 1.3.173–74).

MARGARET

The unhappy Queen Margaret is a poor copy of Richard. In the whole court no one better than she—who scornfully diminishes him to "Dicky"—can understand his unprincipled language and the natural vulgarity of his mind. As a character-type Margaret, too, has few heirs: when Shakespeare writes the third *Henry VI* and *Richard III,* the wheel is turning toward a Puritan internalization of feeling.

Margaret of Anjou—the adulteress arrived from France as bride-to-be to the unwarlike Henry; the daughter of the near-bankrupt Renier, nominal king of Jerusalem and the "Sicils" (*3H6,* 1.4.122)—is sufficiently expert in vulgarity and unhappiness to recognize and embrace the destructive erotic potential of the head-crown short-circuit set in motion by Richard. This is marked by a tiny detail: for both of them the placing of the crown on the head is an act of "paling," with its double sexual connotation of "circling" and "thrusting." "And will you pale your head in Henry's glory / And rob his temples of the diadem / Now, in his life, against your holy oath?" (*3H6*, 1.4.103–5) are her terms of expression for the act of usurpation perpetrated by York senior. "I'll make my heaven to dream upon the crown / And whiles I live t'account this world but hell, / Until my mis-shaped trunk that bears this head / Be round impaled with a glorious crown" (*3H6*, 3.2.168–71) are, conversely, Richard's terms for the long-dreamed rape of the crown. No vulgarity is spared when the crown—whoever is wearing it—enters Margaret's sphere of attraction. Henry still alive, Edward of York, the future Edward IV, sardonically addresses her as to all effects the "King"—"You, that are king, though he do wear the crown" (*3H6*, 2.2.90)—as if to indicate that the crown can be pulled on and off like a pair of trousers.

More clear-sighted than her husband, the unfortunate Henry VI, Margaret understands from the start that the pact of surrender of the throne he has accepted can end in nothing but death. She states this immediately, again with an image involving the head: this time not the ball-head Richard kicked across the floor, but the head of a horse whose reins have been momentarily loosened during a race:

Ah, timorous wretch!
Thou hast undone thyself, thy son, and me;
And given unto the house of York such head
As thou shall reign but by their sufferance.
To entail him and his heirs unto the crown,
What is it, but to make thy sepulcher,
And creep into it far before thy time? (*3H6*, 1.1.231–37)

By opening it to the unbridled horse York, the unwarlike Henry has turned the kingdom into a corral. A racing horse, however, such as that Margaret alludes to, is naturally no ordinary animal. Indeed, horses in general aren't: seldom used in heraldry, horses appear in official portraits of kings and sovereigns to evince their strength and power. The horse is usually linked to aristocratic pomp, of which it is an almost compulsory component within the popular imagination, preparing the way for the modish imitations of the demimonde. A number of celebrated photos show a mounted Coco Chanel with her official lovers, such high society people as Boy Capel, or British aristocrats like the duke of Westminster.

Constitutionally and by dint of her personal history, Queen Margaret belongs to the behind-the-throne aspect of the crown, forerunner of the pseudo-aristocratic demimonde of the nineteenth century, the century when fashion was born in Paris. French by birth, Margaret brings to the court of the Two Roses a sensibility ideally in tune with the bourgeois palpitations of Napoleon III's courtiers, whose skill in the art of conspicuous consumption was to be sanctified by the Great Exhibitions. And since—as Marx, quoting Hegel, famously observed à propos of history's headlong rush that on December 2, 1851, brought Napoleon III to power—all the great events and personalities of history appear twice, the first time as tragedy, the second as farce, in the same way the tragic shadow of the British crown represented in the *Henry VI* sequence by Queen Margaret finds its farcical double in Wallis Simpson, the much-divorced American and queen of England manqué.

WALLIS

Wallis Simpson can be as vulgar as Margaret and as savagely desirous of the crown as Richard. "I shall be queen of England," she had been unable to resist blurting out to Dorothy Cambridge, the wife of one of the duke's cousins, as soon as she received the telegram informing her of George V's serious illness.[19] History wrote a different script. "Naturally Elsie had exquisite taste," commented Diana Vreeland, editor-in-chief of *Vogue* and later special consultant to the Costume Institute of the Metropolitan Museum, whenever the dukes of Windsor and their "increasingly regal" lifestyle came to her mind. Elsie de Wolfe, wife of the press attaché of the British embassy in Paris, had been the duchess of Windsor's consultant in furnishing the Neuilly residence overlooking the

Bois de Boulogne, obtained at a symbolic price from General Charles de Gaulle in 1953 through the good offices of the French government, the same residence Mohamed Al-Fayed would buy for his son Dodi and Princess Diana fifty years later. Neuilly's interior decoration was a reduced regality—a mini-Versailles—and indeed after the duke's death the duchess donated a number of pieces to the royal palace. If Wallis hesitated in front of a particularly important antique, Elsie would encourage her: "Go on! Buy it! Sooner or later it'll come in handy." Clearly, apart from good taste—and again the ultimate source is Vreeland—"Elsie had something which is specifically American. She knew how to appreciate vulgarity."[20]

Vulgarity and vulgarization are, after all, simply accentuated forms of divulgence, and what the Windsors' homes and lifestyle centered on was precisely this: the divulgence of regality at the onset of the new postwar consumer society. This could be read as an early propensity for the ethos of tourism that came into its own in the later twentieth century, with its materialization of symbols as gadgets, amulets for the capacious bags we like to have by us for our perennial, intra- and extraurban, real or virtual traveling.

At Neuilly, the crown is present in the form of a thousand transparent masks: from the gilded crowns beside the entrance lamps to the authentic items from the period of Louis XVI and Marie Antoinette—a high-risk couple if ever there was one—the dispatch box, souvenir of the brief months of his reign, in elegantly distressed red leather with "THE KING" embossed in gold, on display in the entrance hall beside the visitors' book full of prestigious names; the diaphanous nightdress in Wallis-blue silk, the two Ws interwoven in the embroidered monogram on the breast, with above them a crown of regal fleurs-de-lys.[21] At Neuilly, everything speaks of a regality snobbishly (literally *sine nobilitate*) reduced to the level of souvenir, while proclaiming itself as accessible, at least mentally, as a seal of authenticity: " 'You realize,' said the Duke of Windsor to James Pope-Hennessy, 'that there are only three completely royal persons alive now. My sister, my brother and myself.' "[22] And indeed, according to the rigid standards of monarchy, even the blood of Queen Elizabeth II is to be considered somewhat diluted, given that her mother was originally a commoner rather than a royal princess. Pope-Hennessy however—writer, womanizer, and hard drinker—is decidedly less than impressed by Wallis's pseudo-princess-y allure, and would be tempted to class her as The American Woman par excellence, did it not occasionally occur to him to doubt whether she was in fact a woman at all, Wallis too, at times, "stealing the breech" (3H6, 5.5.23–24) from the prince. Wallis the duchess may indeed have had more than an echo of Margaret the queen.[23]

"What a damnable wedding present!" Edward—to his family, David, and now no longer King Edward VIII of England but simply His Royal Highness the Duke of Windsor—had apparently exclaimed on being informed by his brother George VI, on the evening before his wedding, that the woman for whom he had renounced the throne would never be HRH: Her Royal Highness.[24] David knew what store she had set by it, *faute de mieux*—the infinitely *mieux* being of course to be "the queen." Yet there was nothing to be done: so the court had decreed, and so it was to be. Regality remained attached to David-Edward like a second skin, and to the end of his days he would remain His Royal Highness, but Wallis would be addressed as "Her Royal Highness" only within the four domestic walls, where she was paid that homage by her illustrious guests and by her faithful hairdresser Alexandre. In piqued revenge, she had all her purses, six shelves of a precious collection of designer bags, monogrammed with the two intertwined Ws and a golden crown. On New Year's Eve, 1953—the coronation year of the duke's niece Queen Elizabeth II—she took more substantial revenge. The ducal couple honored with their presence the famous Manhattan nightclub El Morocco. At the height of the festivities, among the champagne corks and dancing, ritual favors were distributed, on this occasion small paper crowns. "Bring one for the duke!" the hoarse voice of the duchess was heard to shout. And on the stroke of midnight, as a thousand flashes immortalized the scene, "the coronation's over" she commented somewhat acidly to the photographers.[25]

Yet an infatuation with Shakespeare's kings and their passion for the crown—from which she was hardly exempt herself—must have stayed with her down the years if it is true that in Paris once, during a ball given in her honor by the wife of the owner of the Folies Bergère, someone put a crown of sequins on her head, at which she recited amusedly to an astonished Cecil Beaton, the celebrated line from *Henry IV*: "Uneasy lies the head that wears a crown."[26]

Unless he wear a crown, Margaret mocked. *How sweet a thing it is to wear a crown,* Richard mused. *Uneasy lies the head that wears a crown,* Wallis joked. "To wear" is the verb normally used for both jewelry and general items of clothing. In the rhetoric of sartorial power at the court of Elizabeth I, even with the queen herself, jewels played a large part, even as simple decorations on garments. The new dandy of the late sixteenth century wore velvet breeches on which gold thread would blossom out into small flaming stitches alternating with clusters of pearls. On women, "massive strings of pearls" accentuated the soft circle of the ruff framing their faces. Pearls are to be seen in the hair of the elderly queen in the full-figure portrait by Marcus Gheeraerts the Younger in the National Portrait Gallery in London.[27] The crown, too, is worn as a jewel, simply one that is more significant than all others. No surprise, then, that "to wear a crown," as a formula, recurs throughout *Henry VI, Part Three,* where at one point *two* kings, both nominally in office, outface each other: the anointed Henry of Lancaster—who has very little time left to live—and the self-imposed Edward IV of York. In reality, far more than two heads are actually or potentially crowned in the *Henry VI, Part Three–Richard III* sequence, causing considerable confusion: besides the cowardly Henry, the official king, and Richard of York, king *in pectore,* there are the two Edwards, respectively IV and V; the second one will be king, however briefly, under the "unfashionable" (*R3,* 1.1.22) shadow of his younger brother Richard, the future Richard III, already the ruler in the third *Henry VI.* Over all of them hovers the auratic presence of the Tudor "youth" (*3H6,* 4.6.65), the future Henry VII, who will establish the dynasty of the great Elizabeth, the queen under whose sign Shakespeare is writing. Astonishing, the speed with which his shuttle hurtles its thread between past and present.

Talisman and jewel, object of desire and exchange, the crown accompanies the many nomadic wanderings of *Henry VI, Part Three*: from the court to the various battlefields, from London to Coventry to York. Fortunately, a crown can always be found in the (relatively modest) prop box of an Elizabethan theater company. The list compiled by

Henslowe and Alleyn in 1598 gives: "iii Imperial crownes; i playne crowne."[28] In his capacity as arbiter, Warwick has his work cut out to alternate the crown between Henry and Edward and vice versa:

KING EDWARD Why, Warwick, when we parted
Thou call'dst me King.
WARWICK Ay, but the case is altered:
. . . .

KING EDWARD . . .
Nay, then I see that Edward needs must down.
. . . .

WARWICK [*takes off his crown*] But Henry now shall wear the English crown
And be true king indeed, thou but the shadow. (*3H6*, 4.3.29–50)

The ease of exchange suggests the interchangeability of the heads on which the diadem could rest. The turnover is so rapid as to belie the medieval theory of "the king's two bodies." What is left of it is a fiction, at best a legal hypercorrectness. As a mineral extension of the sovereign body, the jeweled crown manifests, materially as it were, that body's profoundly unitary essence—to the point of consubstantiality—with the unexplored depths of the planet, where the precious materials are found. The wearing of the crown denotes a power extending as far as that demonic netherworld. In his slaving after the crown Richard is, in more than one sense, the "devilish slave" (*R3*, 1.2.90) Lady Anne thinks him to be.

This demonic power is what the slaves in the colonies, like gnomes of the mines, bring up into the sunlight, in the guise of gold, diamonds, rubies, pearls, emeralds: all materials figuring in the design of the variegated crowns available to the ruling dynasty. Henry's inability to resist the temptation of mentally decorating his own crown—however proudly acknowledged as a possession of his heart rather than his head (*3H6*, 3.1.62–64)—with diamonds and Indian stones hints at this geological dimension of kingly power. A memento of the totemic origins of command, the crown seduces through being an object fashioned out of "imperial metal" (*R3*, 4.4.382): a unique metal indeed. Made of such an extraordinary raw material, the crown is, in its very essence, monarchic and imperial rule, and only successively its symbol. As a detached fragment of the immense reserves of imperial metal buried deep in the earth, the crown is simultaneously a particle and a perfectly whole unit of a right of imperium claiming to be one and absolute. This is the reason why it sounds sacrilegious, apart from simply shocking, that Richard should violate the crown with his concrete, material desire, profaning it with a hunger for acquisition that too closely resembles that of the collector of rare pieces.

Richard's fascination with the crown results from the superimposition of the two planes, symbolic and concrete, tied by a knot as difficult to untie as that linking the king's two bodies. This knot underpins Richard's use of "wear": to him alone, among all the pretenders to the crown, is given the capacity for fleshing out the technical expression and externalizing its repressed corporeal component. As the link between the subjective desire for power and power as objectified in the crown, his "wear" is charged with the inborn physicality of both the jewel and the garment, which open the possibility of becoming worn out: alive to the end, though worn by time and fatigue. In their attrition, like human bodies, clothing and jewels learn to become bodies themselves, albeit mute.

Uniqlo, the Japanese fast-fashion chain that occupies a considerable portion of the international low-cost market, states under its site heading Lifestyle Components: "To us, clothes are items the individual chooses to express a personal lifestyle that's exciting and enjoyable. We call this component WEAR." In bringing out the aspects of materiality and caducity incident to the seemingly neutral expression "to wear a crown," in giving individual voice to his own WEAR, in making it the "Component" of a personal, albeit less than exemplary, lifestyle, Richard made a stylistically rash and premature move: he introduced the sacrality of the crown into the fashionistas' territories of costume jewelry.

A jewel, like a garment, is worn in direct contact with the body, the skin, the hair. Sometimes, for more intimate contact, it can be inserted in a deliberately made incision on the surface, as with body piercing or more traditional ear piercing. Beatrjis Lauwaert shaves her hair off and wears her paper crown directly on the newly smooth skin. At other times, the jewel is pinned onto clothing that similarly acts as second skin and has its own places designated to receive these tokens, their design always bearing some more or less direct reference to the traditional symbols of a power that is both temporal and spiritual. Cross, seal, crown, heart: miniaturized into a jewel and worn like a garment, each of these ancestral forms will retain, unbeknownst to the wearer, an element of its sacred and regal origins. Halfway in this process of secularization might be the bracelet with its cross-shaped charms; the crown of rubies above the heart of diamonds and emeralds that the duke gave the duchess for their twentieth wedding anniversary and that she wore till she died; the half-moon powder compact encrusted with a mosaic of precious—Indian?—stones Edward, at the moment *Rex et Imperator*, gave Wallis in December 1936, thus reciprocating the gem-set cigarette case that had been her gift to him the previous Christmas—inscribed "David from Wallis. Christmas 1935"—when he was still Prince of Wales and heir to the throne. On its back, she had had reproduced in enamel a map of their encounters and rendezvous: a mischievous allusion to the solemn map of "The World" marked with the imperial journeys of the Prince of Wales. He took it away with him as a souvenir when he left the court for good, and she later had it hung in his studio in their country house outside Paris.[29]

Historically, as Roland Barthes explained, "as long as wealth regulated the rarity of a gemstone, the latter could be judged by nothing but its price," but in today's world "a widespread liberation of jewelry" has occurred. The copy "is quite open about itself, makes no attempt to deceive, only retaining the aesthetic qualities of the material it is imitating." What is new is that the more jewelry is made out of inexpensive materials, the more it is subjected to the discrimination of style. "No matter how little it costs, the piece of jewelry must be thought about in relation to the whole outfit it accompanies, it must be subjected to that essentially functional value which is that of style." No longer on its own, the piece of jewelry is "one item in a set of links that goes from the body to clothing."[30] Wealth has thus evolved into taste: solidly democratic but decidedly elitist. Yet it would be difficult to object to the crown's jewels as being in bad taste, given that one of their functions was precisely to establish taste. This is the reason why, whether of diamonds or of glass, a piece of jewelry always contains an allusion to dominion. In *The Tempest*, it is said of the king of Naples that "those are pearls that were his eyes" and that "of his bones are coral made," as if to say that even in death, perhaps even more in death, regality claims consanguinity with the precious materials buried in earth and sea.[31] An aspect of regality is still claimed today by pearls and coral, whether real or imitation. Designer bijoux, as testified by the price, signify dominion, neither more nor less than real jewels. Coco Chanel knew all about it: she who, with her legendary mixing of real and fake pearls, paved the way for the use of glass and pinchbeck in the aristocratic empyrean of gold and gems.

"Worn" like any other jewel, the regal crown sets out on the journey that, in the media emphasis on formal events of state, should ultimately promote its metamorphosis into a trinket, as it evolves from miniaturized essence of power into mere allusion to a lifestyle. True, a lifestyle that never loses the atavistic memory of its own sacred origins: never completely expunged, this sacrality can always flare up and turn against a prospective competitor. Just as power is never fully secularized, so the crown will always remain—however remotely—the unsecularized, theological jewel "originated in the ancestral world of the damned" that it is for Shakespeare's English kings.[32] The British crown derives much of its treasure of gems from India, the mythical storehouse of its colonial splendor. When Edward VII made his imperial tour of the subcontinent in 1875, when Edward VIII, still Prince of Wales, retraced his grandfather's footsteps in his legendary eight months' progress aboard the Royal Navy's *Renown*, the maharajahs of Indore, Baroda, Gwalior, Bikaner, and probably scores of other regions vied with each other to literally shower the two royal persons with jewels and precious stones. This was unbounded wealth, not only in realistic but also in ideal terms, precisely because those gems' provenance seemed to signal a power extending over fabulous expanses of time and place, incommensurate with any Western scale. So great was their power of suggestion that they were received as drops of power in the raw.

This may be the reason why the distinction between the jewels personally owned by the sovereign and those owned by the Crown continues to touch a nerve with the Crown's subjects, commoners who have absolutely nothing to gain directly either way. More than by the gems' market value, their imagination is fired by a Marlovian vision of "infinite riches in a little room," materialized, for once, in the "Indian stones" still conserved in the coffers of the Crown.[33] Certainly, in 1921, Edward could not have imagined how many of those stones would go to make up the jewels that, some twenty years on, he would design, melt down, and reset for his beloved and insatiable Wallis. Queen Victoria herself was not immune to the twinkle of precious stones: for her first public appearance to open Parliament after four years of widow's weeds and deepest mourning, she wore the fabulous Koh-i-noor, the five-thousand-year-old diamond donated to her by a Mogul emperor.[34]

But the crown is a harder, more densely significant jewel than even the Koh-i-noor to metamorphose into a trinket, even when worn by a queen. Different degrees of ambiguity are at play. If Margaret's paper crown for old York, as a deliberate desacralization of royal power, contains all the barbaric energy of the crown of thorns, the coronet Queen Victoria bespoke for her "personal use," possibly because irked by the weight of the official jewels, is little more than a piece of costume jewelry in platinum and diamonds.[35] Conversely, the paper crown on Vivienne Westwood's models on her catwalk of 2009–10 takes on the value of a resacralization of haute couture. Seen from another viewpoint though, the crown will manifest an element of trinket frivolity. This element was already active in Richard, for whom the crown was not only an obsession, but also a whim: a fantasy object delicately balanced on the sacred-profane divide, and thus partly a trinket, unknown to him.

Richard wasn't the only one not allowed to pass through the looking glass where the reverse of his optical illusion would have been clear. A number of hints attest to this selective royal blindness, hidden in the folds of various official situations. The elegant circle of diamonds that Elizabeth II wears for the opening of Parliament, for example, contains a bourgeois history of domestic quarrels. Originally it had been among the personal jewels of Princess Alexandra of Denmark, who had married Edward VII, the *boulevardier* king who, at his death, had ordered that his beautiful wife be allowed to keep her favorite pieces; only on the eve of the coronation did she reluctantly hand over to her daughter-in-law, Mary of Teck, the future George V's wife and current queen's grandmother, the precious tiara that today glitters at us on our TV screens from the nave of Westminster Abbey.

Even more to the point: the Windsor jewels might have been expected to go to Prince Charles when he married Diana. This would have been ideal compensation to the heir to the throne for what many observers considered an act of theft, to the detriment of the nation, on the occasion of the abdication. The duchess, however—who in their long years together had been literally covered by the duke in gold and gems considerably exceeding her body weight—did not relent: Wallis refused to hand over anything other than the duke's uniforms and decorations, including the Order of the Garter. It is possible that she never got over the shame of having to appear at an official ball—this was in 1950—wearing on her head merely a sober diamond band, while her beloved David was in full ex-sovereign, ex-emperor regalia. With her relish for jewels, Wallis would have sported a superb diadem, for she was likely, had she been allowed, to have proved most royal; as it happened, the nearest she got to a real crown was this small, though undoubtedly not inelegant, circle.

NOTES

1. William Shakespeare, *Henry VI, Part Three,* 1.1.16. Citations are from *Histories,* ed. Sylvan Barnet, vol. 1 (New York: Alfred Knopf, 1994); references to act, scene, and lines are given in parentheses.

2. A few historical details regarding the succession of English monarchs during the historical period Shakespeare is dramatizing in his English history plays may be of help to the reader of this essay. The years in parentheses are when the monarchs actually reigned.

Richard II (1377–99), the last of the Plantagenets, was the grandson of Edward III (1327–77) and the last king ruling by undisputed hereditary right, in direct line from William the Conqueror. He died childless. In 1399, after a period of social and political unrest caused by his arrogant behavior, he was dethroned by Henry Bolingbroke who reigned as Henry IV. Imprisoned in the Tower of London, Richard died there probably from starvation. As there was no acknowledged rule of succession in the case of failure of the senior male line, his death was followed by a long period of dynastic wars. For the Elizabethans, he was the last truly legitimate king.

Henry IV (1399–1413) was the son of John of Gaunt and the grandson of Edward III. He derived his title from his mother Blanche of Lancaster. He was thus the first king of England from the Lancaster branch of the Plantagenets, the other branch being the York one. The Lancastrians reigned from 1399 to 1461.

Henry V (1413–22) was the son of Henry IV. His military successes in the Hundred Years' War, culminating with his victory at the Battle of Agincourt, brought him close to conquering France. The treaty of Troyes recognized him as regent and heir apparent to the French throne. He married Catherine of Valois, the daughter of the French king. His sudden and unexpected death, at the age of thirty-five, brought to the throne his infant son Henry VI.

Henry VI (1422–61 and 1470–71) succeeded his father at the age of nine months. Two months later, upon his grandfather Charles VI's death, he became king of France, in accordance with the treaty of Troyes. In the years between his reigns as king of England (1461–1470), the crown passed to the York branch of the Plantagenets. Henry's pious and benevolent character and periodic bouts of insanity made him unfit to reign, let alone to take control of the Wars of the Roses, which saw the throne pass back and forth between the rival houses of Lancaster and York. While Henry was a minor, a regency council was formed by his paternal uncles, John, duke of Bedford, and Humphrey, duke of Gloucester. In 1437, at sixteen, Henry was declared of age, and in 1445 he married Margaret of Anjou (Queen Margaret), the daughter of the king of Naples and the niece of Charles VII's queen consort, Marie of Anjou. Henry and Margaret's only son, Edward of Westminster, Prince of Wales, was killed by his cousin Edward, duke of York. In 1461, after a violent struggle, Henry VI was deposed and imprisoned by Edward of York, who reigned as King Edward IV.

Edward IV (1461–70 and 1471–83) was the first Yorkist king of England. He finally overcame the Lancastrians at Tewksbury in 1471. In 1464, he married Elizabeth Woodville (Queen Elizabeth), from whom he had ten children.

Edward V (April–June 1483), son of Edward IV, was assassinated (probably smothered) in the Tower of London at the age of twelve.

Richard III (1483–85), the son of Richard Plantagenet, duke of York, was the last Yorkist king of England. The dynasty of the Plantagenets ended with him. Killed in the battle of Bosworth Field, which ended the Wars of the Roses, Richard was succeeded by Henry Tudor, the initiator of the Tudor dynasty.

Henry VII (1485–1509), the son of Edmund Tudor, first earl of Richmond, derived his claim to the throne from his mother, Lady Margaret Beaufort, a great-grandaughter of John of Gaunt, duke of Lancaster and third son of Edward III. He married Elizabeth of York, the daughter of Edward IV. Though his claim to the throne was tenuous, Henry VII—the last king of England to win his throne on the battlefield—was successful in restoring the power and stability of the English monarchy and was peacefully succeeded by his son Henry VIII, the father of Queen Elizabeth I.

Shakespeare's English history plays reflect the nationalism of England under Queen Elizabeth. They were not composed chronologically. Shakespeare entered history "backwards," beginning from the more recent events and proceeding toward an in-depth examination of the past. Shakespeare's Histories fall into two tetralogies, covering the period from Richard II's deposition in 1399 to Henry VII's accession in 1485. To them should be added Shakespeare's last play, *Henry VIII*, performed at the Globe Theatre in 1613.

Shakespeare wrote the "second" (in terms of linear history) tetralogy first (*Henry VI, Parts 1, 2, 3* in 1589–90 and *Richard III* in 1591) and the first one second (*Richard II* in 1595, *Henry IV, Parts 1 and 2* in 1597–98, and *Henry V* in 1599).

3. Beatrijs Lauwaert, e-mail to author, March 5, 2010.

4. Quoted in Scott Manning Stevens, "Sacred Heart and Secular Brain," in *The Body in Parts: Fantasies of Corporeality in Early Modern Europe*, ed. David Hilman and Carla Mazzio (New York: Routledge, 1997), 269–70.

5. William Shakespeare, *The Merchant of Venice*, 3.2.63–64; references from *Comedies*, ed. Sylvan Barnet, vol. 2 (London: David Campbell, 1996).

6. William Shakespeare, *Richard III*, 1.1.22; references are from *Histories*, ed. Barnet, vol. 1.

7. Suzy Menkes, *The Windsor Style* (Topsfield, Mass.: Salem House, 1988), 150–51, and Suzy Menkes, *The Royal Jewels* (1985; repr. London: Grafton, 1988) have contributed to my thinking.

8. Menkes, *The Royal Jewels*, 245.

9. Stevens, "Sacred Heart and Secular Brain," 264.

10. Ernst H. Kantorowicz, *The King's Two Bodies: A Study in Medieval Political Theology* (1957; repr. Princeton: Princeton University Press, 1997).

11. Walter Pater, "Shakespeare's English Kings" [1889], in *Appreciations: With an Essay on Style* (London: MacMillan, 1920), 199, 186.

12. "The Dialogue of Fashion and Death" (1824) is one of Leopardi's *Moral Tales*.

13. Pater, "Shakespeare's English Kings," 197.

14. Ibid., 190.

15. Roland Barthes, "From Gemstones to Jewellery," in *The Language of Fashion*, ed. Anthony Stafford and Michael Carter (Oxford: Berg, 2006), 59–64.

16. Pater, "Shakespeare's English Kings," 190.

17. Lewis Carroll, *Alice's Adventures in Wonderland* (1865; repr. Harmondsworth: Penguin, 1994), 95.

18. William Shakespeare, *Henry VI, Part Two*, 3.2.410–11; quotation from *Histories*, ed. Barnet, vol. 1.

19. Menkes, *The Royal Jewels*, 96.

20. Menkes, *The Windsor Style*, 16.

21. Ibid., 48.

22. Ibid., 34.

23. Ibid., 78.

24. Menkes, *The Royal Jewels*, 97.

25. Menkes, *The Windsor Style*, 90–91.

26. Ibid., 92. William Shakespeare, *Henry IV, Part Two*, 3.1.31; quotation from *Histories*, ed. Sylvan Barnet, vol. 2 (New York: Alfred Knopf, 1994).

27. Christopher Breward, *The Culture of Fashion* (Manchester: Manchester University Press, 1995), 58, 50–51.

28. Andrew Gurr, *The Shakespearian Stage, 1574–1642* (Cambridge: Cambridge University Press, 2009), 230.

29. Menkes, *The Windsor Style*, 58–59, 190–91.

30. Barthes, "From Gemstones to Jewellery," 62–63.

31. William Shakespeare, *The Tempest*, 1.2.397–99; quotation from *Romances*, ed. Sylvan Barnet (London: Everyman's Library, 1996).

32. Barthes, "From Gemstones to Jewelry," 62.

33. Christopher Marlowe, *The Jew of Malta*, 1.1.37 in *The Complete Plays*, ed. by J. B. Steane (Harmondsworth: Penguin, 1969).

34. Menkes, *The Royal Jewels*, 89–93.

35. Ibid., 18.

4

EARRINGS IN AMERICAN LITERATURE
A SHOWCASE

Cristina Giorcelli

> *My jewelry represents first of all an idea.*
>
> COCO CHANEL

Women have always devoted careful attention to the embellishment of their face. Cosmetics correct the face's imperfections, exalting the color of eyes, lips, and cheeks, and dyes change the color of its frame (hair). Ears beautify the face by providing the proper support for earrings. Close to the face, earrings are immediately visible and create the illusionistic effect of modifying its bone structure (a roundish face will profit from drop earrings; a longish face, from roundish clasp or stud earrings) or of intensifying its colors.[1]

As the language of jewels is "uncommonly fascinating and versatile," in the case of earrings the relationship among color, form, and material is particularly intriguing.[2] Whether made by baroquely intertwined or severely geometrical strings of metals and/or studded with gems, earrings complement the face by adding an inorganic and mineral touch to the softness of skin and hair. In the *Dolce Stil Novo* songs, precious stones often compete with the woman's beauties, thus implying a struggle between the inanimate and the animate.

Pearl earrings may enhance the whiteness of teeth; coral ones may add to the color of lips and cheeks; when made of jet or onyx they may underline the color of dark eyes, or blue eyes when made of sapphires or aquamarines, or green eyes when made of emeralds, or, when made of amethysts, violet eyes, like the celebrated ones of Elizabeth Taylor. Princess Cristina di Belgiojoso, the Italian Risorgimento patriot, who was rich, beautiful, intelligent, and audacious, used to emphasize the darkness of her eyes and hair and contrast the pallor of her skin by wearing, as jewelry, only black bead earrings and black bead necklaces.[3] Even earrings made of gold, silver, or platinum can enliven the face and make it more luminous: women with black hair and dark eyes often choose gold, whereas Nordic beauties underline their opalescent skin and blue eyes with white gold or silver or platinum.

Because what is near the face is likely to be scrutinized with attention, earrings are often very carefully made. Indeed, their "limited size is an invitation to precision and excellence."[4] Earrings are a special kind of jewelry—or jewellery: the word's double spelling betrays, perhaps, its subtly tortuous history.[5] Its etymology comes from the Latin: either from "gaudium" (joy) or from "jocale" (plaything). In both cases, jewels are thus to be considered sources of blissful entertainment. Similarly, the spelling in English of this ornament is mobile and flexible like the ornament itself—it may be "ear-rings" or "earrings" or "ear rings."

According to Richard Klein, "An earring is the purest, vainest, most ephemeral jewel, the one that most closely resembles the airy breath of talk. Earrings talk in the ear. A woman chooses her earrings as a function of what she most wants whispered in her ear."[6] He goes on, "Wearing a ring in the ear tells the world that you like to listen to the sound of your own voice. You want to hear it first! . . . Putting on an earring is a form of seductive narcissism."[7] In his poem "Earrings Dangling and Miles of Desert," Gary Snyder draws attention to Artemisia's/sagebrush's "blue-gray-green" dangling earrings to associate the goddess of the wilderness (Artemis) with the sounds of nature, that is, with knowledge gained through hearing.[8]

As the only kind of jewelry that, when not clasped or attached with a screw, cannot simply be slipped on a part of the body, but necessitates the drawing of blood and thus the infliction of some pain, earrings have a particular characteristic: besides their beautifying virtues, they become a permanent part of the body. If this operation of entering the body emphasizes possession, piercing the lobes is also an apotropaic act: it seemingly wards off bad luck. As Klein has observed, such an act is often considered a rite of passage to mark the end of childhood. Piercing can also be "seen as sacrilegious, a crime against the handiwork of the Lord. Leviticus says: 'You will make no incisions on your flesh, nor will you imprint figures on you.' No piercing, no tattooing. Jews who are tattooed can't be buried in Orthodox cemeteries. To pierce or prick the body intentionally is a form of rivalry with God."[9]

In addition, as G. F. W. Hegel had surmised, piercing also shows human beings' wish not "to remain the way nature made them," but to change/improve themselves according to their tastes, capacities, possibilities.[10] Furthermore, in popular sayings, puncturing the earlobe benefits eyesight. For this reason, acupuncturists consider the earlobe related to vision. Finally, the ear is also a site of fetishism. In the 1950s, Ernest Hemingway underwent a sort of earring crisis when, against his wife Mary's judgment, he wanted to have his ears pierced in order to become a member of the Wakamba tribe in Africa.[11]

Earrings are worn for a number of reasons: to show one's personality, out of vanity, or to pay homage to conventions. Like other jewels, they exist "for pleasure, seduction, and power over others."[12] If, Klein observes, jewels are a form of altruism as their beauty is a gift to the beholder, earrings, while enhancing the wearer's beauty, implicitly submit the beholder to *their* beauty.[13]

From the classical period to the nineteenth century, depending on the precious metals/stones of which they were made, on their shapes, and on the artistry of their manufacture, earrings also revealed status. This is because wearing jewels "was still determined by rules that prescribed when, on what occasion and in what manner a particular piece of jewellery was supposed to be worn. Married women distinguished themselves from unmarried ones with the aid of jewellery."[14] Like other items of jewelry, earrings also stood for special people and memorable moments in the wearer's life.

In ancient cultural traditions, each birthday was believed to be influenced by its appropriate constellation, and each stone had a symbolic meaning, often even a therapeutic value. Relatives and friends would gather at the birth of a baby girl to present, like the good fairies, the newborn with the appropriate gem. The life of a woman from an important family would be punctuated by such recurrences and such objects would then be part of her dowry. In many Mediterranean countries, after her husband's death his widow will wear small round black bead earrings to signify that her mourning will last forever.

Although Simmel claimed that jewelry was the first form of property possessed by women, in antiquity earrings were also worn by men: in Persia, for instance, but also in Europe. William Shakespeare is shown wearing a round earring in a painting attributed to John Taylor, and John Donne wears an earring in the form of a cross in the famous painting by Nicholas Hilliard (or Isaac Oliver). At the beginning of the twentieth century, Ezra Pound, while in London, wore an earring.[15] Until a couple of centuries ago, earrings were commonly worn by sailors, often in the form of hoops. These earrings may have meant that the wearer had sailed around the world or that he had crossed the equator. If a sailor had survived a sinking ship, it was believed that he would often wear one earring in the left ear; finally, according to some, sailors would wear earrings because if their ship was wrecked and their bodies ended up onshore, the person who found them would take their earrings as payment for a Christian burial. For this reason, as they were known to be superstitious, sailors would spend large sums of money on gold earrings. But sailors are also transgressive figures, and earrings worn by males were often associated with sexual transgression.

Earrings have been in fashion since the beginning of recorded time. In the Bible, when Rebecca received the servant of Isaac and gave water to him and his camels, he gave her a gold earring (together with bracelets) because he had recognized in the woman to whom the Lord had led him the proper wife for his master: the mother of a race. The Metropolitan Museum in New York displays a colossal marble head of Athena (ca. 200 BCE), whose ears are pierced for metal earrings. But earrings, as objects that stand for *charis* (charm, loveliness, favor) and for *abrosyne* (refinement), were often attributed to

the paramount wife and mother, Hera, or to Aphrodite. In *Iliad* 14, Hera wishes to seduce Zeus and have him fall asleep so that she can wreak havoc on the Trojans. Thus she dresses beautifully; to the other ornaments, minutely described, she adds a pair of earrings: "in her pierced ears she put ear-rings with three clustering drops."[16] In the fifth Homeric Hymn, Aphrodite is described as wearing "her bright jewelry of pins and twisted brooches and earrings."[17]

In ancient Rome, Cornelia, the mother of the Gracchis, may have prophetically had earrings in mind when, referring to her sons, she said that they were her "jewels." In effect, the two of them had symmetrically tragic destinies.[18] Earrings fell into disuse during the Middle Ages, due to women's imposing headgear that entirely covered their ears. But from the Renaissance to current times earrings have been in fashion. At the end of

FIGURE 4.2 Marble head of Athena (right profile). Greek, ca. 200 BCE. Marble, 19 inches in height (48.26 cm). Purchase, Lila Acheson Wallace Gift, 1996 (1996.178). The Metropolitan Museum of Art, New York, New York, United States. Copyright the Metropolitan Museum of Art. Image source: Art Resource, NY.

the nineteenth century, two different types of earrings became fashionable: in the 1870s they often consisted of small diamond studs, and in the 1890s dangling ones were mostly worn after various methods of fastening them on the ear (especially with a screw behind the lobe) were invented to replace the hook.

The simplest traditional earrings are hoops. Similar to hoops are crescents: hoops that are thicker at the bottom so as to resemble the crescent moon, a recurrent symbol in the Arab world. Hoops are distinctive in the attire of the Roma (so-called gypsies, whose origins were in Egypt), so that women who do not belong to this ethnic group and yet wear them implicitly accept being seen as defiant, Andalusian Carmens, as in Georges Bizet's opera. The other most common, though far more elaborate, type of shape for earrings is the girandole that consists of a stone set in a precious metal from which hang three stones. Should one be inclined to sociological generalizations, one might say that "the girandole . . . was fashionable . . . as women became significantly independent of men—a sign of the more ambitiously articulated speech they wanted to hear in their ear."[19]

Each epoch has its preferred earring shapes, stones, and settings. In the 1950s clasp earrings were the vogue. During the Roaring Twenties, the revolutionary 1960s and 1970s, and from the disquieting 1990s to the present, women have been prone to wearing drop earrings. By dangling, the long pendants provide the face with shades that add depth to its expression and mimicry. Their perpetual movement (and, at times, slight jingle) may allude to the mutability of human life, the heart, and especially the psyche, and therefore to the instability and capriciousness, to the plays of fancy that women, according to convention and tradition, embody and perform. As a consequence, if women wear long earrings, they may implicitly declare their wish to break the rules, to give importance to their freedom, to reinvent themselves at each nod of their head. More than other pieces of jewelry that are quite static, earrings thus talk.

In a necessarily panoramic overview of the presence of earrings in American literary texts from the last decades of the nineteenth century to the present, one must attend to minute references and innuendoes. Compared to other accessories or even to other jewels, earrings may not loom large in these texts: for this very reason, however, they are usually significant.

While in Biarritz, Henry James seems to have absorbed the nearby Spanish atmosphere when he employed some of the topoi of the picturesque: "You can see here and there a trellis and an orange-tree, a peasant-woman in a gold necklace, driving a donkey, a lame beggar adorned with earrings."[20] Though the shape of these earrings is not mentioned, the context (place and condition) suggests that they were probably hoops. James's balanced style requires that both human presences be characterized by jewelry. He endows the man's physical and social disability with earrings possibly to indicate that he is also a racial outcast (a gypsy perhaps?).

At the outset of James's *The Europeans* (1878), Eugenia, Baroness Munster, has gone to the United States with the intention of restoring her fortunes by marrying a rich man.

She is described as possessing "a great abundance of crisp dark hair, finely frizzled, which was always braided in a manner that suggested some Southern or Eastern, some remotely foreign, woman." Her defining characteristic, however, is this: "She had a large collection of ear-rings, and wore them in alternation; and they seemed to give a point to her Oriental or exotic aspect."[21] Although their shape is not specified, the reference may be to large, dangling ones. It will not, therefore, come as a surprise that in the end the baroness, whose father—to add another touch of exotic danger—was born in Sicily (of American parents), will return unmarried to Europe: she is mistrusted by her prospective husband because she is too "remotely foreign" and too much of a liar and a manipulator (in other words, too European or, rather, too much of a Southern European), as implied in the insistence on her distinctive traits, both in her appearance and in her jewelry.[22] Significantly, in a narrative that juxtaposes Europeans (though of American descent) to Americans, numerous references are made to the Orient: Felix, the baroness's cosmopolitan brother, thus comments on the sky near Boston, "[It] is just like Cairo; and the red and blue sign-boards patched over the face of everything remind one of Mahometan decorations" (884); the baroness's American cousin, Gertrude Wentworth, who in the end will marry Felix, not by chance—to forebode the encounter of twin souls—when she first meets him is reading the *Arabian Nights* (894); the baroness herself is said to behave like the Queen of Sheba (898); and the American Robert Acton, who might have married the baroness, lived for many years in China (942). To underline both how different Europeans (who are geographically closer to "the Orient") appear to these well-traveled Americans and how, nevertheless, attracted by these Europeans Americans are, an aura of exoticism pervades the narrative—to which earrings lend the finishing touch.

Again, in James's "The Middle Years" (1893), a secondary, but not unimportant character, a countess who commands the devotion of a young doctor (the novel's coprotagonist), is presented as a massive woman, who looks "vulgar" as she wears "dirty gauntlets" and "immense diamond ear-rings."[23] Nothing more is said of the shape of these earrings: their size loudly bespeaks their cost. As one proceeds in the narrative, one discovers that the countess is the daughter of a baritone (perhaps, Italian?) "whose taste, without his talent, she had inherited."[24] When, "ignorant and passionate" as she is, she discovers that her young doctor spends part of his time with a writer whose novel, *The Middle Years*, he highly regards, she disowns him out of jealousy. Though "generous" and "independent," she is an "eccentric," possessed with "the morbid strain of a violent and aimless will" (343). Her "immense diamond ear-rings" are thus an indication of both her inordinate power and narcissistic lack of generosity.

In James's *Wings of the Dove* (1902), Maud Lowder, Kate Croy's clever and bold aunt, plans a great match for her niece, whom she wants to rescue from poverty. Maud is first presented as a woman with a "prodigious" personality, a veritable "lioness": "majestic, magnificent, high-coloured, all brilliant gloss, perpetual satin, twinkling bugles and shining gems."[25] To complete this gaudy portrait, she is seen as "colossally vulgar" (267). Not by chance Kate names her "Britannia of the Market Place . . . with a pen on her ear" (237). If for Merton Densher, her niece's poor and secret lover, her house speaks of her by "writing out for him . . . the associations and conceptions, the ideals and possibilities of the mistress" (268), her accessories are equally eloquent. At a crucial moment in the narrative, she sits with "her knees apart, not unlike a picturesque ear-ringed matron at a market-stall" (489–90). As she has been associated with commerce from the outset, in this scene, while talking with Susan Stringham, she foresees the possibility of getting rid of Merton Densher by concocting a sort of barter: she will do her best to make him available for the rich heiress Milly Theale, who likes him very much, and thus free her niece. In a novel where almost everybody ends up by deceiving or being deceived by everybody else's cleverness, Maud examines the situation (she has just been told that Milly's doctor wants her to be happy if she wants to go on living) and, like an "ear-ringed" reader of tarots "at a market stall," she envisions a rearrangement of the young people in question. Her earrings are only virtual, but they are the accessory that defines the woman whom Susan sees as an "oracle" (494). In each of these instances, James intends the earrings to show that the characters wearing them lack grace and that their class, sociologically or psychospiritually, is low.

At the beginning of the twentieth century, in the sophisticated and exclusive world of the American expatriates in Paris, famous were the hoops worn by Alice B. Toklas.

Not a beauty and with an upper lip adorned with the shadow of a moustache, she gave herself an exotic air by wearing "gypsy" earrings.[26] As Mabel Dodge describes her, "Alice Toklas ... had a drooping, Jewish nose, and her eyelids drooped ... and the lobes of her ears dropped under the black, folded Hebraic hair, weighted down ... with long, heavy Oriental earrings."[27] Alice's earrings are thus preceded by an insistence on adjectives that refer to her ethnic origins ("Jewish," "Hebraic," "Oriental") and on verbs that through her physical appearance ("drooping," "drooped") anticipate her earrings' shape ("dropped"): they are dangling. Visitors to the Rue de Fleurus couple would often comment on such an adornment. In *The Autobiography of Alice B. Toklas* (1933), even Pablo Picasso is said to see her as someone characterized by "small feet like a Spanish woman and earrings like a gypsy."[28]

In 1914, Djuna Barnes, who lived the spirit of the age with great independence and defiance, in her story "The Terrible Peacock" figuratively captures what earrings stand for. The protagonist (the title's "Peacock") is a "slinky female with electrifying green eyes and red hair, dressed in clinging green-and-blue-silk," who wears "tiny shoes, trim and immaculate; above them a glimpse of thin, green stockings on trimmer ankles."[29] She has fascinated a reporter who, obsessed by her beauty, wants to find out who she is. While his girlfriend metonymically comes to his mind when he sees "a pair of jet earrings dancing before him," memories of the Peacock overlap: "beneath them [the earrings], as the periods beneath double exclamation points, floated a pair of green boots" (32). Indeed, pendants may look like exclamation points that pinpoint a life full of surprises and/or in search of surprises. Because the journalist sees the woman's whole attire as a *written* language (complete with punctuation), it is not by chance that he sees earrings as (black) exclamation marks and boots as (green) dots under them, thus recalling the fashionable art nouveau dangling earrings made, in fact, of onyx and jade.

Especially in the 1920s, with the Jazz Age, earrings became very important; and, among them, pendants enjoyed great popularity. Women started acting more like men: they smoked, drank, dated, drove cars, cut their hair short. As they tended to be slim, their body vanished behind the shimmer of silk and *crêpe Georgette*. The accent was thus on accessories: on their art deco design (often featuring geometrical lines) and their extravagant luxury.[30] In those very years, however, new, less expensive materials such as Bakelite, celluloid, or wood began being widely employed in jewelry. They gave rise to fashion jewelry that started its never-yet-declining course, allowing women of all social and economic conditions to own it. One has but to think of the fake pearls brought to the public's insatiable appetite for jewelry by Coco Chanel in 1924. In addition, with their hair cut "à la garçonne," women, depriving themselves of what St. Paul had called their "crowning glory," had to fill the gap between the bob and the shoulders: earrings did just that and echoed the vertical lines of their dresses adding "a touch of frivolity and femininity to the new masculine look," since they often were made of colorful enamels and/or semiprecious gemstones.[31]

In a 1922 article titled "Eulogy on the Flapper," Zelda Fitzgerald lists earrings as an indispensable ornament for the "flapper." As she comments, "the Flapper awoke from her lethargy of sub-deb-ism, bobbed her hair, put on her choicest pair of earrings and a great deal of audacity and rouge and went into the battle." And afterward she insists, "Now audacity and earrings and one-piece bathing suits have become fashionable."[32] For the New Woman, who conceived of life as a battle that could be contested and won, a moral quality like audacity and an accessory like earrings were a sine qua non: they would pierce their lobes, but also the conformism and philistinism of bourgeois conventions. Such long earrings were what she needed: a stylish and precious weapon—like a pair of spears.

In Willa Cather's *A Lost Lady* (1923), the protagonist, the seductive and intriguing Mrs. Marian Forrester, wears brilliant earrings. Niel, the young man who falls in love with her, "liked to see the firelight sparkle on her earrings, long pendants of garnets and seed-pearls in the shape of fleurs-de-lys. She was the only woman he knew who wore earrings; they hung naturally against her thin, triangular cheeks."[33] These earrings, which had belonged to her husband's mother (38), have a "sparkle," are red ("garnets"), and feature an unusual shape ("fleurs-de-lys").[34] They thus signal the uniqueness of the wearer's vivacious and nonconformist personality (the word used to illustrate their shape is French). On another occasion Marian wears a pair of diamond earrings that "swung beside her pale cheeks." In effect, "her husband had archaic ideas about jewels; a man bought them for his wife in acknowledgment of things he could not gracefully utter. They must be costly; they must show that he was able to buy them, and that she was worthy to wear them" (49). In other words, earrings are a reward gained by a wife for performing her duties well. At the last grand dinner that Marian is holding at her house for the young men whom she is patronizing, she is again wearing "long earrings" that "swung beside the thin cheeks that were none the better, he thought, for the rouge she had put on them" (154). Given her cheerful, strong, and optimistic personality and the fact that she takes life and what it offers without too many qualms or scruples, her wearing long earrings may indicate an easygoing attitude that is as charming as it is infuriating for the conformist Niel.

For Cather, houses and architectural structures often carry symbolic meanings; in this novel she writes that the house in which Marian lives, "stripped of its vines and denuded of its shrubbery would probably have been ugly enough" (8). Because Marian has "thin, triangular cheeks," without her earrings her face too might have been "ugly enough." With regard to women who choose pendants, Marian, the teaser, betrayer, and potential lover of the young and innocent man, with her indomitable spirit—by having inherited "the magic of contradictions" (75) and having "preferred life on any terms" (161)—is the right character for these earrings.

Given their mercurial quality, earrings have often attracted American poets. Emily Dickinson more than once ponders them. In poem 397, she writes:

When Diamonds are a Legend,
And Diadems—a Tale—
I Brooch and Earrings for Myself,
Do sow, and Raise for sale—[35]

Diamond earrings' splendor, their levity, their butterfly-like shades of colors, the artistic ability needed to mount and set them, and their preciousness are celebrated in this and in the following stanza. Their being a pair may also be indicated by the alliteration of the long "a" sound at the end of line 4, followed by a dash to allow for the echo to be heard and absorbed through the sonic texture.

Poem 289, titled "The Lonely House," published in 1890, renders the sense of creeping wonder and odd surprise (stressed by several alternating "where" and "there") felt by two intruders in an abandoned house at night:

> There's plunder—where—
> Tankard, or Spoon—
> Earring—or Stone—[36]

Notice how singular all the objects are, including the earring that generally requires a twin. But, as this item of jewelry has belonged to a "Grandmama" (as specified in the same stanza), in time one of them may have gotten lost or stolen by previous burglars. To the random (and seemingly scattered) kitchen utensils, a few more precious pieces of jewelry are added in the lines that follow. If the "earring" is made of "stone," it may emphasize either the hard or the once comfortable (if the stone is precious) life of the house's inhabitants (an "old Couple").

In a poem from *Tender Buttons* (1914) titled "Book," Stein writes, "Suppose ear rings, that is one way to breed, breed that."[37] As with almost all the poems in this collection the meaning of these words eludes easy interpretation or even paraphrase, because the author plays with language—or muscles the language—to create puns, metaphors, distortions, and even moments of catachresis that compel readers to think about the language per se, not as a vehicle that carries a specific meaning. In effect, she wants her readers to meditate on semantics and look at words in their physicality (shape and sound) in order to induce a less unconscious, mechanical use of language and undermine shared linguistic conventions. In this instance, she splits the word "earrings" into its components and thus turns it into a noun + a verb (a recurrent stylistic characteristic of this volume), and so, perhaps, she hints at something unexpected. In idiomatic usage, an ear that rings indicates that, all of a sudden, somebody is thinking of the person whose ear it is, who, in turn, thinks of him/her. Now, considering that the following "breed" means either rearing or copulating and it is used mostly to refer to animals, when one's ear is ringing it may make one think of somebody and, perhaps, give rise to a mad (beastly?) desire to have a sexual encounter with him/her. Thus, not extravagantly, earrings are connected with sex appeal.

In an untitled poem, Robert Frost, who gave earrings to his lover—the married Kay Morrison, who never divorced or left her husband—played with the word's phonetics and bitterly (he was always very jealous of her) punned by associating "earring" with "erring." After announcing that her (betrayed) "husband" had given her "a ring" (the sign of a bond, fidelity, and virtue, and, should it have featured a diamond, a symbol of perfection, strength, and durability), the speaking voice informs that "But the fellow to whom I'm referring / He gave her an earring for erring."[38] Contrary to the "ring," the "earring" (it is singular, but, because of the two "r"s, it is a sort of *reinforced* "ring") signifies sin for her lover (just as betrayed because of the ambiguous situation they live in). Both men are pathetic, but the earring's giver is even more so as he does not have a status: he is an anonymous "fellow," who, reiterated as "He" in the following line, stands out in his hopeless gullibility as the ultimate dupe.

In "I went into the Maverick Bar" (1974), Gary Snyder compares his Oregon of the 1950s with present-day New Mexico, where travelers—possibly in order not to end up like the protagonists of the movie *Easy Rider* (1969)—appear in public disguising their attire that might show their belonging to a rebellious generation.[39] The speaker affirms: "My long hair was tucked up under a cap / I'd left the earring in the car." These minute elements ("long hair" and "earring") are sufficient to signify a code of behavior that parochial America does not tolerate. But the innocent, rural America of two decades earlier survives in present New Mexico if, in a moment of nostalgia, the speaking voice addresses his country and confesses, "I could almost love you again." The shape of the solitary earring is not specified, although one can guess it is round and pierces the wearer's ear according to the unwritten language of youthful clothing and the nonconformist male accessories of the time.

In a later, delightful poem, "To All the Girls Whose Ears I Pierced Back Then," the sexual meaning of the act of ear-piercing is all too obvious as a girl stands

. . . with clothespins
dangling, setting a bloodless dimple in each lobe
as I searched for a cork & the right-sized needle
& followed the quick pierce with a small gold hoop.
The only guy with an earring.[40]

If this poem sings the rite of sexual initiation and as such is the contemporary version of the love poem that used to employ the sonnet form—here the sonnet is set in two stanzas of seven lines each—the earring serves its purpose: the vocabulary explicitly or indirectly, even by negation, suggests love's pains ("clothespins," "bloodless," "needle," "pierce"). All this happens at a time when the sexual act is performed casually and indiscriminately: as indicated by the poem's epigraph, "for Maggie Brown Koller (among others)," as well as by both the use of a demotic language and the twice-used commercial "&." The only sign of communion between the young girl and the young man who is performing the act of piercing is that both of them seem to wear just one "earring," a singularity that, under such circumstances, is *doubly* expressive.

In 1956, Richard Wilbur wrote the lyrics for Leonard Bernstein's musical *Candide*. One of the songs, "Glitter and Be Gay," is sung by Cunegonde, the young woman who, at the cost of her virtue, lives in luxury and pleasure. But while she wonders whether "Pearls and ruby rings . . . / Ah, how can worldly things / Take the place of honor lost?" immediately afterward, while she puts on her jewelry, she sings: "I rather like a twenty-carat earring, ah ah! / If I'm not pure, at least my jewels are!"[41] If the words serve the purpose of creating a mocking lyricism, the music aptly underlines, with verve, the joking, picaresque atmosphere of this comedy. Cunegonde seems to embody the Marilyn Monroe song "Diamonds Are a Girl's Best Friend." In essence, this is how the musical interprets Voltaire's philosophy.

In Lawrence Ferlinghetti's long (196 lines) visionary 1967 pastoral "After the Cries of the Birds," "guitarists with one earring" appear.[42] Since the eulogy is for the city of San Francisco, capital of the Beat Generation, these "guitarists" immediately recall the artistic and rebellious culture of the late 1960s. Because these "guitarists" evoke Spaniards and Spanish culture, the earring may be the round loop, worn then by those who resisted the status quo.

Charles Bukowski, who rejected all sorts of conformism and disregarded the rules of both polite diction and punctuation, wrote a beautiful poem, "the strangest sight you ever did see," about a racially mixed couple (he is white, she is black) looking for a room to rent in the South:

> she was simply beautiful
> in turban
> long green earrings
> yellow dress.[43]

While we know that the man's pants are "about to / fall from his / ass" and his face is "pinked by the sun and / cheap wine," she looks majestic and stunning. The two complementary colors ("green" and "yellow") of her earrings and dress, while exalting the sheen of her black skin, seem to envelop and isolate her in her perfection. She walks "upright," and "indifferent" to the brutality surrounding her. The earrings, highlighting her face, framed by the turban, make it stand out in a dull and mean world. In Bukowski's poetry, so often devoted to the celebration of mercenary love, earrings frequently return as the proper ornament of prostitutes. In "a man's woman," for instance, we read that "the dream of a man" is a prostitute with a gold tooth, a garter belt, false eyebrows, mascara, and "earrings." After listing all that this woman has to do for him, the speaking voice obdurately concludes:

> just stay one week
> . . .
> and do the thing and go and never come
> back
> for that one earring on the dresser.[44]

The singular earring at the end serves the purpose of underlining the overall, ultimate, and *piercing* squalor.

Another of Bukowski's poems, "this is the way it goes and goes and goes," ends:

so, in the best interest of us all
wave goodbye . . .
as white ladies in pink rooms put on
blue and green earrings,
wave goodbye to me.[45]

The profusion of colors (white, blue, green) and the "pink rooms" seem to indicate that, again, the woman whom the speaking voice is addressing is a prostitute in a brothel. While she and her colleagues are treated with the usual brutality, their showy earrings are seen as *the* necessary accessory of their métier. These earrings are of *two* strong colors, with no further connotation, and are worn by "white ladies," on whom such colors do not have the same illuminating effect as they had near the luster of the black woman's skin in the other poem, thus adding to their vulgarity.

In "The Art of Translation" (1995), Adrienne Rich emphasizes the role of this piece of jewelry:

But say we're crouching on the ground like children
over a mess of marbles, soda caps, foil, old foreign coins
—the first truly precious objects. Rusty hooks, glass.
Say I saw the earring first but you wanted it.[46]

This poem celebrates both translation as a carrying across—the skill that allows people to know what is written in unknown languages ("foreign coins")—and poetry itself as a form of translation of reality into a more perfect form, as a trans-formation, as a metaphor for change.[47] The "earring" (it seems to be the destiny of earrings to often appear in the singular and thus to speak of the impermanence of reality), with its "crushed lapis," may stand for whatever "precious object" is to be found among the "mess" of the world, a "mess" made of a heterogeneous ("marbles, soda caps, foil, old foreign coins") but also dangerous ("rusty hooks, glass") debris. Going back to children's games and the prevarications of a time past, the speaking voice recalls having given up the earring, but not "the words" that she or he had equally found.[48] Later on, she or he buried them but now remembers where to retrieve them so as to mint the language of this poem and convey the importance of this small "object." Possibly, this poem is also reminiscent of William Butler Yeats's "Lapis Lazuli" and the little sculpture that stands for art.

John Ashbery has this item of jewelry as the final word of "A Man Clamored": "You wore a yellow dress and selected earrings."[49] In this poem, the speaker presents a deteriorated social situation (because of continuous "strikes") and a deteriorated natural landscape (because of land's "speculation" in a formerly rural environment). The poem, however, also asserts that, notwithstanding these disruptive conditions, love may still flourish, even if on elusive or wayward terms ("It was a nice beginning for a story / that *might* never end," emphasis mine). The "clamor" in the title may thus stand for two contrary stances: wild protest and boisterous assent. This juxtaposition suits the collection in which this poem was republished, *Chinese Whispers,* and shows how a first suggestion/episode/accident may turn into something entirely different and unexpected (as does any interpretation of any poem/work of art by any individual reader/viewer).[50] This strategy also suits Ashbery's mingling of various tones in this lyric: from resignation and pathos to hope.[51] But the initial presentation of destructive social and natural practices ends—after having gone through the love encounter—in the final line, with a solar ("yellow") and refined ("selected earrings") vision, thus bringing a ray of light to an otherwise bleak panorama. Who is "you," then? Pronouns are always slippery in Ashbery's poetry, but here, I would venture, "you" is not the poet, the reader, or the lover, but an apparition, a miraculous entity who stirs our bruised hopes. This rapid and felicitous line stops on the word "earrings," thus giving it a special relevance, while the adjective "selected" emphasizes the attention and care paid in the choice of this jewel (as in the word's choice). If the vision is contingent, accidental, and fleeting, this is the law of our life that, in Ashbery's view, is always in flux and flow. The earrings' shape or color or material is not specified: what one (implicitly) knows is that these earrings cannot but be precious as they brighten the whole poem.

Finally, in a poem published posthumously, "Elephant Ears," Denise Levertov celebrates (once more) her Welsh mother, Beatrice, who had the soul of a poet and, like her daughter, had big ears. But while the daughter has "given up wearing earrings," because of her lopsided ears,

> At the age I am now, she still wore her various pairs
> Of beautiful earrings with confidence.

Because in the Buddhist tradition big ears stand for wisdom, she wonders whether she might not call upon Buddha or Ganesh to enlighten her about the possibility of finally acquiring it and to plead:

> For the *chutpza* to dangle jewels
> From long and uneven lobes?[52]

In American literature, earrings—with their shape, material, shades of color, and the very fact that they get mentioned—contribute to a distinctive understanding of their wearers, their stances, and the environment in which they are enmeshed and from which they emerge. Often, they are pendants, alerting readers that characters will be gaudy, or sexy, or untrustworthy, or devious, or rebellious, or indomitable. No small task for such small objects.

NOTES

1. Coco Chanel's quote in the epigraph is from Patrick Mauriès, *Les Bijoux de Chanel* (London: Thames and Hudson, 1993), 25.

2. Marjan Unger, "The Language of Jewellery," in *Fashion and Accessories*, ed. Jan Brand and José Teunussen (Arnhem: ArtEz, 2007), 68.

3. She was a friend of Margaret Fuller's. See Cristina Giorcelli, "A Humbug, a Bounder, and a Dabbler: Margaret Fuller, Cristina di Belgiojoso, and Christina Casamassima," in *Margaret Fuller:*

Transatlantic Crossings in a Revolutionary Age, ed. Charles Capper and Cristina Giorcelli (Madison: University of Wisconsin Press, 2007), 195–220.

4. Unger, "The Language of Jewellery," 67.

5. According to the *OED*, the word comes either from "jeweller" or from "jewel": in the former case, the importance is given to the creator, in the latter to the object.

6. Richard Klein, *Jewelry Talks: A Novel Thesis* (New York: Pantheon, 2001), 200.

7. Ibid., 192.

8. Gary Snyder, *Mountains and Rivers without End* (Berkeley, Calif.: Counterpoint, 1996), 127–29.

9. Klein, *Jewelry Talks*, 176.

10. Cited in Klein, *Jewelry Talks*, 170.

11. See Carl P. Eby, *Hemingway's Fetishism* (Albany: State University of New York Press, 1999), 178. In *Ernest Hemingway: A Life Story* (New York: Scribner's, 1969), 517–18, Carlos Baker mentions this moment in the writer's life but does not refer to an earring.

12. Martine Elzingre, "Fading Borders: Jewellery and Adornments and Their Relation to Fashion and the Body," in Brand and Teunussen, *Fashion and Accessories*, 79.

13. Klein, *Jewelry Talks*, 76.

14. Minke Vos, "Fashion Jewellery," in Brand and Teunussen, *Fashion and Accessories*, 178.

15. Hugh Kenner, *The Pound Era* (Berkeley: University of California Press, 1971), 236. In *Ezra Pound, the Solitary Volcano* (New York: Anchor Press, 1987), John Tytell specifies that Pound wore "a singular turquoise earring" (5).

16. Homer, *The Iliad*, trans. A. T. Murray, 2 vols. (London: Heinemann, 1924), 14:183.

17. *Hesiod, the Homeric Hymns, and Homerica*, trans. H. G. Evelyn-White (London: Heinemann, 1977), lines 162–63.

18. See Cristina Giorcelli, "*(Talking to)* Lucia Odescalchi, Grazia Borghese, Cristina Rotondaro Dal Pino: Princely Jewels in Rome Today," in *Abito e Identità: Ricerche di storia letteraria e culturale*, ed. Cristina Giorcelli, vol. 9 (Rome: Ila Palma, 2009), 27.

19. Klein, *Jewelry Talks*, 203.

20. Henry James, *Portraits of Places* (1883; repr. Boston: Houghton, Mifflin, 1911), 176.

21. Henry James, *The Europeans* (New York: Library of America, 1983), 877. Henceforth page numbers will be given in parentheses in the text.

22. Let us recall that in *William Wetmore Story and His Friends* (Boston: Houghton, Mifflin, 1903), 1:161, James uses the adverbs "orientally, exotically" to refer to Princess Cristina di Belgiojoso (see note 3), whose character, in his judgment, was affected by a sort of "cabotinage," by an element of showing off—the same to be found in this baroness.

23. Henry James, "The Middle Years," in *Complete Stories, 1892–1898* (New York: Library of America, 1996), 338–39. Henceforth page numbers will be given in parentheses in the text.

24. For the ways in which James characterizes Italians in his works, see my "Beguiling City, Bewitching Landscape, Bewildering People," *Henry James Review* 33, no. 3 (Fall 2012): 216–32.

25. Henry James, *The Wings of the Dove* (New York: Library of America, 2006), 236. Henceforth page numbers will be given in parentheses in the text.

26. Alice B. Toklas also liked to present earrings as gifts; see letter by Fania Van Vechten to Alice in *Letters of Gertrude Stein and Carl Van Vechten, 1913–1946*, ed. Edward Burns (New York: Columbia University Press, 1986), 1:230.

27. Renate Stendhal, ed., *Gertrude Stein in Words and Pictures* (Chapel Hill, N.C.: Algonquin Books, 1994), 62.

28. Gertrude Stein, *The Autobiography of Alice B. Toklas* (New York: Modern Library, 1993), 30.

29. Djuna Barnes, *Smoke and Other Early Stories*, ed. Douglas Messerli (College Park: Sun and Moon Press, 1982), 25, 27. Henceforth page numbers will be given in parentheses in the text.

30. See Cristina Giorcelli, "Wearing the Body over the Dress: Sonia Delaunay's Fashionable Clothes," in *Accessorizing the Body: Habits of Being 1*, ed. Cristina Giorcelli and Paula Rabinowitz (Minneapolis: University of Minnesota Press, 2011), 33–53.

31. Daniela Mascetti and Amanda Triossi, *Earrings: From Antiquity to the Present* (London: Thames and Hudson, 1999), 132.

32. Zelda Fitzgerald, "Eulogy on the Flapper," in *The Collected Writings*, ed. Matthew Bruccoli (New York: Scribners, 1991), 391. Originally published in *Metropolitan Magazine*, June 1922.

33. Willa Cather, *A Lost Lady*, with historical essay by Susan J. Rosowski (Lincoln: University of Nebraska Press, 1997), 37. Henceforth page numbers will be given in parentheses in the text.

34. Earrings with garnets and pearls were fashionable in the mid-nineteenth century (ibid., 277).

35. Emily Dickinson, *The Complete Poems*, ed. Thomas H. Johnson (London: Faber and Faber, 1970), 189.

36. Ibid., 134.

37. Gertrude Stein, *Tender Buttons* (New York: Claire Marie, 1914), 28.

38. Robert Frost, *Collected Poetry, Prose, and Plays* (New York: Library of America, 1995), 559. See Jeffrey Meyers, "An Earring for Erring: Robert Frost and Kay Morrison," *American Scholar* 65, no. 2 (Spring 1996): 219–41.

39. Gary Snyder, *Turtle Island* (New York: New Directions, 1974), 9.

40. Gary Snyder, *Danger on Peaks* (Washington, D.C.: Shoemaker, 2004), 64.

41. Richard Wilbur, *Collected Poems: 1943–2004* (New York: Harcourt Books, 2004), 469.

42. Lawrence Ferlinghetti, *The Secret Meaning of Things* (New York: New Directions, 1968), 38, line 153.

43. Charles Bukowski, *The Pleasures of the Damned: Poems, 1951–1993* (New York: Ecco, 2007), 144.

44. Charles Bukowski, *Mockingbird Wish Me Luck* (Los Angeles: Black Sparrow Press, 1972), 138.

45. Ibid., 141.

46. Adrienne Rich, *Midnight Salvage, 1995–1998* (New York: Norton, 1999), 5.

47. Let us just recall that Rich knew several foreign languages.

48. As for Wallace Stevens, for Rich, too, this "is a world of words to the end of it." Wallace Stevens, *The Collected Poems* (New York: Alfred A. Knopf, 1954), 345.

49. John Ashbery, *As Umbrellas Follow Rain* (Lenox: Qua Books, 2001), 6.

50. This is the British name of the game "Telephone" in the United States. Ashbery had already mentioned this game in "Portrait in a Convex Mirror."

51. See David Perkins, *A History of Modern Poetry: Modernism and After* (Cambridge, Mass.: Harvard University Press, 1987), 632.

52. Denise Levertov, *This Great Unknowing* (New York: New Directions, 1999), 15.

5

BUTTONS, BUTTONS, AND MORE BUTTONS!
Margherita di Fazio

In antiquity, buttons were used only as ornaments. They acquired their present function in the thirteenth century, when close-fitting clothes and narrow sleeves came into fashion.[1] The term derives from the medieval French *bouton*, originally meaning sprout or bud.[2] Generally small discs or spheres, they are sewn onto the border of a piece of clothing, joining it to another by passing through the corresponding buttonhole.[3]

Early buttons could be made of precious materials, but also of copper or brass.[4] More recently, buttons used in millinery, dressmaking, and tailoring, but also for linen, gloves, and shoes, were made of different materials (precious or common metals, mother of pearl, ivory, bone, glass, crystal, wood, leather, horn, jade, porcelain, and all kinds of plastic, particularly Bakelite), each manufactured with a different technique: turning, pressing, punching.[5]

Sometimes buttons are real works of art.[6] In the nineteenth and early twentieth centuries, buttons of precious metals were further enriched either by etching, hand painting, or the addition of other precious ornamentation. In the late nineteenth century, buttons of natural or artificial material became articles of design. For instance, some American-made buttons resemble plates of fruit; one holds an apple, a pear, a strawberry, and a few vine leaves and grapes; another, a pile of cherries.[7] Recently, buttons have been used to create costume jewelry: large buttons of white mother-of-pearl might be made into a necklace; a large brooch might consist of many small iridescent mother-of-pearl buttons.[8] Buttons have become collectors' items: from the mysteries of the button box, present in every home (where buttons of all kinds, taken from old clothes, were kept for possible further use or for sentimental value), to collections of rare specimens or representative models from one particular period.[9] Buttons can be the object of great passion (so much so that the French king, Francis I, had a black velvet gown made with 13,600 gold buttons sewn onto it, to wear for a meeting with a sultan), but also an object of hatred.[10] This antipathy can degenerate into a phobia (called *koumpounophobia*) from which one person out of every seventy-five thousand suffers.

For men's elegant evening wear, cufflinks were often of the same design as the buttons on the shirt front. They first appeared around the end of the sixteenth and beginning of the seventeenth centuries but are now rather rare, apart from formal wear.[11] The

FIGURE 5.1 Marie Antoinette button, ca. early nineteenth century. Miniature, hand-drawn, under glass with a gold circle on brass with eight white sapphires and eight metal rosettes. From the collection of Il Museo del Bottone, Sant'Arcangelo di Romagna, Italy. Printed by permission of the museum.

cuff, instead of having a button on one side and a buttonhole on the other, has two buttonholes through which one element of the cufflink is passed, thus linking it to the other half. Cufflinks can be made of precious materials and can be variously ornamented (with the owner's initials, the badge of a club, and so on).

How to explain the mystery of these male and female fastenings? Buttons on men's clothing are sewn onto the right side with the buttonholes on the left, while on women's garments, the buttons are on the left. This difference survives in modern times, although fashion tends more and more toward androgyny. Why this disparity? There is no certain answer to these questions; we can relate only the commonly held, and not very convincing, hypothesis that in times in which men used to go about armed, they needed to have the right hand free, even when dressing, to grab a sword or a dagger swiftly.

This tiny item is also useful in idiomatic phrases: "to buttonhole someone," meaning to keep talking to someone for a long time about a boring subject (it doesn't take very long to sew on a button, but making a buttonhole is a tedious job); "not worth a button" probably arises from the fact that the buttons now in daily use are easily lost and easily replaceable; again, one is "buttoned up" when overly cautious and not talking freely, while "to unbutton" can mean to confide, to open up and tell all. The contrast between *button* and *butt* (a large 600-liter barrel) has been liberally used in puns and wordplay; for example, the seven dwarfs, in the Italian version of their cheerful "Silly Song," sing these verses: "A contrast that's quite frantic / I can't believe at all / A butt is so gigantic / and buttons are so small!"[12] Umberto Eco uses the amusing parallel of butt/button in his "translation" or rather "rewriting" of Raymond Queneau's *Exercises in Style*. When speaking of a button, he adds: "But I don't mean an enormous wooden container for fermented liquids."[13] Beyond the scope of tailoring, the term is used for small round objects similar to buttons: in botany (from which, as we have seen, the term originates), in the areas of medicine, electricity, mechanics, fencing. To describe power, the button room is the control room. The word is the same but not its meanings; the button of a flower has evidently nothing to do with a coat button, and the button of a doorbell has nothing in common with the buttons on our jacket. And a bolt—a roundish object serving to join mechanical parts, and so, like buttons, used to close a gap—is very different from the buttons on a blouse or vest.

This semantic slippage opens buttons to artistic imagination. How not to recall the two memorable scenes in *Modern Times* in which Charlie Chaplin, as an alienated worker deranged by the stultifying repetitiveness of his work on the assembly line, continues to perform the gesture of screwing bolts even when he is no longer at work and attacks the buttons decorating the back of the shapely secretary's skirt or the gigantic ones on the front of the dress of a buxom lady who is sedately walking along the street? Here, two apparently incompatible fields have come together. So, too, with Russian Futurism on the cover of the "transrational book" *Zaumnaja Gniga* by Alexej Kručenych (1915): on the ace of hearts proudly and visibly glued to the front cover, a button, a big, white, real button, is attached.[14]

LITERARY BUTTONS: A RHAPSODY

In fiction, buttons appear in the description of characters' clothes and serve to underline significant details. Buttons made of gold and diamonds can be given as a parting present: "'Cousin,' said Charles, 'may I offer you these two buttons? They can fasten ribbons around your wrists; that sort of bracelet is much the fashion just now.'"[15] They can be of semiprecious stones: Don Giovanni Ussorio's "jewels, precious and gaudy, sparkled even on his thumbs, and a cornelian button fastened the bosom of his shirt over the centre of his chest."[16] Metal buttons appear frequently: "You had a jacket with gold buttons that were your nightmare, for everyone teased you about them," says Enrico Lanti to an old schoolmate he meets after many years at a Carnival party.[17] The newly married couple arrives, "he in his tail-coat with golden buttons and a solitaire diamond in his shirt-bosom."[18]

Golden buttons are so bright and conspicuous that they can become the main feature of a character. At the Age of two, the heroine of a novel by Carolina Invernizio is kidnapped by a harridan in the confusion of a market. Brought up in the Turin underworld, she is initiated to a life of crime.[19] The child is called Gold Button because she wears a coat, made by the woman who holds her in her power, "full of gold buttons." Also, her beautiful wonderfully blond hair is worn wound round her head "like a large button." A few years later, now older, Gold Button manages to escape captivity and makes her appearance in Turin society circles: she is a beautiful young woman, fascinating, exquisitely elegant, married to an equally elegant man. Her name is now Marien, but the writer still uses the namesake Gold Button and tells readers, creating a kind of complicity with them, that "we shall always call her by that name."[20]

Color is also important, as is the divergence in color between buttons and clothing (in *Madame Bovary* when little Charles, awkward and confused, enters the class "[he is wearing] a jacket of green cloth with black buttons")[21] or their clashing disharmony (in *The Bastard of Istanbul* when "she was wearing a fluffy green outfit adorned with salmon stripes and purplish buttons. She looked like a dwarf Christmas tree decorated by someone in a state of frenzy").[22] At other times, we are told their numbers: from the quantity of buttons shining on uniforms (in "On Account of a Hat," Sholem Shachnah does not look at the physical traits of the person lying asleep on the bench, but sees and describes only the buttons of his uniform, and for the whole length of the tale thinks of the man only as "Buttons"),[23] to the various types on coats or gloves.[24]

The single button, mentioned in passing, directs attention elsewhere. In the dramatic scene in *Malombra*, for example, Marina does not stop to think about the button, but about the glove and the person who wore it in the past: "The glove, the kind with a single button, was small, slender and long; it had the feel of a live person; it still contained, so to speak, the spirit of the delicate hand that had once worn it."[25] But it could also be an important accessory, worthy of admiration and description. Benvenuto Cellini recounts a commission from Pope Clement VII, who demanded:

a button for my priest's cope, which has to be made round like a trencher, and as big as a little trencher, one third of a cubit wide. Upon this I want you to represent a God the Father in half-relief, and in the middle to set a magnificent big diamond ... together with several other gems of the greatest value.

Cellini explains that he

had put the diamond exactly in the center of the piece; and above it God the Father was seated ... giving the benediction. ... All around I set a crowd of cherubs in divers attitudes, adapted to the other gems. A mantle undulated to the wind around the figure of the Father, from the folds of which cherubs peeped out.[26]

Italo Calvino's representation of the button, a single button, is not connected to a real object, but to its painted reproduction. This little masterpiece—the result of a particular way of "seeing" the world, of analyzing and classifying it—presents us with the quintessence of the button. Here, in precise language, the small object stands out: its roundness, the raised edge, the holes for the thread, the thread itself that contrasts with the material of the button, which, in turn, contrasts with the qualities of the cloth onto which it is sewn. Every element is seen with crystal clarity, its entirety is a poetic representation. At dawn, the light breaking on the horn surface of the disc, the button becomes "a mirror, its imperturbable circumference registering the world's tumultuous image," while the gradual waning of light and the descending dusk restore it to its solid opacity. And again:

Natural openings—caves in the rock, volcanic craters, the orifices of the human body— have all the mystery of routes leading to the obscure forces of the being. Not so the holes in buttons: clear-cut, regular, symmetrical, central, they stand for reason—at its most everyday: practical reason, sufficient reason—and they make the button a button.[27]

In literary texts, buttons are more than just sewn onto clothes and accessories. In addition to discharging this primary function, they perform other, secondary ones to create character. As Flaubert tells us, speaking of Emma: "She had, like a man, thrust between two buttons of her bodice, a tortoise-shell eyeglass."[28] This sentence, especially the expression "like a man," reveals explicitly the contradiction in Emma's character that led Charles Baudelaire to see an adultress as "a worthy hero . . . in the guise of a disgraced victim . . . a virile soul in a charming feminine body."[29]

And there is more. A row of buttons is a place in which to insert the fingers of a hand in an attitude of meditation or deep thought; this gesture is noticed by the guests of the hotel in Luigi Pirandello's novella "From the Nose to the Sky," as senator–professor Romualdo Reda, the illustrious chemist and member of the Lincei Academy, walks calmly toward the woods from whence he will never return: "At a certain moment, when he felt ready, he got up and, without a word, without looking at anyone, two fingers stuck between the buttons of his waistcoat, he started to walk, quietly and gravely, though so small a figure, along the lane that went towards the Conventino woods."[30]

At times buttons completely forget to perform their task of connecting the borders of clothes and take on other functions: "Beneath the profusion of sapphire charms, enamelled four-leaf clovers, silver medals, gold medallions, turquoise amulets, ruby chains and topaz chestnuts there would be on the dress itself . . . a row of little satin buttons which buttoned nothing and could not be unbuttoned." Buttons here have a purely decorative function, in line with Odette de Crecy's ostentatious taste. They are only one of the multitude of ornaments on her dress described by Proust with ironical admiration.[31]

Buttons do not fully and impenetrably close, like zippers; they leave spaces. Gabriele D'Annunzio's Andrea Sperelli makes a small gesture, born of the habit of passion and from the wish to stress the deep tie that unites him to his lover. At the moment when Elena is leaving him, explaining herself, Andrea interrupts her again and again with denials, "taking her hand, and with his fingers between the buttons feeling for the flesh of her wrist."[32] In Alfredo Panzini's story "La Cagna Nera" (The black bitch), during an afternoon walk with the school headmaster and his wife, two people with whom he is not on familiar terms, the hero—a young impoverished earl now teaching in a village school—is teasingly prompted by the woman to court the wife of another teacher; she underlines the suggestion by "tweaking his overcoat button."[33] We are told nothing more about her. But this gesture implies that she means more than she says and is suggesting, in a rather coarse way, that he need not look far afield; if the young man wants female company, it is available right in front of him.

In other instances this act is typical of the behavior of a character. Giovanni Episcopo goes to Via Montanara to ask for the hand of Ginevra in marriage, to the house of her mother, the "official pawnbroker, authorized by decree of the Royal Police." The woman consents readily enough, but he is made uncomfortable by her behavior: "When she spoke to me, she came too near, she touched me continually: now giving me a light push, now tweaking a button on my coat, now brushing a speck of dust from my shoulder, now picking a hair, a thread off my clothes."[34]

The gesture is also appropriate to the rude psychology of M. Grandet, Saumur's wine merchant, a rich miser who invariably profits from every situation. He had learned (from a Jewish man, who had successfully swindled him) to put his hand to his ear and to stammer conspicuously during business talks. This behavior, especially the stammer, would induce his interlocutors to help Père Grandet out of his difficulties by finishing his sentences, and in so doing to lose sight of their point. During a bout of stammering, Grandet "seized the banker by a button and drew him into a corner of the room."[35]

The button's counterpart, the buttonhole, that opening in the material that permits the button to perform its function, is also essential. Button and buttonhole live in proximity, defining the basic complementarities of some elements in our world. Carlo Dossi notes: "Man and woman complete each other, like a button and its buttonhole, like a violin and its bow, like a seed and the earth."[36] Buttonholes appear in literary texts when buttoning or unbuttoning clothes is mentioned, as, for example, in some passages by Gianna Manzini and Alberto Moravia.[37] Before they were machine sewn, buttonholes were difficult to make. In *Little Women* the sisters express their future resolutions by promising "I shall learn to make buttonholes and attend to my parts of speech."[38] The buttonhole often marks an opening in the left lapel of a coat. This buttonhole is useless for buttoning, having no corresponding button, but it serves to break the monotony of a man's attire and to add something to a woman's dress, because flowers or decorations can be pinned to it. Gentlemen can sport anything from a generic flower to a gardenia, a camellia, a carnation, or a rose in many forms: red, perfumed, tea, wild, or a rosebud. Women may have their coats and jackets adorned with violets and lilies of the valley. Other decorations are a gentleman's prerogative and are nearly always military.[39]

Cufflinks generally indicate elegance and sophistication.[40] But they also emphasize other aspects, rougher and less refined, like the humble poverty in Federico Tozzi's novella "The Shadow of Youth." Old Luigi, confronted by Livio—who is coldly determined to break off a timid but profound relationship—does not rage or scold, but painfully accepts the situation. Indeed, he thanks the young man for having come of his own volition to return the letters he had written and is painfully conscious of the inadequacy of his own clothes: "He [is ashamed] of his old shoes and his suit, that is soiled by long service. He [pulls back] the cuffs of his shirt, with the fake gold cufflinks, that keep slipping out."[41] In Carlo Emilio Gadda's *Acquainted with Grief,* after the obligatory obeisance of the waiters in restaurants and after the heavy meal that they consider extremely gratify-

FIGURE 5.2 Hundreds of buttons in the interior of Il Museo del Bottone, Sant'Arcangelo di Romagna, Italy. Created and curated by Giorgio Gallavotti. Printed by permission of the museum.

ing, the diners are full of themselves. They continue to sit, smoking with their elbows on the table, "perhaps gazing at themselves in the mirror of the others' pupils. In full exploitation of their cuffs, and of their cufflinks."[42]

Cufflinks, moreover, signal belonging, as in Romano Bilenchi's *Il bottone di Stalingrado* (*The Stalingrad Button*) where Bruno's cufflinks are engraved with the symbol of the hammer and sickle, despite the Fascist victory. As they are considered a provocation, a Fascist group decides to give him a "severe public lesson." Bruno's friend Marco, who has overheard the brutal scheme, however, intervenes. Taking the incriminating cufflinks from Bruno's shirt, he replaces them with the ones his mother gave him when he passed his grammar school exams—thus interweaving a mother's love, leftist ideology, political rivalry, and friendship.[43]

THE BUTTON AS PROTAGONIST

A button is a button, that is, it serves its purpose as a button, being sewn onto diverse parts of clothing to hold them together. Thus it is not positioned at random on clothes and accessories but follows two fundamental rules: the obvious one of *necessity* (closing the gaps that must be closed), and that of *order*, not so apparently indispensable, but equally constrictive. From *order* follows *symmetry*. Buttons closing the front of a shirt— or a coat, dress, or jacket—are generally all of the same shape and size and sewn firmly at the same distance from each other (or in pairs, or other combinations at regular intervals), forming a harmonious uninterrupted row (of course, the case of the single button is different). If there is a button on one pocket of a coat, there must be a button also on the other pocket; if the tips of the collar are buttoned to the shirt, the buttons must be two small identical ones for each tip; if one cuff of a woman's dress is closed by a button, the other cuff must be closed by an identical button. The two or three buttons decorating the right sleeve of a man's coat must correspond to the two or three buttons decorating the left sleeve, and so on.

But sometimes this habitual and soothing regularity is broken, because a button is missing. In the orderly row, an alarming gap has appeared. Why is the button missing? Three scenarios:

1. The button has fallen off accidentally; we don't know when or where.
2. The button has fallen off because of unintentional clumsiness.
3. The button has been removed intentionally.

THE BUTTON HAS FALLEN OFF ACCIDENTALLY; WE DON'T KNOW WHEN OR WHERE.

We perceive this circumstance as negative. The wearer of an article of clothing with a button missing (unless it was detached in fortuitous circumstances and is immediately repaired), or with a button dangling and about to fall off, is considered slovenly and possibly not quite trustworthy.[44] But the interpretation is often not so superficial. Especially for poets. Especially when the poet is Alexander Pushkin:

> In winter in his last years, he would stroll along the Nevsky Prospect in a slightly shabby top hat and a long bekesh [a man's winter overcoat with fur lining and lapels], similarly timeworn. Since he was the darling of the Muses and the poet favored by the gods, lingering curious glances pursued him. The more attentive onlookers noted with surprise that in the back, where thick folds of material were gathered at the waist, Pushkin's bekesh was missing a button.[45]

This is how Serena Vitale introduces the subject in her book *Pushkin's Button,* in which, among other things, she underlines the poet's impatience with court fashions, noting that at times he dressed with no regard for the codes of aristocratic dress (or even purposely ignored them), such as the necessity for the hat to match the suit or the need to wear not the bourgeois tuxedo, but the one designed specifically for the office of *kamerjunker* of the Czar. It is one thing to refuse to wear clothing felt to be an imposition by an establishment one does not love; it is quite another to go about habitually with a button missing.

What is the reason for this omission, this defect, in Pushkin's coat? Vitale rejects Kolmakov's suggestion ("the button's absence bothered me whenever I encountered Alexander Sergeevich and noticed it. Clearly, they were not looking after him"), for it is unthinkable that a Russian aristocrat should not have a bevy of servants at his disposal to do anything that was necessary (nor was it in the order of things that his wife should not see to it). Vitale, in fact, thinks that the absence of the button was a "ray of light in Pushkin's gloomy kamerjunker career, a mocking symbolic comment, a grinning coded message from the Russian Empire's very last dandy," transmitted across the years. As she argues, "L'exactitude est la politesse des cuisiniers." In her opinion, Pushkin's missing button speaks of poetry and freedom. Actually, it is poetry itself. "Mocking the etiquette of prosody, freeing the line from servile metrical obeisance," it is a verse that becomes "ever new and mobile, changeable, unpredictable, whimsical, boundlessly elegant and free." She demonstrates this graphically. A regular verse is constructed like this: —/—/—/—/. Pushkin's back-belt, instead, goes its own original and daring way: —/--/--.[46]

The history of the buttonless overcoat belt does not end here. We meet the bekesh again on January 27, 1837, the day of the duel that will prove fatal to the poet.[47] Pushkin has dressed carefully: a new tail coat, dark vest, shirt, black trousers. At one o'clock, he is ready to leave for the meeting with his second to discuss the time and the rules of the duel that afternoon. He tells his servant to bring him his bekesh; he puts it on and starts for the stairs. But he returns immediately and asks for his long fur coat. Why does he refuse the bekesh? And more especially, why does he turn back? Vitale tells us that Russians believe that to cross the threshold twice, reentering after having just gone out, is an omen of disasters to come. Pushkin was very superstitious and normally would have avoided returning immediately. But Pushkin wants to fight with the utmost concentration. His inflexible determination is to kill D'Anthès, and nothing must interfere with this. Not even a shiver of cold that might cause the arm to tremble. So it is better to wear his warmest clothes. Given Vitale's comparison of Pushkin's half-belt without a button to the joyous freedom of verse, the symbol of poetry, a symbol of Art's transgressive song, the coat must not be present at this bloody and implacable event, the duel.

A missing button is the mark of Pushkin and his coat. The presence of a button is now the mark of his rival D'Anthès after their duel. The poet has been wounded in the spleen and will die at home, after two days of painful agony. D'Anthès gets off lightly with a wounded arm. But here we discover a long-standing controversy. Eyewitness accounts mentioned a button: the bullet passed through the fleshy part of the right arm but was stopped by one of the buttons holding his trousers to the suspenders. Later, to support the suspicion of a plot—according to which the duel was not accidental, but deliberately organized to get Pushkin out of the way—the rather incredible hypothesis was proposed that the officer had worn some protection under his uniform: a coat of mail, or even a cuirass.

THE BUTTON HAS FALLEN OFF BECAUSE OF UNINTENTIONAL CLUMSINESS.

A small gesture that is part of daily life, fiddling with a button and inadvertently weakening the thread until it breaks, can take on grave significance. It can even be indicative of the collapse of a whole system of values. Don Filiberto Fiorinnanzi, one of Luigi Pirandello's rational characters, after years of intense meditation had reached a vision of existence that allows him to live a relatively tranquil life:

> Quite some time ago he had risen to the stature of a paragon of composure and restraint, in his way of conducting business, in his contributions to the discussions that arose in the pub or the barroom, in all his actions, even in his way of dressing and walking. And God knows how much it cost him to keep his long coat, that was rather old but looked so grave and dignified, buttoned right down even in summer.[48]

So Filiberto Fiorinnanzi pursued a precise equilibrium, not only in his own life and actions but also in everything and everyone that surrounded him. It pained him to see someone walk along the road with his tie outside his collar or his jacket unbuttoned, or if the municipality did not promptly change the bulb of a street lamp, or if someone stole. It was torture for him to see how Meo Zezza, one of Marchese Di Giorgi-Decarpi's "ministers," robbed his master. The marchese was exceedingly organized and administered his property (which was divided into lots, each comprised of ten holdings headed by a "minister") with enviable competence, so much so that "every year the students of the commercial high school were brought by their professors to study the structure of that administration as a paragon of its kind."[49] How was it possible, wondered Filiberto, that the continuing and exorbitant thefts of that "cagliostro" (swindler) eluded such a precise and balanced system? He could not resign himself to it, and in the end he decided to denounce these goings on. With great patience and even greater determination he went through all the complicated necessary paperwork and at length was admitted, after having had to wait a few days, to the presence of the marchese. But his vehement and detailed accusations were received coldly. He was listened to with an appearance of great boredom and detachment, and haughtily dismissed. The Marchese Di Giorgi-Decarpi was not only already aware of the thefts (his perfect administration could not have overlooked them) but actually abetted them, for the lands administered by Meo Zezza brought in much more than the others. While the other "ministers" pocketed their salaries and did not bother to raise the profit of the land, Zezza, who stole part of the harvest, had an interest in raising its yield and consequently had to care for it very diligently.

Filiberto Fiorinnanzi had to face a real defeat: the order on which he counted so much was here actually inverted, and his rigorous system totally destroyed. His prostration found a symbolic expression in the button of his long coat. While the marchese was speaking, Filiberto had twisted this button so many times that it had come off in his fingers. But what was the use of it now? Even order in dress was no longer necessary. Filiberto Fiorinnanzi, experiencing the subversion of all his values, could very well walk the streets with a button missing.

Why intentionally remove a button, or a whole row of buttons? There can be many reasons: to let out or take in an article of clothing; in exchange for newer and shinier ones; to save them when an article of clothing is being thrown away. But, as ever, in literature there are other, impractical, motives.

In *The Stalingrad Button* by Bilenchi, a button is removed voluntarily by Hans, a young Austrian forced after the Anschluss to fight in the German army. The Wehrmacht is now fighting in Italy, and Hans is stationed in Tuscany. One afternoon, crawling through the underbrush, he comes upon Marco and Giulia, two young partisans who, in a shed in the woods, are reading, or rather studying, an essay by Marxist philosopher Antonio Labriola. Although fighting on opposite sides, the three freely discuss their situations. Hans confides his thoughts and his hostile feelings toward the Nazis. He takes a small metal button from his pocket; it is battered but still displays in relief a hammer and sickle above a five-pointed star. He gives it to Marco, saying: "I took it from the sleeve of a soldier killed in Stalingrad; I thought it would bring me luck." Then he adds:

His body lay for days in front of our position in the middle of the road. One night it disappeared. His comrades must have taken it away. Now I give you this button to remember me by. That boy, whether he was Ukrainian or Siberian, also died for us. Without all those dead Russians, whose bodies were withered and stiffened by the cold, there would have been no future for anyone in the world.[50]

He gently pats Marco's back and leaves. The button, with its own specific significance, has been taken from the uniform as a lucky charm and then given as a memento. It is also the symbol of the unification of different peoples (from a Russian soldier it passes to an Austro-German soldier and then to an Italian resistance fighter), in deliberate contrast to the bloody divisions of war.

In the story "The War of the Buttons" by Louis Pergaud, buttons are intentionally and furiously torn off in the war game played by generations of boys from two rival villages,

FIGURE 5.3 Button commemorating the political detente between the United States and the Soviet Union, created in 1972 on the occasion of the first linkup of the space shuttles belonging to the two superpowers. From the collection of Il Museo del Bottone, Sant'Arcangelo di Romagna, Italy. Printed by permission of the museum.

Longeverne and Verlans.[51] The aim is to tear off as many buttons as possible and leave clothes unfastened, even torn, until they fall miserably from the body and finally slide to the ground. Battles follow a prescribed code of warfare, with commanders and troops engaging each other ritualistically. In the first phase, the opposing forces face each other from a distance, screaming war cries (insults and curses). In the second phase, advancing guardedly, they throw stones by hand or with slings. The third phase is a furious hand-to-hand fight; prisoners can be taken and be submitted to the ultimate humiliation: the tearing off of their buttons.

The text describes in detail an unbuttoning at the hands of the Longeverne faction (the story is told from their point of view) and then by the Verlans boys, who manage to capture and humiliate the enemy's commander Lebrac. After this humiliation, he endures a further ordeal when he returns home with his clothes held together by pins, thorns, and bits of string: he will be bitterly scolded by his mother and beaten by his father.

Lebrac tries to prevent the loss of buttons by using a surprise tactic: the whole Longeverne group goes into battle stark naked. This tactic achieves the desired result, but battles must be fought with clothes on. To avoid the family beatings, Lebrac organizes a store: a small treasury of buttons, elastic bands, hooks, some bought and some taken from the enemy, to repair the ripped clothing.[52] The sister of one of the boys (who is also the commander's sweetheart) mends the boys' clothes when necessary.

The boys prove to be resourceful, intelligent, and quick-witted in this game. Schooltime and family life are barely tolerated and are seen as constraints from which to escape as quickly as possible. The story is, in fact, about two wars: between the boys of the two factions, and against the grown-ups (to elude their vigilance, escape their punishments, and cut out a space free of them). The boys' world is a world apart, built contrary to the rules of grown-ups: its secret existence is made possible through subterfuge and lies. This is the significance of the buttons in the game: tearing buttons off, ripping clothes open, undressing others and themselves means defying the rules of the adult world. It means uncovering the secret that must remain hidden under clothes, the mystery of the body.[53] This violent removal not only destroys the rules of *order* and *symmetry*, but also that of *necessity*, completely annihilating the function of the button.[54]

AN ABERRATION: A MISSING BUTTON SHATTERS THE HARMONY OF BUTTONING

But what if, on the contrary, disharmony is at the source of an unbuttoning? What if it was the tailor who didn't (or couldn't) observe the fundamental rule of order and symmetry? What if a jacket or coat presents an anomaly, one that does not go unobserved, as we read in *Exercises in Style*?[55]

The opening passage, "Notation" (the starting point for the ninety-nine "variations"), introduces "the button" when the protagonist of the first episode (which takes place on an S line bus) is talking to a friend in front of the Gare Saint-Lazare.[56] The friend tells him, "You should add a button to your overcoat," and shows him where, at the fitting at the waist, and tells him why (although the author is silent on this point). His friend has observed an error in the ordering of buttons and thinks that it should be put right and order reestablished. This is the case with most of the variations. The reader, following this dialogue, is made aware that *the coat is a button short.*

This is the case, as I pointed out, with most of the variations but not all. Here and there, the verbs and expressions used are not always the same: for example instead of "add," or "attach an extra button,"[57] we find the term "move," and the expressions "put higher up," or "out of place," and so on.[58] *In these cases, the presence of the button is taken for granted.* Is the button missing or misplaced? Either way a sense of insecurity and uncertainty is not easily remedied. Such is the button's power.

NOTES

1. The use of buttons made it possible to detach the sleeves from the body of a dress, and thus wash them separately. Sleeves were the part of a dress most likely to get dirty, and so they could be washed more often than the whole dress (which was an arduous task). See Chiara Frugoni, *Books, Banks, Buttons and Other Inventions from the Middle Ages*, trans. William McCuaig (New York: Columbia University Press, 2003), 105.

2. From the vulgar Latin *botonnes*, apparently similar to *botones* and *botontini*, signifying heaps, mounds of earth (*Vocabolario degli Accademici della Crusca*, fifth printing, vol. 2 [Florence, 1886]). For the origin and history of buttons, see Salvatore Battaglia, *Grande Dizionario della Lingua Italiana* (Turin: UTET, 1962), vol. 2; Rizzoli-Larousse, *Enciclopedia Universale* (Milan: Rizzoli, 1966), vol. 2; Aldo Duro, ed., *Vocabolario della Lingua Italiana* (Rome: Istituto della Enciclopedia Italiana Treccani, 1986), vol. 1.

3. Other ways of uniting two parts of clothing include snaps, zippers, hooks and eyes, velcro.

4. In the past, buttons were made and sold by goldsmiths, and because women spent so much on them, they were subject to sumptuary laws. See Chiara Frugoni, *Medioevo sul Naso* (Bari: Laterza, 2010), 102. In "Novella CXXXVII," a judge, Amerigo degli Amerighi from Pesaro, appointed to enforce the sumptuary laws, found it difficult to oppose their specious justifications in defense of their ornaments. He lamented, "Gentlemen, I have spent most of my life studying reason, and now, when I thought I had learned something, I find I know nothing, for in attempting to forbid your women's ornamentation, as you instructed me to do, I am confronted by reasons I never found written in any law book . . . ; I will relate some of them: My notary . . . finds many buttons worn on the front. He says to the wearer: 'You cannot wear these buttons.' and she answers: 'Yes, Sir, I can, for they are not buttons, but small bowls, and if you do not believe me you can look, they have no stem

and no holes.'" Franco Sacchetti, *Il Trecentonovelle* (Turin: Einaudi, 1970), 337 (my translation). The author conceived the outline of his collection in 1385, began writing it in 1391, and completed it in 1397–98.

5. The materials are very important. Le Couteur and Burreson repeat a theory that chemists used to circulate with great amusement: the buttons on the uniforms of Napoleon's army were made of tin, and so, in the freezing Russian winter of 1812, they lost their integrity and crumbled, leaving the soldiers in considerable difficulties. Could Napoleon's defeat in Russia be due to his buttons? Penny Le Couteur and Jay Burreson, *Napoleon's Buttons: How 17 Molecules Changed History* (London: Deep Books, 2004).

6. The relationship between art and buttons is underlined, with elegant irony, in a short publication that is divided into two parts: "The Influence of Buttons on the Development of Art" and "The Influence of Art on the Development of Buttons." See Pietro Coccoluto Ferrigni (alias Yorik son of Yorik), *I bottoni nell'arte e nella Storia* (1903; repr. Naples: Colonnese, 1992).

7. See Bina Pagano, *Bottoni, Buttons* (Milan: Motta, 2002), 397.

8. In 1991, Giorgio Gallavotti founded the Button Museum in Sant'Arcangelo di Romagna, collecting specimens from 1700 on, divided into three sections (history, materials, curiosities).

9. An instance is Alberto Riva's collection, from the end of the nineteenth century, exhibited in Palazzo Pitti's Costume Gallery from December 2007 to April 2008. See Dora Liscia Bemporad and Caterina Chiarelli, eds., *Appesi a un filo: Bottoni alla Galleria del Costume di Palazzo Pitti* (Livorno: Sillabe, 2007).

10. Nowadays, when monarchs no longer wear such magnificent clothes, the glory of clothes resplendent with buttons has been taken over by artistic installations. We could mention the works of Nick Cave, especially the Soundsuit NC10.016, entitled *Mannequin* (duffy, iron structure, beads, buttons, fabric), at the Rome Macro Museum in 2010–11, with its disquietingly humanoid shape.

11. See Leonardo Volpini, *I gemelli da polso* (Milan: Motta, 2001), 13. "In the formal suit, that is in the uniform of modern men in leadership roles, the shirt is the backdrop for exalting the exhibitionism of a tie and of that semi-occult category, the cufflinks, that are not often in outrageous evidence, but are generally discreetly unprepossessing" (8–9) (my translation).

12. *Snow White and the Seven Dwarfs*, Walt Disney, 1937. The Italian translation of the "Silly Song" by Rastelli, Panzieri, and Devilli completely changed the sense of the original text to maintain the rhythm and the "silliness."

13. Raymond Queneau, *Exercises in Style* (1947; repr. New York: New Directions, 1981). I am using Umberto Eco's translation from the French: Introduction to *Esercizi di Stile* (Turin: Einaudi, 1983), 43 (my translation).

14. Vladimir Markov, *Russian Futurism: A History* (Berkeley: University of California Press, 1968), 324.

15. With these words Charles, leaving for the Indies to seek his fortune, gives his cousin the two buttons that, it will be discovered, are made of diamonds. Also his uncle receives a pair of cufflinks (while his aunt receives a gold thimble). See Honoré de Balzac, *Eugénie Grandet* (1833; repr. Radford, Va.: Wilder Publishing, 2008), 103.

16. Gabriele D'Annunzio, "The Countess of Amalfi," in *Tales of My Native Town*, trans. Rafael Manellini (Garden City: Doubleday, Page, 1920), 15.

17. Giovanni Verga, *Eva* [1873], in *Una Peccatrice, Storia di una Capinera, Eva, Tigre Reale* (Milan: Oscar Mondadori, 1980), 260 (my translation).

18. Giovanni Verga, *Mastro Don Gesualdo* [1889], trans. D. H. Lawrence (London: Jonathan Cape, 1925), 343.

19. Carolina Invernizio, *Bottone d'Oro* (1912; repr. Milan: Editrice Lucchi, 1989).

20. Ibid., (my translation). On the theme of glittering buttons, see the story of *King 33 and his 33 Gold Buttons*. The king is so tall that he needs thirty-three buttons (gold ones, of course) to close his mantle. Claudio Imprudente, *Re 33 e i suoi 33 bottoni d'oro* (Molfetta: La Meridiana, 1994). Even lusterless buttons often appear in children's stories. Perhaps it is their round shape that catches the imagination, because it can be put to many uses: the wheel of a cart, a snail's house, the piggies' plate (Sara Fanelli, *Button* [London: ABC, 1994], illustrated by the author), even the eyes of various characters, as in Neil Gaiman's *Coraline*, illustrated by Dave McKean (London: Bloomsbury, 2002), made into an animated film in 2009. Here, buttons take on a negative connotation, because those who live and operate in the land of evil have button-eyes.

21. Gustave Flaubert, *Madame Bovary*, trans. Lydia Davis (New York: Penguin, 2010), 1.

22. Elif Shafak, *The Bastard of Istanbul* (New York: Penguin, 2008), 43.

23. Sholom Aleichem, "On Account of a Hat," in *A Treasury of Yiddish Stories*, ed. Irving Howe and Eliezer Greenberg (New York: Viking Press, 1954), 114.

24. Gloves, for example, can have one, two, three, or more buttons. According to Luigi Capuana, who, analyzing Verga's works, compares Nedda, the poor olive-picker, "her poor moleskin dress torn and dirty, her bare feet caked in mud, her face baked by the sun and lined by suffering," to the

heroines of his previous novels, whose names were full of charm, whose figures were "covered in silks, velvets, and lace . . ., *gloves with thirty-two buttons,* and satin ankle-boots with enormous heels." Luigi Capuana, *Verga e D'Annunzio,* ed. Mario Pomilio (Bologna: Cappelli, 1972), 73 (emphasis and translation mine).

25. Antonio Fogazzaro, *Malombra* (1881; repr. Milan: Oscar Mondadori, 1984), 100–101 (my translation). In this key scene, Marina discovers by chance, in the secret compartment of an ancient cabinet, a letter from her ancestor Cecilia and some objects belonging to her: "a prayer-book, a tiny mirror with a silver frame, a lock of blonde hair tied with black ribbon, a glove." The letter convinces Marina she is Cecilia's reincarnation, and the girl takes upon herself the sad duty of revenge.

26. *The Autobiography of Benvenuto Cellini,* trans. John Addington Symonds (New York: Collier and Sons, 1910), 94, 92.

27. Italo Calvino, "The Button" in "The Painter of Absense," in *Image, Eye and Art in Calvino: Writing Visibility,* ed. Birgitte Grundtvig, Martin L. McLaughlin, and Lene Waage Petersen (London: Legenda, 2007), 282. The other studies are "The woman's shoe," "The man's shirt," "The pillow," all objects painted by Domenico Gnoli. Other works by him depict buttons: as a detail on a man's shirt collar (*Giro di collo,* 1966; *Chemise,* 1966); as a gigantic presence on a suit (or coat), half hidden by the material of the buttonhole (*Unbuttoned Button,* 1969); as a central vision on a rectangle of cloth from a coat or overcoat (*Bouton,* 1966). Gnoli's paintings depict various objects, and details of objects: the tie, the lock of hair, the zipper, the tip of a woman's shoe. His vision tackles the problems of essence and knowledge by selecting and magnifying reality, and in so doing provokes wonder and disconcerting bewilderment.

28. Flaubert, *Madame Bovary,* 20.

29. Charles Baudelaire, " 'Madame Bovary' of Gustave Flaubert," in *Baudelaire: Selected Writings on Art and Artists,* trans. P. E. Chavet (New York: Penguin, 1972), 250–51.

30. After a long search, his body is found in the woods, perfectly composed, with no apparent cause of death (an odd thing is noticed: "from the high crown of the horse-chestnut a nearly invisible spider's thread had fixed itself to the tip of the little Senator's nose"). Luigi Pirandello, "Dal naso al cielo," in *Novelle per un anno* (Milan: Mondadori 2001), 1:435 and 438–39 (my translation).

31. Marcel Proust, *Within a Budding Grove,* vol. 2 of *In Search of Lost Time* [1913–27], trans. C. K. Scott Moncrieff and Terence Kilmartin (New York: Modern Library, 1998), 268.

32. Gabriele D'Annunzio, *The Child of Pleasure* (1889; repr. Boston: L.C. Page, 1906), 61.

33. Alfredo Panzini, "La cagna nera" [1895], in *Opere scelte*, ed. Goffredo Bellonci (Milan: Oscar Mondadori, 1970), 687 (my translation).

34. Gabriele D'Annunzio, *Giovanni Episcopo* (1891; repr. Milan: Oscar Mondadori, 1979), 32 (my translation).

35. Balzac, *Eugénie Grandet*, 85.

36. Carlo Dossi, *La desinenza in A* (1884; repr. Milan: Rizzoli, 2002), 296 (my translation).

37. "Adelina draws near to me; her fingers play with the buttonholes of my vest; she buttons it up." Gianna Manzini, *Il valtzer del Diavolo* (1947; repr. Milan: Mondadori, 1953), 175 (my translation). "He himself, with a quick gesture that wanted to help out my awkwardness, drew the lapels of my blouse over my breast and fitted each button into its buttonhole." Alberto Moravia, *La Romana* (1947; repr. Milan: Bompiani, 1955), 48 (my translation). The English translation doesn't mention buttonholes, just buttons. Moravia, *The Woman of Rome*, trans. Lydia Holland (New York: Farrar, Strauss and Giroux, 1949).

38. Louisa May Alcott, *Little Women* (1868; repr. New York: Dell, 1987), 143. Later, in Jo's journal kept for her mother and Beth, she "was thanking [her] stars [she]'d learned to make nice buttonholes" (404).

39. A black button can be sewn onto a buttonhole as a sign of mourning.

40. Cufflinks, often made of precious metals, are sophisticated accessories, typical of dandies. Domenico Modugno's 1955 song "Il vecchio frac" presents a vivid image of their clothing: "The man in tails" walks slowly through the sleeping town: "On his head is a top hat, / two diamonds on his cufflinks, / a crystal cane, / a gardenia in his buttonhole / and on his white vest / a *papillon*, a blue silk *papillon*" (my translation).

41. Federico Tozzi, "L'ombra della giovinezza" [1919], in *Le Novelle* (Florence: Vallecchi, 1963), 2:736 (my translation).

42. Carlo Emilio Gadda, *Acquainted with Grief*, trans. William Weaver (New York: G. Braziller, 1969), 168. He goes on: "Ardent dreaming, souls of the young, mostly runners in offices, of the young and hairdresser-working classes, dreamed of arriving at this: some day! 'From the Apennines to the Andes.' With that cigarette between index and middle fingers, that little yellow glass on the table, that cuff, those cufflinks."

43. Romano Bilenchi, *Il Bottone di Stalingrado* (1972; repr. Milan: Rizzoli, 2001), 27 (my translation).

44. To prevent losing the button, remove it. When young Grisha fiddles with his "plump hand" with a button on his coat, until it is hanging by a thread, his mother tears it off and puts it in her pocket. Leo Tolstoy, *Anna Karenina* [1873–77], trans. Richard Pevear and Larissa Volokhonsky (New York: Penguin, 2000), 66.

45. Serena Vitale, *Pushkin's Button*, trans. Ann Goldstein and Jon Rothschild (Chicago: University of Chicago Press, 2000), 75. Using various documents—diplomatic dispatches, letters, diaries, memoirs, secret police reports—of nineteenth-century Russia, with its intrigues, its gossip, its meanness, Vitale's book is a historical reconstruction of the motives and events that led Pushkin to the fatal duel.

46. Ibid., 106.

47. The duel was between Pushkin and his brother-in-law Georges de Heeckeren. Of French origin, he was called D'Anthès, but he had taken the name of his adoptive father, the Dutch Minister Baron de Heeckeren. He was an officer in the *Chevaliers Gardes*, the knights of the Guard of Her Majesty the Empress of all the Russias, serving in Petersburg. Rumor had it that the poet's beautiful wife, Natalie, was partial to the young knight's charms, but there were two sides to the gossip: D'Anthès was seen as capable of any base trick; Natalie was blamed for being frivolous, silly, and an incurable flirt. Scandal was warded off by the marriage of D'Anthès to Ekaterina Goncharova, Mrs. Pushkin's sister, so he became the poet's brother-in-law and legitimated his visits to Pushkin's house. But then there were anonymous letters, and the rumors worsened. The poet was jealous, had a fierce temper, and challenged the young officer.

48. Luigi Pirandello, "Il bottone della palandrana," in *Tutt'e tre*; see *Novelle per un anno*, 1:297 (my translation).

49. Ibid., 299.

50. Bilenchi, *Il Bottone di Stalingrado*, 66–67.

51. Louis Pergaud, *La Guerre des boutons: Roman de ma douzième année* (Paris: Mercure de France, 1912). I am using the Italian version and translating from it (Milan: Mondadori, 1978). The book became famous because of Yves Robert's 1962 film.

52. Tintin is the treasurer. He takes his role very seriously and compiles the *Statement of the Longeverne Army*, subdividing with care the sum the boys have mustered: "*Shirt buttons*, 1 sou. *Coat and cardigan buttons*, 4 sous. *Trouser buttons*, 4 sous. *Hooks to hold trouser backs*, 4 sous. *Sugar loaf string to be used as breeches*, 5 sous. *Elastic for garters*, 8 sous. *Bootlaces*, 5 sous. *Jacket hooks*, 2 sous. Total, 33 sous. Emergency fund, 2 sous" (ibid., 144).

53. Gianni Celati, in the Introduction to the 1978 Italian version of Pergaud, stresses this fundamental aspect of the narrative. He discusses the function of buttons: "Buttons on clothes exist to enclose the body, so that the body does not come into direct contact with the outside, except on certain covert occasions" (ibid., 18). "They are imposed by the grown-ups, and the boys violate their rules through their game" (6) (my translation).

54. Who wins these two wars? The boys, of course. But although in the war between peers, the victory, though variable according to the changing fortunes of the field, is clear, in the war across generations, victory is more complex, because of the passing of time, as generations follow each other. The winners today will be losers tomorrow. And this is declared openly in the last sentence of the novel. A boy, La Crique, "moved, thinking sadly of the coming snow, and maybe with a foreboding of lost illusions, let fall these words: 'And to think that, when we are grown up, we might be as stupid as they are!'" (my translation).

55. Queneau, *Exercises in Style*. The title page of the Italian edition reads "Translated by Umberto Eco." But more than a translation it is a demonstration of Eco's linguistic prowess. He says that more than a question of translating, it was one of understanding the rules of the game. On the jacket there is a reproduction of *Objet Dada*, a picture by Jacques Carelman, author of the surprising *Catalogue d'objets introuvables*, 1969. Among other elements, a delicate female left hand appears in the foreground, of which only four fingers are visible. On the ring finger, completely decontextualized, there is a red button with a raised edge and four holes.

56. The "variations" pertain to the field of rhetoric, but not exclusively. See Eco, Introduction to *Esercizi di Stile*, x.

57. In French, *ajouter* (ibid., 10); *mettre un bouton supplémentaire* (ibid., 2).

58. In French, *déplacer* (ibid., 26); *remonter* (ibid., 98); *bouton mal placé* (ibid., 126).

6

CURSE OF THE CORSAGE

FEMMES FATALES AND THE CAN-DO GIRL

Charlotte Nekola

Why would bad women bother to wear flowers? Flowers—in the form of corsages, bridal bouquets, and gifts for loved ones—belong to the territory of good women, like sweethearts, prom dates, fiancées, brides, and devoted mothers. Bad women, like the femmes fatales in film noir, prefer cigarette holders, mink coats, diamonds, sequined nightclub gowns, ankle bracelets, and kimonos that conceal little revolvers. Yet some of the most famous cinematic femmes fatales sport fluffy camellias in their suit lapels and flowers in their hair. Or they plunge flowers seductively into the V-necklines of their blouses. When they had cigarette holders and revolvers, why would they need flowers, too?

My interest in this subject is not purely academic. I have always been in love with femmes fatales, a passion conceived by watching films noirs on TV as a child in the 1950s. I would be in the living room watching Ida Lupino or Barbara Stanwyck snarl and blow smoke rings around their men. In the kitchen, my mother was stirring pot roast or dutifully checking on biscuits. I took the black-and-white films on TV to be a sort of documentary of life's possibilities and the snarly femmes fatales seemed to have a much more exciting life than my mother's. Every detail of their diabolic costumes intrigued me: the cigarette cases, the shiny halter dresses, the white fur capes. Each detail moved

FIGURE 6.1 Charlotte Nekola, *Curse of the Corsage*, 2013. Pigment print of assemblage, 24 × 20 inches.

them from street to nightclub or ocean liners and maybe to the electric chair. But the flower's role in this trajectory was much less clear than diamonds or minks or pearl-handled revolvers. In fact, despite repeated viewings over fifty years, I never noticed them until recently.

So I watched my well-worn repertoire of films noirs again, looking for the femme with the corsage, or a flower in her hair, or one whose signature might be a certain vase of flowers. Concentrating on the years 1940–53, which spanned from the earliest films noirs to the return of American soldiers from the Korean War, I looked at a broad swathe of films that featured prominent femmes fatales who favored flowers, and then very closely at *Mildred Pierce,* a film in which corsages and flowers marked important junctures all through the film. Then I took another route, exploring the iconography of corsages in the context of wartime fashion history. In 1941, the United States was on the verge of entering World War II, caught between knowing about the devastation of the war abroad and not wanting to know. On December 7, 1941, Pearl Harbor was attacked, and the decision was made. By 1945, the United States had become a country transformed by war and immersed in wartime culture, abroad and at home. The world for women included the rationing of food and goods for clothing, civilian aid leagues run by women, women in the armed forces, mothers and wives hoping for soldiers to return, women joining the domestic workforce in greater numbers than before, and women occupying jobs like riveting airplanes together and working in munitions plants that had previously been dominated by men. What could be the role of the luxurious corsage, an accessory doomed to die, not sensible and reusable, in this new world?

I sought the images projected by the fashion industry for these years, as reflected in two major periodicals, *Vogue* and *Glamour,* as well as on-screen images, to see if I could find connections that would explain the significance of the gardenias or camellias or orchids for the femme fatale. By surprise, the investigation sparked new insights about the history of women, work, and the aspirations of a new kind of screen woman—and real women—whose success did not depend on a corsage.

FILM NOIR FLOWERS

In the world of film noir, a femme fatale is the heartless, selfish woman who can break any rule she wants. She does not have to wait to receive a corsage or flower as a gift. She can accessorize herself. A giddy Miss Wonderly, for example, in *The Maltese Falcon* brandishes a fluffy gardenia corsage as she lies shamelessly to detective Sam Spade. Very early in *Mildred Pierce* we find Veda, whom we might call the "daughter fatale," still toting a flower in her hair even after she killed the guy who is both her lover and stepfather.

The flower can identify the deceitful femme fatale and can also mark an important moment of deceit. The heroine of *The Letter* coyly plucks a flower from a vase and plunges it into the V-neck of her blouse. It instantly becomes a self-made corsage to side-track herself and her lawyer; she's guilty of her lover's murder. All of these femmes fatales have accessorized themselves with corsages. The corsage is part of their costume, not a love token. When contemplating the true character of a femme fatale, part of the suspense lies in wondering how bad, how heartless, can she really be? The corsage is a clever distraction—the femme's boyfriend or rescuer, detective or lawyer, or the film viewer, might think, *why, couldn't this gorgeous creature be just like any other woman, a sister, a sweetheart, who loves flowers and dresses?* The corsage is, simply, an accessory to their crime.

In this way, corsages can be used as subterfuge: Surely little venomous Veda, selfish to the core, could actually be a sweet young debutante under that camellia. Surely Miss Wonderly, looking like a confused schoolteacher who forgot to take off her corsage, is just a mixed-up girl underneath. Surely Leslie, looking gay and beautiful as she seizes the flower from its vase, is projecting innocence, not guilt, to fool the lawyer who's half in love with her.

FIGURE 6.2 Bad Brigid O'Shaughnessy in motion, corsage and cigarette on full display. *The Maltese Falcon* (directed by John Huston, Warner Bros., 1941).

According to the 1969 *Dictionary of Costume,* the corsage is

a small bouquet of flowers worn on the shoulder or bosom, or carried in the hand. Also, the décolleté bodice of an evening gown. With the growth of the florist industry and the refrigerator, . . . the corsage became a dress accessory. Fresh Parma violets were succeeded by gardenias, orchids, and camellias, formerly considered "fast." At a dance, flowers were generally worn at the waistband of a dress, the lapel of a coat, or pinned to a muff. In the 1920's, with drooped, loose waistlines, flowers were pinned on the shoulder.[1]

This definition is provocative. The flower pinned on a bosom, or the plunging neckline of an evening dress, makes obvious reference to the woman's body, as if pointing to her sexuality. The idea that certain flowers were "fast" is fascinating; they carried connotations of loose sexual mores before the flowers were even pinned on. Emily Post's *Etiquette* from 1940 underscores the questionable moral fiber of a corsage. In her "glossary," the author defines the corsage but adds that it is "vulgar" to call this accessory a corsage, and that the preferred term would be "flowers to wear."[2] Presumably this fine distinction originates somewhere in the deep subconscious associations of women and flowers, of décolleté bodices and what lay underneath.

In the wartime 1940s, corsages could refer back to the more luxurious 1920s, with dances and dizzy nightclub prowls, suggesting decadence. A fashion magazine, such as *Vogue* from the early 1940s, shows corsages worn as accessories to an outfit, like jewelry or a hat, but it is doubtful that *Vogue*'s vision corresponded to the everyday reality of anyone but the very rich, who could afford a perishable, soon-to-die accessory like a corsage for everyday use. The film femme fatale radiates this kind of luxury: she does not have to wait for a gift; she is not on a budget; she is her own special occasion. Apparently, gardenias, orchids, and camellias, all popular with femmes fatales, already arrived with a bad reputation: they were "fast." "Fast" girls were not "nice"; flowers used promiscuously could convey a message.

The authors of noir screenplays certainly played with the conventions associated with corsages and flowers. In *The Blue Gardenia,* a nice girl gets a "Dear Jane"—a letter of rejection from her Korean War soldier fiancé—and decides in revenge to go out for a wild night. She accepts the invitation of an obviously not nice man on the make, has too many Polynesian cocktails, and pins on a blue gardenia corsage as her decadent spree accelerates. Now she is "fast." Later that evening, the man won't give up when she refuses his advances, and she knocks him unconscious—maybe dead—with a poker from the fireplace. It was an act of self-defense that could look like murder. She flees the scene of the crime, but the blue gardenia had already fallen on the floor; it becomes a key detail and a clue that links her to the crime. It stymies her attempts to prove herself innocent. This heroine is no femme fatale, just a nice girl who made a mistake, and the blue gardenia taunts her. A true femme fatale could manage her corsage.

Other examples of flower or corsage as icon dot the landscape of pulp novels and the films they became. It was a camellia that almost fell out of the murdering Veda's hair in the film *Mildred Pierce* as she clutches her chenille bathrobe to herself and appears to be a worried schoolgirl. No doubt, flowers were signifiers. According to the 1949 Bantam Books pulp cover of Alexandre Dumas's *Camille,* his novel told the story of Marguerite Gautier, "The Lady of Camellias" who was "luxuriously kept by the richest men in Europe."[3] She was a bad woman who liked "fast" flowers.

Add to the list of suspicious flowers dahlias and magnolias. In the film *The Blue Dahlia,* an unfaithful World War II wife buys armfuls of blue dahlias and puts them in a vase. Her soldier husband arrives home from the war to find his wife the queen of a bungalow party shack, with a new boyfriend and a confused story about the death of their child. When he confronts her, she plucks out the petals of the dahlia viciously, as if each one signified her guilt. The dahlias come to represent her infidelity and selfishness—and perhaps the unspoken funeral in the house.

In the United States, magnolias come loaded with a different set of associations. They grow freely in the American South and were the luxury trees for the front lawns of plantations—status symbols of wealth gained on the back of slavery. White Southern belles decorated themselves with magnolias in their hair and on their ball gowns, if we believe the lore of movie staples about the South like *Gone with the Wind*. African-American author Bucklin Moon titled his novel *No Magnolias*—an obvious protest against Southern history. The book dramatizes race issues. On its cover, the heroine wears no corsage, no magnolia, only a challenging stare and a serious white blouse. She looks as if someone were taking her photo, and she wanted to stare right through the photographer. In this case, a magnolia is a corsage to be repudiated.

Perhaps orchids are the most decadent of the "fast" flowers in the noir world, because they are grown in hot houses, at great expense. Giving a girl an orchid could evoke a response like "ah" or "ooh," as if she had just been given an engagement ring: an investment has been made. A contract like marriage could be coming. But luxurious orchids are at the same time what fancy men, bad men, give to ladies from sheer extravagance, as a show-off, as when Mildred Pierce's rotten boyfriend first attempts to win her with orchids.

Orchids can also be the pet hobby of rich fanciers who can afford their own hothouses, as in Raymond Chandler's *The Big Sleep*. Here, detective Philip Marlowe meets his new client, the dying general with two decadent daughters, in a hothouse choked with orchids: "The air was thick, wet, steamy and larded with the cloying smell of tropical orchids in bloom. . . . The plants filled the place, a forest of them, with nasty meaty leaves and stalks like the newly washed fingers of dead men."⁴ It is as if these morbid orchids are the corsages the two daughters will always wear, as they constantly both flirt with and lie to Philip Marlowe. Indeed, there is a dead man rotting underground nearby. No wonder the orchid stalks remind him of the "newly washed fingers of dead men," a flower with a death grip. Later the general confesses: "I seem to exist largely on heat, like a newborn spider, and orchids are an excuse for the heat" (9). So the orchids are both death and life, but still hideous to the general: "They are nasty things. Their flesh is too much like the flesh of men. And their perfume has the rotten sweetness of a prostitute" (9). By the book's end, we know that the general might as well be talking about the "rotten sweetness" of both of his daughters. Both tried the seductive ploys of the femme fatale on Philip Marlowe; one was an impulsive murderer, and the other played coy to cover up for her. Once any corsage is made, it is on its way to death. But in the world of *The Big Sleep*, it is as if the flowers are already dead even while still living, and living is the same thing as rotting.

The sepulchral orchid makes other odd appearances in noir film and literature. In the film *Conflict*, a husband wants to murder his wife so that he can marry his wife's sister. But he's only dreamed about it so far. When he finally decides to contact a hit man, he picks up the phone and tells the operator, "Get me ORCHID" and follows with the rest of the telephone number. Perhaps calling the "orchid" exchange is the equivalent of pinning on a corsage. It is his corsage moment, dressing himself up before the kill, signaling further descent into rottenness. In Cornell Woolrich's noir novel *I Married a Dead Man*, the desperate heroine adopts an extravagant lie: she assumes the identity of a dead man's wife as a trade for financial security. But the weight of this huge fabrication unravels her more and more. At one point her nerves fray, and the big black telephone receiver she's holding falls on her shoulder, "clinging there wilted, defeated, like some sort of ugly black hard-rubber orchid worn for corsage."[5] The telephone turns into the flower of evil, an ugly black orchid. Woolrich's phrasing, "worn for corsage," is peculiar—as if the act of wearing a corsage is a deliberate act of deception, some kind of dirty trick that women can play, like using cheap perfume. It reminds us of Emily Post's condemnation of "corsage" as "vulgar." Cornell gives the heroine—a desperate unwed mother-to-be—the tool kit of a femme fatale, including deception and an imaginary corsage, but makes it a revolting corsage that eats away at her conscience. Like the general's orchids, her corsage is rotten.

Perhaps it is merely the twin face of flowers that make them such unstable metaphors, standing in for purity or decay, depending on the occasion—rituals for both weddings and funerals. Orchids seem to offer a special fetish, as they are not common to either weddings or funerals—too lavish, too decadent. Flowers have never been entirely pure. They can flip both ways. Think of Hester Prynne in Nathaniel Hawthorne's *The Scarlet Letter*, rebelliously embroidering flowers around the letter "A" she was forced to wear in penance for adultery. She made her own corsage; she changed the meaning of the "A" with the decor of proper matrons, the stuff of sentimental needlepoint pillows and flowered aprons. Or we might say she changed the meaning of the sentimental by throwing a scarlet "A" into a field of flowers. Certainly flowers, anywhere, have a nascent reference to Eve, the one blamed for ruining the Garden of Eden; after all, first comes the flower, then the fruit.

Even the pure-sounding white rose of the fairy tale "Beauty and the Beast" is not spotless, according to Joseph L. Henderson in Carl Jung's *Man and His Symbols*. When the merchant father leaves for a journey, his daughter Beauty asks only for a white rose instead of jewels as a present, a request usually taken as a sign of her humility. But it proves to be a special, difficult request. The father steals the white rose from the Beast's garden—the flower moment. His theft unleashes the Beast's anger and sets in motion a brutal punishment: his daughter must come to live with the Beast, who instantly falls in love with her. Three months later, Beauty has fallen in love with her "animal man" as Henderson calls him. The rose is complicated: "cruelty and kindness combined." It brings on pain—her father's disease, the Beast's near death, her initial repulsion for the Beast, and the transference of her loyalty from father to Beast.[6]

A flower, then, may intrinsically signify pain and pleasure, the death of childhood and the birth of sexuality. A femme fatale's corsage could certainly be a badge of pride, her self-proclaimed sexual pride. If the flower is sex, she will wear the flower, quite boldly, as Hester Pyrnne wore her A, as Veda wore her camellias. Georgia O'Keeffe showed us that flowers are infinitely sexual, like the throat of an iris, unfolding and unfolding. Even Hawthorne allowed Hester Prynne to appropriate flowers to show that her "sin" might simply be part of the natural world. Beauty wanted "just a rose," but she was really asking for a lot of trouble. The femme fatale's use of the corsage can also be complicated. She can hide behind its seeming innocence like Miss Wonderly in her "schoolgirl act." She can decorate herself, like Veda in *Mildred Pierce,* so she can have it all ways: look the innocent birthday girl, blow out the candles on her cake, kiss and kill her mother's husband, all in one night.

The 1945 film version of *Mildred Pierce* begins with gunshots. We see the interior of a well-appointed beach house. Oddly, the camera lingers on a highly stylized, art-deco era painting of a flower on the wall, our first clue to the poisonous corsage/flower that dances through the film.

The film cuts to Mildred's house, where Veda waits. There's a commotion: the police have arrived at her grand house. Veda appears to be pulled out of bed, wrapped in a white chenille bathrobe, her hair a little mussed, her eyes the perfect imitation of a confused child wakened from a bad dream—even though she's just shot her lover and stepfather dead. Only one detail is off—a big camellia is still in her hair, drooping a little now, the very same camellia she wore to her birthday party that very night, the same camellia she wore when she killed her stepfather. It looks like the flower in the painting in the beach house.

Soon the film flashes back to the beginning of the whole sordid story. In a sun-washed

FIGURE 6.3 Veda in her chenille bathrobe, corsage still in her hair, after she shot Monty. *Mildred Pierce* (directed by Michael Curtiz, Warner Bros., 1945).

suburb of Los Angeles, two sisters walk home from school, Veda tall and prissy, Kay a bouncy tomboy. Their home is a "Spanish" style stucco house that has its own corsage outside—a giant palm tree, voracious looking. Inside, their house is a stage set of domestic middle-class tranquility: a piano to play, big drapes, a mother baking pies in the kitchen.

But trouble looms in the little stucco paradise: the mother feverishly bakes pies to sell to neighbors to make money. It's the Depression: the father has lost his job, the mother nags him to find another one, and the father has a more sympathetic woman friend. Who knows how soon the piano, the drapes, and even the house might be repossessed? The giant palm outside underscores the fragility of the stage-set house. The house could blow away, but the giant palm would still be there, to mock the space left behind.

Veda, the big sister, lives in a world of her own aspirations, chiefly gleaned from magazines. She rigs herself up like a flower before she goes to bed, her hair in a ribbon with a big flowery bow, in a flowery peasant-style nightgown. The sight of her flower child overwhelms Mildred with love, and she tries to kiss Veda goodnight, but Veda says, "But let's not get sticky about it." No bee will find this self-made flower.

One afternoon Mildred comes home from work and finds prim Veda playing the piano and Kay dressed up like a South American nightclub dancer, wrapped up in silk shawls, bracelets, flowers in her hair, smeared with lipstick—a miniature version of Carmen Miranda. Flowers are part of the little girl's mantrap costume, fashioned by Veda, and Mildred can't bear it.

Soon after, Kay will die of pneumonia, the tragic victim of nature. Mildred arrives very late on the deathbed scene, because she's just been lured to the beach with her new boyfriend, playboy Monty Beragon. In return for being a fast woman and an absent mother, she must forfeit a child. Later, inexplicably, we see barely a moment of Mildred mourning. Instead, zesty Mildred immerses herself in the gritty business of opening her first restaurant—chickens, light fixtures, cash register, and grease. For the restaurant's opening night, Monty brings her some "fast" orchids—but working woman Mildred's orchids wind up in the trash.

It is the daughter Veda, not Mildred, who becomes the recipient and wearer of cor-sages. In the novel, after the restaurant's very successful opening night, Veda bubbles over about meeting Monty for the first time. She asks Mildred:

"Did you tell him about me?"

"Yes of course."

"Then he asked for Ray [Kay's name in the novel], and when I told him about her, he turned perfectly pale, and jumped up, and—"

"Yes, I know."

"And mother, those orchids!"

"You want them?"

"Mother, Mother!"

"All right, you can wear them to school."[7]

Monty is "perfectly pale" like orchids—and like the pale dead sister, who's been skipped over quickly for a "fast" flower. And now the flower will shamelessly be worn to school. It is Mildred who mind-reads Veda's desire to *wear the flowers*. This flower moment mir-rors one of many moments of complicity between mother and daughter in the declara-tion of endless desire.

Mildred is soon part of a triangle, in both book and film, made up of a greedy daugh-ter, a greedy boyfriend, and herself. They all pass through a flurry of buying the kind of clothes and cars and cigarette cases that suit Veda's new country-club life. But Monty himself is broke. Eventually, he must do the unthinkable: ask Mildred for money. He has thought to wear a carnation in his buttonhole for the occasion—his corsage. The carna-tion denotes deepening debauchery in the triangle. As Paula Rabinowitz notes, the se-ductive gigolo in Henry James's *Daisy Miller* specialized in wearing different bouton-nieres—the man's version of a dangerous corsage—while escorting Daisy to her doom.[8]

Soon Veda learns to use the corsage as a prop, whether she needs to look like a dam-aged young lady or a lascivious nightclub singer. She first tricks a rich, naive society boy into a sham marriage, claiming to be pregnant. His parents insist on an annulment, which Veda had planned for all along as a business deal for herself. For the legal proceedings, she decks herself out in a somber black dress with a prim white corsage. Once Veda has the money and gets home, she flops on the couch, laughs maniacally, and confesses that she's not really pregnant, still wearing her serious dress and corsage. The corsage marks another level of debasement, one that even Mildred can't bear. They fight. Veda: "I got the money, didn't I? . . . with this money I can get away from you. You and your chicken and pies and kitchens and everything that smells of grease." Mildred: "Get out before I kill you." The corsage hasn't fooled her.

In Veda's next incarnation, she's covered in flowers, and not much else. She's run away from home and become a nightclub act. Her barely there costume with a vaguely Polynesian look sports a huge shoulder-to-arm corsage, and flowers trail through her hair. She's sunk to a new level—nightclub tramp. Mildred lures her away with a new life: a grand house, Monty for a stepfather. Veda comes home. For a brief time, all seems marvelous. Now Veda will create herself again, as the debutante birthday girl. She floats into her party in a dress with layers of white chiffon, a confection like a fairy queen. Oddly, there's an oversized flower portrait in the party room—a hint of poisonous flower in the air. Veda completes her outfit with a big camellia worn in her hair.

The camellia is still there when Mildred catches Veda and Monty in a long kiss, and still there when Monty taunts Veda: "What? Did you think I'd marry a rotten little tramp like you?" And it is still there when Veda pumps several bullets into Monty. In the end, Veda is a rotten tramp, Mildred's orchids linger in the garbage or are handed over to her daughter to wear in school, and Monty's festive boutonniere is used for sponging money. In each case there is rot—recalling Chandler's orchids like dead men's fingers. Corsages, after all, are only a few days away from becoming rotten themselves. For Mildred, Veda, and Monty, flowers are accessories of evil. Flowers originate in the same natural world that produces blazing sunlight, giant palm trees, and stunning beaches, a world so big and bright that it cannot be trusted.

FIGURE 6.4 [FACING] "U.S. Male" issue, cover of *Glamour*, April 1942. Accompanying a serviceman appeared to be a sanctioned use of the corsage, though these seem made of fabric, not flowers.

Glamour

U. S. MALE ISSUE
Meeting – Amusing –
Dressing for – Working for –
and Marrying – Men

April, 1942   For Young Women – The Way to Fashion, Beauty and Charm   PRICE 15 CENTS
20 CENTS IN CANADA

1945: the year that *Mildred Pierce* came out and the year that World War II ended. The world was not big and bright; lines had been drawn everywhere and dark, obscene missions accomplished. Veda's refusal to do anything useful, to work, as her mother had done, as millions of military and civilian women war workers were doing, heightened her depravity. With her leisure life, camellias, and chiffon, with her contempt for "pies and chicken," she was easy to hate.

Back in early 1941, *Vogue* offered fashions for nightclubs and cruise ships, country-club fetes and exotic travel, and still trilled about flower fashion accessories. But by 1945, in both highbrow *Vogue* magazine and working women's *Glamour,* most women in America were in uniform.[9] The dominant fashion in both publications was the suit, with many variations, that in turn was a variant on the military uniform. Corsages, as accessories, dropped out of sight quickly after 1942—wearing one might have been something like dining on caviar and champagne when everyone else was getting by on rations. It might have been unpatriotic.

How much *Vogue* reflected everyday life was and still is elusive, since the fashions are so haute in style and price that they seem fantasy material. *Glamour* declared its allegiance to the working girl—and they did not mean streetwalkers; they meant the women who were taking up war-related work and other respectable jobs. It was soon subtitled, "For the Working Girl." In addition to modestly priced fashions, *Glamour* offered serious reading material. Articles appeared on how to get a raise, the history of women and work, how to outfit a cramped hallway apartment into a cozy nest, how to spruce up old garments to make them look new. One article even proclaimed that "Women's Place Is in the World," predicting that the recent influx of women into the workplace could make a permanent, radical change in the American workforce.[10]

In 1941, eleven months before Pearl Harbor, *Vogue* certainly had its eye trained on the war in the rest of the world. The January 15 issue ran articles on "Germans over Paris" and an essay from Madame Chiang Kai-Shek on "Chinese Women Mobilized for War."

Yet domestic life in the United States appeared unruffled in "A House like a Summer Garden," while "Flower Show, 1941" showered women with fanciful flower hats. Articles like "Made for Miami" and "Southwest Passage" implied that travel plans need not be forsaken. The article on Chinese women mobilizing for war sat alongside the fashion features called "Under Twenty—Yen for the Chinese" and "China-boy Shorts, China-girl Tunics."[11] It was as if world turbulence were merely inspiration for fashion ideas. Its article on the Germans in Paris was chiefly a lament about how dreary Paris fashions had become.[12] *Glamour,* born in 1942, aimed itself toward spunky, patriotic American young women doing their duty in one way or another—whether taking a new job in the city, working as a volunteer nurse or in a munitions factory, or waiting for a boyfriend or husband to come home from the war.

Broadly, in the beginning of 1941, in the world of *Vogue,* flowers dotted the fashion scene liberally—on hats, in bouquets, as corsages—not just for night life, but also for a polished daytime look with a suit. Corsages were not always special gifts; they embellished even a sporty town-and-country look, fantasy or not. The *Vogue* fashions of early 1941 were dramatic and plush—featuring broad shoulder pads, cinched-in waists, elaborate decorations, attention to details like tiny pleats on a blouse or rhinestone studs on a gown, expensive fabrics like brocade and velvet, and yards and yards of fabric when called for. It was the wardrobe of femmes fatales.

In previous years, *Vogue* had looked to Paris as the fashion capital, the major source of inspiration. But the German occupation of Paris had already abruptly changed that enthusiasm, and the center of fashion shifted to New York.[13] The February 1, 1941, issue of *Vogue* moved the theme to everything American, devoting itself to "USA Fashion on Its Own." Cultural features looked at articles on "American Indian Art," a muralist who specialized in American main streets, and an essay called "America" by Robert Sherwood. Fashion turned to "Suits in the U.S.A," "America Delivers the Goods," and "United States Control."[14]

By 1942, fashion had to adjust to the rationing of fabric as well as the loss of Paris. The opulence of a femme fatale's wardrobe would have been severely challenged by

1942's fabric restrictions: "A fitted coat could be 43 inches (109 centimetres) long have a sweep of 72 inches (183 centimetres). Coat sleeves could not be dolman, leg-of-mutton, or any bias cut, or have cuffs."[15] How then, could femmes fatales, notorious for their jobs singing in nightclubs, costumed always in lavish gowns, go to work? No wonder they turned to crime—No sweep? No bias cut? No sequins? Impossible!

The modest goals of March 1942 *Glamour* articles confronted rationing, thrift, and shortages: "Clever Ways with a Needle" and "Nellie the Beautiful Hoarder," for example. And perhaps this parsimony extended to the rationing of glamor for national security: "You've a Date with Defense" or "My Fashion Autobiography, by Bonnie Budget." "Be Physically Fit for National Defense" fell into the "Beauty" section.[16] The featured fashion staple was the suit, the uniform for civilian women. A 1943 advertisement for Hockanum Woolens underscored the crossover between military style and civilian adaptations of military style: "In all six wars . . . Hockanum Woolens of superlative quality have been supplied, as now, for the Uniforms of the Armed Forces and for Civilian Clothes on the Home Front."[17] The ad portrays two demure women, one with downcast eyes, one with a hat and veil, showing off a wool suit and a wool coat, each cut more for utility than for flair, posed soberly in front of a "Buy War Bonds" sign. These were patriotic clothes, sturdy, useful, and plain—certainly not the dream stuff of femmes fatales.

And what of flowers, and corsages, in this schizophrenic atmosphere, yearning toward the luxe life while reporting on training Chinese peasants? Early in 1941, *Vogue* ran a big feature called "Flower Show, 1941," recommending indulging a passion for everything *fleur:*

Last year, you may have owned ONE flower hat. This year, just ONE will never appease you. . . . you'll want the hat rack to be a Grand Central Palace Flower Show. You'll want to wear your new turban trellised with pansies, your sailor suit bunched with anemones. Heavy, sweet roses above your brow, violets under your chin, tulips over your ears. You'll want to wear flowers with your furs, your tweeds, town tailleurs, your dinner-suits.[18]

Apparently, certain flowers had been released from their onus of being "fast" in this enthusiasm, and the *Vogue* fantasy extended the use of flowers and corsages to every sort of clothes or accessory a woman might own—but how many of their readers really had "town tailleurs"?

The rhapsodic praise of flower power continues with bringing the bee to the flower: "Men will sigh with relief. Flower hats are always men-pleasers. No male author ever described a heroine without putting a flower in her hair" (46). It was a broad claim—that no male author "ever described a heroine without putting a flower in her hair." Apparently this author was not thinking of Ma Joad in *The Grapes of Wrath*. But it raises an interesting question: how much was the costume of the femme fatale a construction of men—male authors, male directors, male wardrobe consultants?

The *Vogue* article goes on to play with the language of war to promote its thesis on fashion flowers: "No Male Defense holds out long out against a face under a Flower hat" (46). Certainly the idea of "Male Defense" had double meaning; it was the last spring without the United States being formally involved in the war, and perhaps the last spring to be flirtatious with flowers. These 1941 hats offered luxury: "a red rose on a turban of pink silk" (47), "crushed parma violets, purple and lavender" (48), "pansies, an enormous cluster of them—trellis one side of the back-of-your-pompadour turban" (48). This last hat is absurd, one and a half times as high as the woman's face. The women in the photos appear like store mannequins, incapable of rolling a bandage or digging a trench or using a gun. Perhaps it was the flower's last hurrah.

It was difficult to find any hint of a corsage in *Vogue* or *Glamour* for the rest of 1941 or 1942, unless it was the cover of *Glamour* dedicated to "The U.S. Male." Here, twin models in twin outfits including polka-dot gloves and red rose corsages each hold one arm of the same serviceman. The corsages are so identical and flat that they appear to be made out of fabric—practical, reuseable accessories, not soon-to-rot corsages. Jump to 1945, and there were no flowers or corsages to be found in *Vogue* or *Glamour,* until the *Glamour* Easter issue in March 1945. *Glamour* ran an article called "Easter Comes on April First." Here, the utility suit meets the flower: "What will you wear? A suit, of course

... and flowers."[19] But the flower corsages are not gay, or flamboyant, or seductive. The women who wear them look almost identical, all in suits, like uniforms, all in pillbox hats, two of them with eyes demurely downcast, the third cheerfully admiring the corsage and suit combo of her comrades in arms, and every single woman on her way to church on the arm of an officer in uniform. The rapacious, dangerous flower of the femme fatale, in this prescription, was now tamed.

SOME CAN DO WITHOUT FLOWERS

By 1945, the visual message of *Vogue* and *Glamour* had practically merged, with only one fashion dominating each publication—the suit, without corsage. True, the fabrics, the cut, and the cost of the suit may have varied between the two publications, but the mandate looked the same: be in uniform, be ready, have the "can-do" look of a woman who can work or help her country or forgo luxury. These were stylish but sensible suits, not clingy sequined nightclub suits but a versatile, well-cut, movable suit—civilian versions of the uniforms that thousands of women in the armed or civilian forces were wearing for wartime effort. Perhaps even the uniform was a bit glamorous; during the war, American designers were admired worldwide for American women's service uniforms.[20] The crossover between the suited civilian and the servicewoman, combined with rationing, implied that a thrifty patriotic woman might not own more than one suit, so she best choose a classic.

Looking at this radical jump from the haute couture, glamorous, decorative woman to the suited-up, ready-for-action competent woman between 1941 and 1945, I suddenly remembered another interesting woman in many films noirs or film noir variants. Though the deliciously wicked femmes fatales of the 1940s had always dazzled me first, another compelling woman sometimes appeared. I call her the "can-do" woman who goes to work in her can-do suit. Sam Spade, for example, had his devoted secretary Effie in the 1941 film version of *The Maltese Falcon*. She wore a suit, rolled Sam's cigarettes,

FIGURE 6.5 "Approved by U.S. Males," advertisement for Sacony suit, *Vogue*, March 1, 1945. Why did the "can-do" suit need male approval?

sat on his desk, and answered his midnight telephone calls. Miss Wonderly, the femme with all her exquisite looks and corsages, landed in prison. But Effie got to get up and go back to work. Ida in *Mildred Pierce* was the ever-sensible business manager who kept her head, her job—and her tailored suits. Lovely flowers sent Veda to jail.

Other film noir variants like *Phantom Lady, Cat People,* and *Saboteur* used the conventions of film noir—the dark look, the shadows, the doomed man, seduction. But the day was saved—and the man was saved—in each by the woman in a can-do suit. She beats the fatale force in the end. In *Phantom Lady,* two women occupy the role of femme fatale. The first woman is already dead; she had been a faithless wife obsessed with her own jewels, boyfriends, and nightlife. The police quickly accuse her earnest engineer husband of the murder. A "phantom lady" offers his only hope for an alibi. She's the other part of the fatale force: a woman he picked up in a bar who was wearing a fur hat so huge and outrageous that it might have appeared in 1941 *Vogue*—a sort of obscene fur corsage. But she completely disappears, and our hero is quickly bound for the electric chair.

The hero's can-do woman is his secretary, so clean and sincere that her nickname is "Kansas." Despite all obstacles, can-do Kansas barges through every piece of evidence at her own risk, including finding the phantom lady, posing as a cheap pick-up girl to get evidence from a sleazy musician, and almost getting killed by the true killer. Her boss goes free. What about her? A promotion? A new career as a detective? All we know is that a marriage proposal arrives through her Dictaphone.

Jacques Tourneur's 1942 *Cat People* is horror noir with patriotic touches. As it opens, a beautiful but sad woman muses by the panther cage at Central Park Zoo, when she's not working as a fashion designer. An all-American ship engineer falls for her, but she has a few peculiar flaws that inhibit a true marriage. First, due to a curse inherited from her birthplace, an evil village in enemy Serbia, if she kisses a man, he will die, or so she believes. So on their honeymoon night, separate bedrooms. Second, she has odd uncontrollable aggressive moments, as when she bats at her pet canary like a cat would, until it dies. Third, the curse she suspects seems confirmed at her wedding dinner at a Serbian restaurant. Like a conventional bride, she looks radiant in a suit and a corsage. But a cat-faced woman glittering in sequins who passes by the table and murmurs "moire sestre"—my sister, in Serbian—soon destroys her joy.

So the heroine appears half can-do woman and half femme fatale. On the can-do side, she does have a job, and suits, and she does warn her husband. On the femme fatale side, her suits come with a lot of fluffy accessories and a wedding corsage, strange inhibitions and half-truths. Meanwhile her husband starts to spend those frustrating sexless evening hours at work. Right beside him is his right-hand coworker Alice, always ready to work cheerfully, wearing her plain tailored work suit night and day. Alice has always been secretly in love with him. She calls herself "a new kind of other woman"—presumably one who has her own job, her own paycheck, a can-do kind of other woman who can see the light of day and speak her own mind, not financially kept by a man in a secret love nest. Eventually, sensible Alice helps her man find out the truth—his Serbian corsage-wearing wife really *is a panther.*

Alfred Hitchcock's 1942 patriotic thriller *Saboteur* gives us ample opportunity to see the can-do suit in action—in fact, the same suit, through the entire film. *Saboteur* is not a noir with a doomed ending. But it does involve a hapless hero falsely accused of sabotage at a munitions plant and uses noir aesthetic conventions. The hero has to run for his life against a sort of "collective fatale," a group of saboteurs. Together they calmly blow up dams, munitions plants, and new warships.

The traitors have framed the hero Barry; he must run. His escape leads him to a lonesome house in a forest. A charming blind man, who refuses to judge Barry as a criminal, answers the door. The man's visiting niece Patricia arrives also, wearing her can-do suit. She works as a photographer's model. Her image looms over patriotic billboards promoting milk, or the war effort, all over the highways of the United States. Like other Hitchcock helper women, she suspects Barry's guilt at first, but he tricks her into helping him escape.

So her can-do suit is at first a sort of defense uniform, and later a lab coat as the working girl examines the evidence, and later becomes a comrade-in-arms uniform when she begins to help and trust him—and fall in love. Thrifty and true to the war effort, she wears the same suit through the whole film, even as she finally chases the real saboteur to the Statue of Liberty and barely escapes falling off of it. Had the film gone on to her inevitable thrifty wartime wedding to Barry, she doubtless would have been wearing the same suit—without flowers.

This brings us back to the idea of *permission to wear the flower.* A patriotic bride had permission, as did the patriotic girlfriends in uniform in the *Glamour* 1945 Easter fashion spread. The femme fatale asked no permission, even in times of war. In fact, the bad wife of the returning soldier in *The Blue Dahlia* bought herself all the blue dahlias she wanted, which came to represent her infidelity, selfishness, and lack of patriotism.

Although the movie of *Mildred Pierce* was vaguely set in the Depression, its fashion look conformed much more to the deluxe fashions of *Vogue* magazine in early 1941. The film came out in October 1945. By this time, film audiences were thoroughly steeped in the iconography of the uniformed or can-do suited woman versus fur-clad glittery glamor queens with huge shoulder pads, recalling prewar 1941. In this view, Mildred was bad, retrograde, though tempered by early scenes of her as a worried wife baking pies for money, pounding the pavements looking for work, or learning how to be a waitress. But her daughter Veda was completely bad, with no redeeming history. In *Mildred Pierce*, it was Mildred and Mildred's tart-mouthed assistant Ida who wore the can-do suits. Daughter fatale Veda, however, used corsages and flowers as props whenever it suited her latest incarnation of herself: ruined innocent, nightclub tramp, reborn debutante, and fiancée of her own stepfather.

For the 1945 audience, Veda's manipulation of the flower could, consciously or not, easily add another shade of meaning to her depravity. In addition to her shocking selfishness, her flowers were unpatriotic! And Veda never wore a sensible can-do suit. Her suits had velvet collars or lavish glittery brooches on the lapels (like jeweled corsages), cinched-in waists, and tight skirts—not suitable for the nation's defense.

The thrill of watching the can-do suited woman was seeing her solve her crime, jump into action, go to work, walk home alone, all without corsages. But Hollywood could think of no more interesting future for them than a promise of marriage. Even the great actress and maverick director Ida Lupino, whose courageous films about unwed mothers, paraplegics, career-crazed tennis stars, rape victims, bigamists, and other outcasts challenged the conformist 1950s, though they raised riveting social problems, resorted to the same perplexing ending—married happily ever after.

The can-do women were principled, fearless women who did not wait around for orchids, camellias, or magnolias. They did not expect to win by tricks. They could not really be targets for woman hating or metaphors for death; they were not rotten to the core. They did not casually sport corsages as props to disguise their true nature. They offered something else, for a time, even if in the end they did not receive anything in return from the Hollywood scripts, as unconventional as themselves. But the thrilling potential of the can-do woman, her corsage thrown to the wind, still buzzes in the air.

1. Ruth Turner, *Wilcox Dictionary of Costume* (New York: Charles Scribner's and Sons, 1969), 85–86.

2. Emily Post, *Etiquette: The Blue Book of Social Usage* (New York: Funk and Wagnalls, 1940), 32.

3. "About THE COVER," Alexandre Dumas, *Camille* (New York: Bantam Books, 1949), front inside cover copy.

4. Raymond Chandler, *The Big Sleep* (New York: Vintage Crime, 1992), 7. Further citations appear in the text.

5. Cornell Woolrich, *I Married a Dead Man* (New York: Penguin, 1994), 19.

6. Joseph L. Henderson, "Ancient Myths and Modern Man," in *Man and His Symbols*, ed. Carl G. Jung (New York: Doubleday, 1969), 138.

7. James M. Cain, *Mildred Pierce* (New York: Alfred A. Knopf, 1941), 194.

8. Paula Rabinowitz, "Coda: Seen and Obscene," in *Fashioning the Nineteenth Century: Habits of Being 3*, ed. Cristina Giorcelli and Paula Rabinowitz (Minneapolis: University of Minnesota Press, 2014), 277–86,

9. In the Fashion Institute of Technology Library in New York, where bound volumes of fashion magazines still exist, I turned every page of *Vogue* from January to July in 1941, before the United States entered the war in December. I reasoned that these months, coming into spring, Easter, and summer, would be the most likely to feature corsages. I looked at the same months in 1942 for *Glamour*, after its birth in January 1942. I then jumped to 1945, for both magazines, for the same months, after America was saturated in wartime culture and about to deal with the problem of the returning soldiers, looking for corsages as accessories, or if not in sight, generalizing to flowers.

10. Samuel Grafton, "Women's Place Is in the World: How to Make Today's Hard Work a Permanent Chapter in History," *Glamour*, February 1942, 27.

11. Table of Contents, *Vogue*, January 15, 1941, 3.

12. By an Eye-Witness, "Germans over Paris," *Vogue*, January 15, 1941, 60–61.

13. Jonathan Walford, *Forties Fashion: From Siren Suits to the New Look* (New York: Thames and Hudson, 2008), 61–62.

14. Table of Contents, *Vogue*, February 1, 1941, 3.

15. Limitation Order issued by the Civilian Production Administration, quoted in Walford, *Forties Fashion*, 69.

16. Table of Contents, *Glamour*, February 1942, 3.

17. Hockanum Mills advertisement, quoted in Walford, *Forties Fashion*, 70.

18. "Flower Show, 1941," *Vogue*, January 15, 1941, 46. Further citations appear in text.

19. "Easter Comes on April First," *Glamour*, March 1945, 116–17.

20. Elizabeth Ewing, *History of Twentieth Century Fashion* (Totowa: Barnes and Noble, 1986), 148.

7

SCHIAPARELLI'S CONVULSIVE GLOVES

Victoria R. Pass

In the 1930s, designer Elsa Schiaparelli (1890–1973) was famous for the unique accessories and embellishments that she designed to accompany smart suits and chic evening gowns. Schiaparelli's design sensibility was closely aligned with the artistic theories of surrealism. In fact Schiaparelli's accessories were the flourishes that transformed her chic looks into what I call strange glamor, an aesthetic based on the surrealist principals of the uncanny and convulsive beauty in fashion. The psychological experience of the uncanny can be evoked through the conflation of things that are irreconcilable: reality and fantasy, the actual world and the dream world. A classic example of the uncanny is a familiar image in the world of fashion, the mannequin—a figure that conflates human and nonhuman, animate and inanimate. Convulsive beauty is an aesthetic principal formulated by the "pope" of surrealism, André Breton (1896–1966), and defined as a series of strange and uncanny encounters, or paradoxes that elicit a physical reaction in the viewer, often shock. Schiaparelli's strange glamor used this principal of shock elicited through the uncanny to bring attention to the constructed nature of the sexualized body. She drew on the uncanny potential inherent in clothing to confuse fabric and flesh, object and subject, dead and alive to create some of her most striking designs.

The glove, with its potential to connect the animate and inanimate—the glove with the hand itself—is one of the key surrealist images of the uncanny and plays a central role in Schiaparelli's strange glamor. It was also deployed by many surrealist artists, including Breton in his novel *Nadja*. In Schiaparelli's hands, so to speak, gloves were used to transform not only an ensemble but also the woman wearing it. Easy to put on and take off, gloves provided the perfect vehicle for altering the body. The young surrealist Meret Oppenheim (1913–85) understood their potential as well. She designed dozens of uncanny accessories, some of which were purchased and reproduced by Schiaparelli, while others existed only in sketches. Like Schiaparelli's designs, these accessories destabilized the identity of the wearer and undermined conventional notions of attraction and sexuality.

STRANGE GLAMOR

An illustration by Cecil Beaton of Schiaparelli's first showing in her new atelier on Place Vendôme appeared in the March 15, 1935, issue of *Vogue*. The image shows a model, who bears a strong resemblance to Schiaparelli, sauntering down a flight of stairs in a smart suit, her hat cocked jauntily to one side:

> down the stairway festooned in blue velvet, steps a terse figure—the epitome of spring 1935. Her hat marches aggressively ahead of her, its blue felt visor rolled amusingly. Her blue wool suit, punctuated with red-and-green buttonholes, has the military briskness of Vienna before the War. Her blouse of white silk, froths at the neck and wrists with Binche lace and wears a heart insignia.[1]

The woman in Beaton's sketch is bold and unrestrained, her ensemble full of the contradictions fashion followers had come to expect from Schiaparelli. The militarism of the suit, with Schiaparelli's signature wide shoulders and long lean skirt, is contrasted with the feminine flourish of the blouse with its lace cuffs and collar and a playful heart with an arrow through it just below the neckline. Schiaparelli matches the masculine bravado of martial tailoring with the doodle of a love-struck girl.

SCHIAPARELLI (Bergdorf
Goodman): In Schiaparelli's
new house in the Place Vendôme, down the stairway festooned in blue velvet, steps a
terse figure—the epitome of
spring 1935. Her hat marches
aggressively ahead of her, its
blue felt visor rolled amusingly.
Her blue wool suit, punctuated
with red-and-green buttonholes,
has the military briskness of
Vienna before the War. Her
blouse, of white silk, froths at
the neck and wrists with Binche
lace and wears a heart insignia

FIGURE 7.1

Cecil Beaton, "Paris

Openings," *Vogue,*

March 15, 1935.

The woman wearing the suit is also somewhat incongruous. Not the pretty young girl
we expect in the fashion illustration but a more mature, unusual-looking woman who,
in this ensemble, encapsulates the idea of strange glamor, an aesthetic in fashion that
flourished in the 1930s, created through dissonance and through the contrasts on which
Schiaparelli's designs thrived: masculine and feminine, day and night, hard and soft, traditional and revolutionary. Strange glamor was certainly not Schiaparelli's invention
alone, but she is perhaps the designer who embodied it most fully, particularly in her
own personal style, which was closely associated with her work as a designer. Schiaparelli was not classically beautiful but was instead classified as a one of the *jolies laides,*
a "good looking ugly."[2] Her clothes were made for women like her, not to hide their

unusual features but to draw attention to them, making these women's look shocking. This interest in shock is what sets Schiaparelli's work apart from her contemporaries and links it with the notion of "convulsive beauty" so central to the surrealist project. This shared aesthetic connects Schiaparelli with surrealism.

For Schiaparelli, strange glamor was not concerned with glossy young prettiness or with the sweet androgyny of the flapper of the preceding decade. It is eccentric, challenging, individual, and mature. It is the glamor of Joan Crawford, Greta Garbo, Marlene Dietrich, Tallulah Bankhead, and Katharine Hepburn, all of whom were dressed by Schiaparelli. These women—along with ethnic beauties who rose to fame in the 1930s such as Anna Mae Wong, Dolores Del Rio (who was dressed by Schiaparelli), Dorothy Lamour, Hedy Lamarr, and Rita Hayworth—were changing the standards of pale blonde beauty in Hollywood.[3] In high society, Schiaparelli devotees Daisy Fellowes, Millicent Rodgers, and Wallis Simpson (later the duchess of Windsor) also exuded strange glamor.

Strange glamor is best demonstrated through several examples. In its Hollywood incarnation, Joan Crawford is particularly instructive, since her look changed from that of a young flapper to the mature aesthetic of strange glamor.[4] In a photograph from 1927, Crawford poses as the classic flapper, hair cropped under a cloche, bee-stung lips, gaze askance, body in a slouched pose.[5] In a photograph of Crawford by Edward Steichen from 1932, she wears a pleated dress and patterned coat by Schiaparelli and stares directly at the viewer.[6] Crawford faces us head on, sitting straight on the back of a modern chair. Her body is shaped by the coat that gives her the classic high broad shoulders and nipped-in waist she became famous for. Her glamor is bold and constructed, right down to her notorious plucked eyebrows. A photograph of Tallulah Bankhead from *Harper's Bazaar* in 1934 illustrates the contrasts inherent to strange glamor. Bankhead's stern glare in the photograph stands out against the fluffy white wool of her bunny hat and the bib collar of her Schiaparelli jacket.[7]

What made Schiaparelli's strange glamor so unique was her engagement with André Breton's concept of convulsive beauty. Breton, as writer and theorist, placed himself at the head of the mainstream surrealist movement. Writing many of the key texts that defined the movement, he wielded the power to decide which artists belonged to the movement. Those artists who were excommunicated by this Marxist pope of surrealism were often involved with fashion or other commercial endeavors, such as Salvador Dalí in 1939. Despite his distaste for fashion, Breton's concept of convulsive beauty found expression in clothing. Dilys Blum explains that "the acceptance of new concepts of female attractiveness during the 1930s had a parallel in the surrealists' challenge to existing notions of beauty . . . beauty implied harmony, but convulsive beauty took pleasure in being shocking, with an emphasis on dissonance and discordance."[8] Schiaparelli's strange glamor was symptomatic of a wider cultural embrace of the kinds of beauty that attracted the surrealists, those created through contradiction rather than unity.

Breton ends *Nadja* (1928) with the statement, "beauty will be CONVULSIVE or it will not be at all."[9] The classic example of convulsive beauty is the chance encounter. Breton writes in *Mad Love* that the Comte de Lautrémont's famous encounter between a sewing machine and an umbrella on a dissection table "constitutes the very manifesto of convulsive poetry."[10] Breton's description of convulsive beauty links aesthetic response to erotic pleasure. Breton identified the merging of two things—that is, when they move beyond Lautrémont's encounter to become one object or being—as *l'érotique voilée* (the veiled erotic).[11] This merging is often of the animate with the inanimate, as is the case with the surrealist fascination with mannequins. Man Ray used Meret Oppenheim as a model to explore this concept in one of his most famous photographs, *Erotique Voilé* (ca. 1933).

German-born Meret Oppenheim moved to Paris in 1932 from her home in Switzerland and by 1933 began to meet several of the surrealists including Alberto Giacometti and Hans Arp. In her early twenties, she was a generation younger than the surrealists and a true product of her times. Embracing the freedoms of the New Woman to explore her sexuality outside of marriage and procreation, she was seen by the male establishment of surrealism as the embodiment of the primitive woman/child, the *femme enfant*, a naive and unconventional woman fully in touch with her primal instincts and thus with her subconscious.[12] This kind of woman played the role of muse for many of the surrealists. Breton's novel *Nadja* expresses his fascination with a *femme enfant*, and even includes some of her drawings, prized by Breton for their convulsive beauty.

The young Oppenheim was thus the ideal model for Man Ray, who photographed her standing nude behind a printing press, her left arm coated in ink. The handle of the press's crank is situated just above her pubic region, and the top of the crank and its shadow obscure her breasts, accentuating Oppenheim's androgynous body. The phallic handle convulses her body between masculinity and femininity and allows her organic form to meld with the machine. The brilliant merging of masculine and feminine, human and machine created through Oppenheim's pose and Man Ray's lighting and framing create a powerful image of Breton's concept of *l'erotique voilée*. This is not simply the encounter between woman and machine, but the merging and mixing of the two.

This unlikely combination also evoked one of the most important elements of convulsive beauty: shock. According to Breton, convulsive beauty "consists of jolts and shocks, many of which do not have much importance, but which we know are destined to produce one *shock*, which does."[13] Within convulsive beauty, shock can manifest itself as an unexpected erotic charge or unstable amalgamation of movement and stillness. Hal Foster explains that "shock is an alternative route to the unconscious," which is why it was so important for surrealists such as Breton.[14] Shock affects a viewer in a visceral way; it is a bodily reaction and it is what makes convulsive beauty convulse.

Shock tactics were crucial to Schiaparelli's practice and her creation of convulsive beauty and strange glamor. Shock practically became a second signature for Schiaparelli in 1937 when she created her signature shade, shocking pink, and the perfume *Shocking*. Schiaparelli even took the name for her autobiography, *Shocking Life*, where she wrote about her discovery of this new color and perfume name:

PLATE 2 [FACING] Gattinoni, "Santa Teresa d'Avila," Fall–
Winter 2006 Collection. Courtesy of Gattinoni Couture.

PLATE 3 [ABOVE] Charlotte Nekola, *Curse of the Corsage*, 2013.
Pigment print of assemblage, 24 × 20 inches.

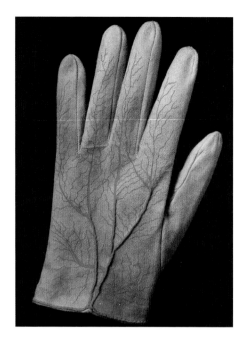

PLATE 4 [LEFT] Meret Oppenheim, silkscreened leather gloves, edition created for *Parkett,* 1985. Copyright 2013 Artists Rights Society (ARS), New York / ProLitteris, Zurich.

PLATE 5 [BELOW] Meret Oppenheim, *Fur Gloves with Wooden Fingers,* 1936. Fur gloves with wooden fingers in a Plexiglas box. Galerie Hauser & Wirth AG, Zurich. Copyright 2013 Artists Rights Society (ARS), New York / ProLitteris, Zurich.

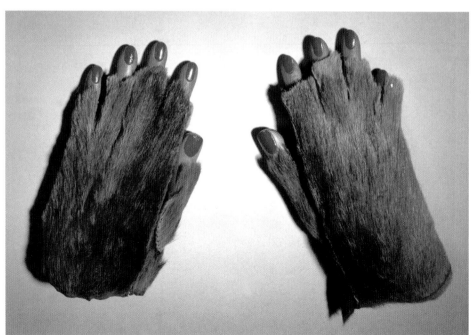

PLATE 6 Frida Kahlo (1907–54), *Self-Portrait on the Borderline between Mexico and the United States*, 1932. María Rodríguez de Reyero Collection, New York. Private collection, New York. Photograph: Erich Lessing / Art Resource, NY. Copyright 2014 Banco de México Diego Rivera Frida Kahlo Museums Trust, Mexico, D.F. / Artists Rights Society (ARS), New York.

PLATE 7 [ABOVE] Tarrah Krajnak, *Untitled*
(from *Strays*), 2012. Pigment print, 6 × 9 inches.
PLATE 8 [FACING] Tarrah Krajnak, *Rosary in Hand*
(from *Strays*), 2012. Pigment print, 6 × 9 inches.

PLATE 9 Prilidiano Pueyrredón, *Portrait of Manuelita Rosas*, nineteenth century. Oil on canvas, 199 × 166 cm. Museo Nacional de Bellas Artes, Buenos Aires.

The colour flashed in front of my eyes. Bright, impossible, imprudent, becoming, life-giving, like all the light and the birds and the fish in the world put together, a colour of China and Peru but not of the West—a shocking colour, pure and undiluted. So I called the perfume "Shocking." The presentation would be shocking, and most of the accessories and gowns would be shocking. It caused a mild panic amongst my friends and executives, who began to say that I was crazy and that nobody would want it because it was really "nigger pink." "What of it? Negroes are sometimes strikingly smart."[15]

In shocking pink and her perfume *Shocking*, Schiaparelli married a number of different themes that had defined her fashion: the natural world, exotic cultures, and surrealism. Schiaparelli saw her new shade of pink as deriving from cultures outside of Europe, which have often influenced her fashions. The bottle for *Shocking*, designed by artist Leonor Fini (1908–96), a close friend of Oppenheim, was based on the torso of Mae West and had a sex appeal that was certainly shocking to some. The fragrance too was shocking, formulated for the classic Schiaparelli woman: "no shrinking violet would be attracted to the warm, sensual animalistic notes of ambergris, civet, and musk and the fruity spicy tones patchouli and vetiver blended with such classic perfume ingredients as rose, jasmine, syringe, magnolia, and gardenia."[16] Perfume expert Jean-Marie Martin-Hattemberg went so far as to call *Shocking* "the first sex perfume."[17] Frida Kahlo, an exemplar of strange glamor herself, was a fan of the perfume. At her 1953 retrospective in Mexico, she was confined to her four-poster bed that had been brought to the opening, the pillows laced with *Shocking*.

UNCANNY GLOVES

In *Nadja*, Breton conflates gloves with women, imagining the leather as female flesh allowed it to take on a life of its own. Gloves were a particularly potent site for the conflation of woman and object, as even the plainest glove was already endowed with the potential for evoking the uncanny. Breton talks about his uncanny feeling at a woman removing her sky-blue glove: "I don't know what there can have been, at that moment, so terribly, so marvelously decisive for me in the thought of that glove leaving that hand forever."[18] The same woman also possessed a bronzed glove that Breton uses to illustrate this page. In this passage, a hand is confused with a glove and a bronze sculpture. In *Nadja*, "intimacy is always mediated, for Breton, by the displaced objects of desire, those objects— be they Nadja's glove, her clothes, or the city itself—on which he focuses attention."[19] Glove and woman are made one: leather turns into female flesh so that the glove takes on a life of its own. We can also see this theme reflected in a number of fashion magazine covers from this period, which also animate gloves. These include surrealist Giorgio de Chirico's cover of the November 15, 1937, issue of *Vogue* where gloves appear in a surrealistic still life, and another *Vogue* cover from February 15 of the same year, by Raymond De Lavererie, in which a glove comes to life to feed a grape-shaped brooch to a bird.

The glove's close connection to the body is integral to Schiaparelli's playful designs. Many of her gloves were rather simple, using her favored bright colors, contrasting colors, or unusual details such as slashing. These gloves could act to highlight hands, such as a 1936 pair in "wine suede with pale blue binding outlining the fingers like a neon light sign."[20] Other gloves created a jarring effect through a contrast in color. A pair of fingerless gloves in Schiaparelli's signature shocking pink seem to float on the field of a black evening cape in an illustration by Jean Cocteau for the December 1936 issue of *Harper's Bazaar*.[21] Brightly striped gloves with fur cuffs for a 1937 collection appear to slice the hand up, with each finger a different shade of brown.[22] These gloves had the uncanny effect of making strange the familiar shape of the hand. Schiaparelli used the contrast of gloves with the garments they accompanied to create a disruption or disjuncture of a glamorous look, effecting Breton's desired convulsive beauty and aesthetic of shock. For example, handkerchief gloves that look like bandages were paired with elegant evening gowns for autumn 1937. These gloves evoke a damaged body in startling contrast to the embellished surfaces of the dinner suits and evening ensembles. Schiaparelli also employed unusual colors and finishes for gloves, such as a pair of green doeskin gloves with gold kid ruffles running down the fingers for summer 1939. Curator Dilys Blum connects these gloves to the signs and symbols Schiaparelli would have known from her childhood in Italy, the horn-shaped *cornicello* amulet, as well as the sign of the *mano cornuta*, or the horned hand used to ward off the evil eye "or indicate a man has been cuckolded."[23] Other gloves included signature Schiaparelli "gadgets," such as compacts or matches, in hidden compartments that enhanced their value.

Schiaparelli's best-known gloves are probably those embellished with red snakeskin nails, which she designed to be worn with her bureau drawer suits and coats made in collaboration with the surrealist Salvador Dalí for winter 1936. The bureau drawer suits and coats were inspired by a recurring theme in Dalí's paintings and sketches: female bodies penetrated by drawers. According to Dalí, "The drawers include everything—Freud, Christianity, the possibility of penetration into the interior of a human being with its secret compartments all full of meaning."[24] In Dalí's works, these drawers were a means of visualizing the revelation of a woman's subconscious. The drawers penetrate and expose the female subject while simultaneously turning her into an object: a piece of furniture. Schiaparelli's suits and coats, by contrast, bring the bureau to life using rectangular patch pockets that mimicked drawer fronts embellished with knob-shaped buttons. Schiaparelli's drawers were all closed; some were real pockets, and others were a tease, being of no use whatsoever.[25] The suits and coat followed Schiaparelli's principle of day wear—codified by her biographer Palmer White—as armor. White argues that Schiaparelli's clothes worked to "protect the New Woman from counter-attacks by the male."[26] Schiaparelli transforms fabric into the wood of a bureau, and only the woman wearing the suit knew which pockets could actually be used.[27] Adding to this modern armor were the gloves Schiaparelli designed to accompany these ensembles made of black or white suede with colored snakeskin nails.[28] Schiaparelli's gloves confuse leather and skin, teasing viewers.

In the same collection Schiaparelli also included gloves in "surrealist pastel suedes with the veins of the hands painted on" that may have been inspired by a sketch by Meret Oppenheim.[29] In 1936, her father was forced to give up his practice as a doctor in Germany because his name sounded Jewish. With her financial support gone, Oppenheim began selling her jewelry and fashion designs to Elsa Schiaparelli, among others.[30] One of the best known of the designs was a fur bracelet that was shown with the same Winter 1936 collection as the bureau drawer suits.[31] This was the only design Oppenheim acknowledged selling to Schiaparelli, but a number of her sketches, including one for gloves embellished with veins, bear a striking resemblance to accessories in several Schiaparelli collections.[32] In 1985, Oppenheim collaborated with *Parkett,* a German art magazine, to produce an edition of these gloves that resemble the description of the gloves in Schiaparelli's collection.

Whether the design was Oppenheim's or not, it reflected a theme that fascinated both women: the notion of bodily transparency or the body turned inside out. Schiaparelli's earliest collections of knitwear in the late 1920s and early 1930s included "a skeleton sweater that shocked the bourgeois but hit the newspapers, which then took little notice of fashion. White lines on the sweater followed the design of the ribs so that women wearing it gave the appearance of being seen through an X-ray."[33] The idea resurfaced later in 1938, again in collaboration with Dalí, as the Skeleton Gown. The long clinging black matte jersey dress featured padded sections that seem to reveal the wearer's skeleton. Thwarting the fantasy of being able to see through clothing, these designs reveal the macabre interior of the body. Fashion critics Caroline Evans and Minna Thornton, in a feminist analysis of Schiaparelli's oeuvre, argue that the artifice and theatricality that she embraced in her designs allow women to control the masquerade of femininity.[34] Caroline Evans rightly connects "Schiaparelli's playful attitude toward the body" to Joan Riviere's argument about the masquerade of femininity, "for it articulates female identity as a matter of surface, or appearance, destabilizing the idea of an essential femininity."[35]

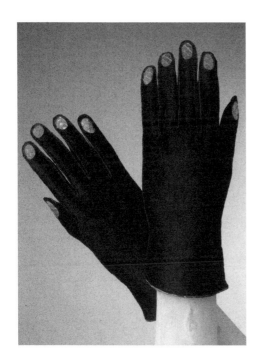

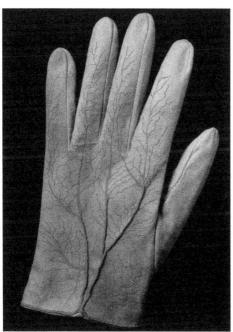

FIGURE 7.2 [TOP] Elsa Schiaparelli, woman's gloves, winter 1936–37. Black suede, red snakeskin. Philadelphia Museum of Art, Gift of Mme. Elsa Schiaparelli, 1969.

FIGURE 7.3 [LEFT] Meret Oppenheim, silkscreened leather gloves, edition created for *Parkett*, 1985. Copyright 2013 Artists Rights Society (ARS), New York / ProLitteris, Zurich.

Schiaparelli's destabilization of femininity in her fashion is part of the wider surrealist project to question the notion of a unified consciousness and identity through an exploration of the subconscious. By tricking the eye in her designs, Schiaparelli allowed her customers to reveal the way that the entire spectacle of femininity is constructed.[36] By thwarting the voyeuristic gaze of the viewer, these garments provide a kind of armor for the wearer, making the viewer self-conscious of his desirous gaze.

Oppenheim created a template for gloves embellished with the bones of the hand in 1936 and revisited the theme in 1964 in *X-ray of My Skull*, an X-ray of her profile adorned in jewelry. All of these striking images of strange glamor reveal the delicate inner working of the human body. The soft blue suede gloves are infused with blood through delicate veins. They are given life though the detailed embellishment, both glamorous and deathly. Schiaparelli continued to use gloves as a means of toying with the viewer's expectations. Perhaps the most striking and provocative of Schiaparelli's gloves was a pair

FIGURE 7.4 Marcel Vertès, "Spinach Is Fashion," *Harper's Bazaar*, September 15, 1938. Schiaparelli's gloves with golden claw fingertips are at upper left.

of black evening gloves designed for her Winter 1938–39 collection with golden metal claws. The gloves literally allowed a woman to let her talons show, evoking the image of the femme fatale but in a temporary form. The spectacle of putting on or taking off the animalistic claws underlines the constructed nature of the image of the femme fatale.

GLOVES FOR THE FEMME ENFANT

Other gloves took the conflation of woman and animal even further. *Harper's Bazaar* describes one pair in 1938: "Schiaparelli's humor persists. Bright red snakeskin inserted between the fingers of black antelope gloves to make your hands look like little paws."[37] Other pairs employed fur to look like paws. In 1935, Schiaparelli used several different materials including wildcat fur, seal pelt, and Persian lamb to create "gloves . . . as bulky as a hackney driver's and the most exciting accessory of the year."[38] These elbow-length gloves covered the top of the arm and hand with fur, using suede for the underside, creating the look of animal arms. They mocked the surrealist *femme enfant,* the primitive woman more animalistic and childlike than men.

Oppenheim may have been seen by surrealist men as the embodiment of the *femme enfant,* but like Schiaparelli she relished undermining the stereotype. While many of her accessory designs exist only in the form of sketches, her 1936 sketch of fur gloves is a notable exception. The sketch shows a female hand with red varnished nails sprouting fur.[39] In the pair of gloves that resulted from the sketch, Oppenheim used wooden fingertips with red nails to evoke the feminine hand emerging from the fur mitts. These gloves, like Schiaparelli's, highlight the conflation between gloves and skin, in this case taking the conflation one step further to combine woman and animal through the inclusion of the lifelike fingertips with their chic red nails. Oppenheim's gloves are brought to life in a disturbing and uncanny way. It is easy to imagine Schiaparelli's gloves, once removed from the wearer's hands, retaining their uncanny charge, as do Oppenheim's, appearing to be the disembodied paws of some hunted animal.

FIGURE 7.5 [TOP] Schiaparelli gloves in wildcat and suede shown on lower left, *Très Parisienne*, February 1935.

FIGURE 7.6 [LEFT] Carl Erickson, Schiaparelli silver fox gauntlets worn with a black wool suit and quilted felt hat, *Vogue*, October 1, 1935.

Both Schiaparelli and Oppenheim continued to explore the image of the primitive woman, most often in accessories meant to be removed in public, always underlining the construction of this surrealist ideal. Oppenheim sketched a high-heeled shoe with a fur-covered vamp and red varnished toes emerging at the tip in 1936, and around 1942 she sketched a hat with the gaping mouth of a dog rising from the crown, its tongue hanging down the wearer's nose. Schiaparelli produced a series of remarkably similar hats. In 1936, she showed a hat with a blue-eyed fox perched on the crown.[40] The Winter 1938–39 collection, which also included the claw gloves, featured another fox-topped hat with a long tail that wrapped around the neck of the wearer as well as a lavishly jeweled muzzle for a fox stole.[41] Here the wild creatures are tamed by the wearer, worn as though pets.

FIGURE 7.7 Meret Oppenheim, *Fur Gloves with Wooden Fingers*, 1936. Fur gloves with wooden fingers in a Plexiglas box. Galerie Hauser & Wirth AG, Zurich. Copyright 2014 Artists Rights Society (ARS), New York / ProLitteris, Zurich.

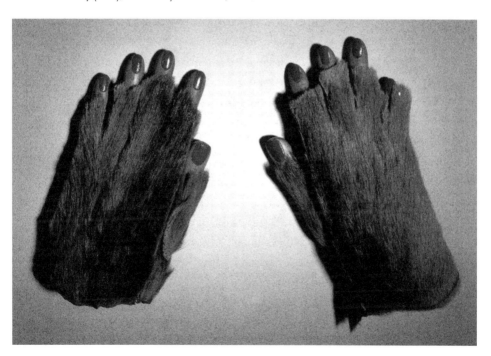

Another ensemble from this collection presents an alternative reading of Schiaparelli's fur accessories. The designer paired a wildcat fur coat with a hat featuring a wildcat face perched atop the wearer's head and the creature's legs and paws draping down from the hat and tying around the wearer's neck.[42] The woman wearing this extraordinary ensemble appears as a huntress wearing the skin of her prey in triumph. At the same time, the woman appears to transform into the wildcat. This oscillation between the femme fatale huntress and the primitive wildcat *femme enfant* directs the viewer's attention to the way the spectacle of fashion constructs the sexuality of the woman wearing it. Once the coat and hat are removed the woman is suddenly divested of the animalistic sexuality of the ensemble. This ensemble destabilizes the identity of the wearer; her sexuality vacillates between naive and threatening.

The similarities between Oppenheim's and Schiaparelli's fur accessories expose the ways in which these designs move beyond the uncanny to create images of convulsive beauty. These accessories transform the wearer into an animal, but through a liminal, transitory accessory, made to be taken off. This is particularly true of the fur gloves. Both Oppenheim's and Schiaparelli's fur gloves move beyond being simply uncanny accessories—playing up the conflation of live female hand and dead fabric or leather glove— to become convulsive accessories. Meret Oppenheim's most notorious use of fur in a surrealist object, *Fur-Lined Tea Cup, Saucer, and Spoon* (1936) (or as Breton dubbed it *Le Déjeuner en Fourrure*), placed alongside Schiaparelli's contemporary gloves reveals convulsive beauty.

Notably, Oppenheim's sculpture was inspired by a fur-covered bracelet she had designed for Schiaparelli in 1936. In one of the canonical stories of modernism, Oppenheim recalled that in a conversation with Picasso and Dora Maar at a cafe, Picasso admired the bracelet and said "Think of all the wonderful things you could cover in fur!" Looking at the teacup on the table at that moment, Oppenheim had the idea for the object.[43] She bought a tea cup, saucer, and spoon at a Paris department store and covered them in exotic Chinese gazelle fur. The object is both alluring and disgusting.[44] The tactile lushness of the fur invites the viewer to handle the object, and the hollow organic forms of each of the parts of the tea set combined with the pleasurable sensation of the fur evoke the vagina. The idea of tasting the fur cup or spoon in the mouth is revolting, but might also evoke the pleasures of oral sex. The tactility of this object, and the way it makes the familiar table setting strange and erotic engages with convulsive beauty on the deepest level in that the object itself evokes such powerful physical sensations. Even in a museum setting where we are not permitted to touch the object itself, our imagination takes over, creating the sensation of the fur cup in our hands and on our lips. Oppenheim's surrealist object underlines the eroticism of fur, making it at once alluring and repellant.

Turning back to Schiaparelli's exuberant fur gloves, it is clear the utility of warm fur for winter gloves has been exceeded by the sensual pleasure of the fur and the shocking images of a chic woman with the arms of a wild animal. Schiaparelli plays on the idea of the primitive instincts of the woman she dresses escaping the confines of her conservatively tailored suits and smart dinner dresses. This combination of primitive fur with civilized fashion mocks the surrealist image of the *femme enfant*, because this woman can remove her wild paws at any time. She too undermines the eroticism of fur. The gloves invite touch, and yet the appearance that they are not simply gloves but paws, claws, or talons warns viewers to keep their distance. Taking a cue from the original utility of gauntlets, from which some of these fur gloves took their shape, they act to protect the body on a number of levels.

Schiaparelli's designs exploit the surreal and erotic potential of gloves. She used them to transform women into femmes fatales or animals. Schiaparelli's gloves are conflated with hands, as they are in the work of Breton. Using the transient quality of gloves, Schiaparelli's spectacle reveals the working of the surrealist construction of the *femme enfant* and femme fatale in the same way Meret Oppenheim's objects do. Schiaparelli undermines the image of the femme fatale, making her viscous talons easily disposable. Both Oppenheim and Schiaparelli bristle at the limits of these identities. Schiaparelli, most likely in occasional collaboration with Oppenheim, gives women the option of adopting these personae at will, and then disposing of them as easily as removing a pair of gloves.

1. "Paris Openings," *Vogue*, March 15, 1935, 56.

2. Dilys E. Blum, *Shocking! The Art and Fashion of Elsa Schiaparelli* (Philadelphia: Philadelphia Museum of Art, 2003), 153.

3. Sarah Berry, *Screen Style: Fashion and Femininity in 1930s Hollywood* (Minneapolis: University of Minnesota Press, 2000), 95.

4. Schiaparelli biographer Palmer White called Joan Crawford, "the embodiment *par excellence* of the Schiaparelli Lady." Palmer White, *Elsa Schiaparelli: Empress of Paris Fashion* (New York: Rizzoli, 1986), 108.

5. The image is reproduced in Peter Cowie, *Joan Crawford: The Enduring Star* (New York: Rizzoli, 2009), 37.

6. The photograph appeared in "Miss Crawford of Hollywood," *Vogue*, October 15, 1932, 65: "This is one of Schiaparelli's typically extraordinary combinations—a dark hyacinth-blue lacy knitted woollen dress with a jacket of heavy matelassé crêpe in white and heliotrope. It is not too big for her—it is meant to look that way." It is reproduced in William A. Ewing and Todd Brandow, eds., *Edward Steichen: In High Fashion, the Condé Nast Years, 1923–1937* (New York: W.W. Norton, 2008), 210.

7. The photograph is by Von Horn, *Harper's Bazaar*, December 1934, 81.

8. Blum, *Shocking!*, 152.

9. André Breton, *Nadja*, trans. Richard Howard (New York: Grove Weidenfeld, 1988), 160.

10. André Breton, *Mad Love (L'amour Fou)*, trans. Mary Ann Caws (Lincoln: University of Nebraska Press, 1987), 9, 123.

11. Briony Fer, "Surrealism, Myth and Psychoanalysis," in *Realism, Rationalism, Surrealism: Art between the Wars* (New Haven: Yale University Press, in association with the Open University, 1993), 216.

12. Artist Daniel Spoerri, who met Oppenheim in 1954 in Bern, explained, "she was a garçonne—she really had that. With her gamine air, her short hair, and exceptional attractiveness she completely corresponded to the beauty ideal of the avant-garde of that time [the 1930s]." Belinda Grace Gardner, "'She Was Incredibly Open for Everything': 'Trap' Artist Daniel Spoerri Retraces His Friendship with Meret Oppenheim," in *Meret Oppenheim: From Breakfast in Fur and Back Again*, ed. Thomas Levy (Bielefeld: Kerber Verlag, 2003), 44.

13. Breton, *Nadja*, 160.

14. Hal Foster, *Compulsive Beauty* (Cambridge, Mass.: MIT Press, 1993), 49.

15. Elsa Schiaparelli, *Shocking Life: The Autobiography of Elsa Schiaparelli* (1954; repr. London: V & A Publications, 2007), 89–90.

16. Richard Howard Stamelman, *Perfume: Joy, Obsession, Scandal, Sin; A Cultural History of Fragrance from 1750 to the Present* (New York: Rizzoli, 2006), 213.

17. Jean-Marie Martin-Hattemberg, "Elsa Schiaparelli: Senteurs surrealists, flacons d'extravagance," *Parfums & Senteurs* 4 (October 2000): 73. Quoted in Stamelman, *Perfume*, 213.

18. Breton, *Nadja*, 56.

19. Fer, "Surrealism, Myth and Psychoanalysis," 183.

20. "Tales of Details," *Vogue*, September 15, 1936, 152.

21. See *Harper's Bazaar*, December 1936, 64.

22. See "Madness in the Hand," *Harper's Bazaar*, October 1937, 146, and "Collection Caviar," *Vogue*, September 15, 1937, 98.

23. Blum, *Shocking!*, 207. The same collection also included several symbolically inspired motifs such as St. Peter's keys embroidered in pearls and prints of angels, annunciation lilies, and hands joined in prayer.

24. Cited in Robyn Gibson, "Surrealism into Fashion: The Creative Collaborations between Elsa Schiaprelli and Salvador Dali" (PhD diss., RMIT University, Melbourne, 2001), 187. Gibson cites Carlton Lake, *In Quest of Dali* (New York: Putnam Sons, 1969), 25.

25. "Pockets are the outlet this season for the individual imaginative quirks of the couturier. Schiaparelli's touch of surrealism in her bureau-drawer pockets is the sort of thing we mean. Obviously, Salvador Dalí is responsible for this—and it's not a bad idea, if they only held something." "Tales of Details," 153.

26. White, *Elsa Schiaparelli*, 96–97.

27. Robyn Gibson, "Schiaparelli, Surrealism, and the Desk Suit," *Dress* 30 (2003): 51.

28. "Tales of Details," 150.

29. Ibid., 150. Blum, *Shocking!*, 123.

30. Alberto Giacometti may have introduced Oppenheim to Schiaparelli, as he and his brother Diego had already been working for her on designs for the furnishings of her Paris salon. Alberto Giacometti also designed buttons and brooches for Schiaparelli. Whitney Chadwick, *Women Artists and the Surrealist Movement* (London: Thames and Hudson, 1985), 122; Blum, *Shocking!*, 122.

31. The sketch is dated to 1942–45 and reproduced in Levy, *Meret Oppenheim*, 96. See also Blum, *Shocking!*, 142.

32. Blum, *Shocking!*, 122.

33. Schiaparelli, *Shocking Life*, 46–47.

34. Caroline Evans and Minna Thornton, "Fashion, Representation, Femininity," *Feminist Review*, no. 38 (1991): 55.

35. Caroline Evans, "Masks, Mirrors and Mannequins: Elsa Schiaparelli and the Decentered Subject," *Fashion Theory* 3, no. 1 (February 1999): 7.

36. Evans and Thornton, "Fashion, Representation, Femininity," 55.

37. "Schiaparelli Hands out a Frenzy of Excitement," *Harper's Bazaar*, March 15, 1938, 133.

38. "Leopard and Sealskin," *Vogue*, October 1, 1935, 63.

39. Thanks to Ursula Ehrhardt for translating the text on this sketch for me. The sketch is reproduced in Christiane Meyer-Thoss, *Meret Oppenheim: Book of Ideas; Early Drawings and Sketches for Fashions, Jewelry, and Designs* (Bern: Verlag Gachnang & Springer, 1996), 35.

40. "Fur Furore," *Vogue*, October 15, 1936, 104.

41. "Spinach Is Fashion," *Harper's Bazaar*, September 15, 1938, 72–73.

42. One of these ensembles is in the collection of the Metropolitan Museum of Art (accession number: 2011.64a, b) and was part of the 2012 exhibition *Schiaparelli and Prada: Impossible Conversations*.

43. As recounted by Oppenheim in Margot Mifflin, "An Interview with Meret Oppenheim," *Women Artists News* 11 (September 1986): 30.

44. Janine A. Mileaf, *Please Touch: Dada and Surrealist Objects after the Readymade* (Hanover: Dartmouth College Press, 2010), 146.

8

FROCK AND BRACELET IN OMEROS

Maria Anita Stefanelli

HELEN ON THE CATWALK

In Derek Walcott's *Omeros*, Helen, a reincarnation of the beauty sparking the Trojan wars and a living emblem of Saint Lucia, wears a yellow dress that belonged to Maud, the aging Irishwoman wife of Major Plunkett, a retired British officer.[1] It might have been the brilliant invention of a fashion designer, capable of harmonizing the architectonic creations of the Italian designer Roberto Capucci (who strives, in homage to nature, toward perfection and harmonic proportions) with the chromatic explosions of the Caribbean painter Dunstan St. Omer (boyhood friend and the artistic alter ego of Walcott).[2] Seated beside his wife, who is lost in her memories of the past, in front of a Guinness,

Plunkett saw the pride of Helen passing

in the same yellow frock Maud had altered for her.
"She looks better in it"—Maud smiled—"but the girl lies
so much, and she stole. What'll happen to her life?"

"God knows," said Plunkett, following the butterfly's
yellow-panelled wings that once belonged to his wife,
the black V of the velvet back, near the shallows. (*Omeros*, 29)

Obsessed with his scheme of writing the history of this island that, because it has been long claimed by different countries, has earned the title "Helen of the West Indies," the old soldier distinguishes geometric animal shapes in the frock worn by the beautiful native girl. Translating one of the details of the frock's architecture (the line of contrast between black ebony skin and the chromatic effect of the material, covering a range of yellows from gold to pale lemon and buttery shades) into typescript, Major Plunkett detects in it the sign of the flight of the *Fregata Magnifica*, a sea bird with black plumage and pointed wings, that is the cue, as we read in Walcott's poem recalling his school years, "The Latin Primer," for a meditation on cultural and geographic borders, where he writes: "that slowly levelling V / made one with my horizon."[3]

V is also an abbreviation that (setting aside terms that are out of context like *vector, velocity, very, verse, versus, vice, vide, voice, voltage, volume, vowel*) moves semantically from the anatomy of the female back (a pun on the back of a page with *v* meaning *verso*) to the desire to trace, in a postcolonial perspective, the mark of a native Nike: *Victory*. Plunkett, for whom *V* means merely an annotation in the margin of a page, is startled by the way the frock hangs on the ebony body (that has already been likened to the catlike "padding panther," in connection with Saint Lucia's recent fight for independence) and by other potential references. The female figure, image of an identity that overruns all demarcations of nationality, race, and culture, has its literary and artistic origins in another poem, "The Light of the World," in which the poet glimpses a beautiful woman in one of the island's ubiquitous public minibuses:

> I could see where the lights on the planes of her cheek
> streaked and defined them; if this were a portrait
> you'd leave the highlights for last, these lights
> silkened her black skin; I'd have put in an earring,
> something simple, in good gold, for contrast, but she
> wore no jewelry.[4]

Silk, as material, carries the glossiness of skin into the ekphrasis the poet creates by transforming the passenger on the bus into a vivid and detailed representation—an homage to the art of rhetoric, revealed through gender, which here does not describe a work of art but is the verbal evocation of an existing person.[5] The poet completes the imaginary portrait of the woman with a golden accessory, predisposing the reader to see what he is seeing; but although she carries herself majestically and her head (as in Helen's case) is "nothing less but heraldic," the person on the minibus does not wear any jewelry. The poet's wish is therefore frustrated, and the potential portrait is not to be completed with the accessory. But the description is appropriately in harmony with the concept of *energeia,* which makes it possible for the reader to see not only what is described but also—as in the ekphrasis of Achilles's shield in the *Iliad*—what is not.[6]

The poet resorts to the license of not showing an object directly but of making the reader conscious of a shape introspectively through an act of perception qualified by its ethical as well as its aesthetic value.[7] The earring recalls the tight circular cuffs that bound the wrists of the slaves, and gold signifies the financial value of human merchandise; it is stuck through the earlobe to emphasize, by the prick necessary for its first positioning, the abuse of possessing another's body.[8] A novel Venus emerges from the everyday life of the island, one identified with the tiny nation-island itself. The poet draws on a mythical-historical-artistic figure in a famous painting for his personal and local version of the woman representing liberty:[9]

When she looked at me, then away from me politely,
because any staring at strangers is impolite,
it was like a statue, like a black Delacroix's
"Liberty Leading the People," the gently bulging
whites of her eyes, the carved ebony mouth,
the heft of the torso solid, and a woman's,
but gradually even that was going in the dusk,
except the line of her profile, and the highlit cheek,
and I thought, O Beauty, you are the light of the
world![10]

A yellow frock falling in classical folds and leaving the breast bare, a red Frisian cap on her head like the male figures around her, a red sash tied around her waist with the ends flying, the woman leans forward holding the French flag in her right hand, the weight of the body balanced forward, toward the observer, on one naked foot, opening the way to the truth of the Revolution against the lies of the Bourbon regime: Liberty.

Walcott's creation is less faithful to her original classic namesake (the Helen abducted by Paris, whose name recalls the unlucky fate of the French fleet in the Battle of the Saints). Instead, she advances on silent feet in quest of a job, her proud head wrapped in a madras headdress (madras—the material of the national costume) and her face an ebony mask.[11] She wears clothes of various origin and displays a haughty mien that contrasts with her desperate situation, but she resembles a waif with bowed head—"she seemed to drift like a waif" (*Omeros*, 29)—and speaks a hybrid Creole on the borderline of grammar and history.[12]

From Helen rises the elegant flight of a butterfly that draws, with the beating of its wings, three triangular shapes in the air (two for the wings and one for the back), which first fan out, then adjust to flight, settling symmetrically in pairs at the sides of a central velvet plane. The flight suggests the difficulty of capturing her. The frock merges with the butterfly that, in moving, continually traces triangles in the air and recalls Saint Lucia's national flag, designed by Dunstan St. Omer. It is dominated by three triangular shapes, posed vertically one inside the other, evoking in their isosceles stylization the twin Piton mountains of Soufrière, proud landmarks of the island to which Helen's breasts are compared, and the inner equilateral triangle, the people's aspiration to a harmonic order.[13] The triangles are white, black, and yellow, gesturing to the cultural and ethnic influences of the population: white and black match each other, while yellow takes on all the possible shades of the various African and Asian minorities. The flag's monochromatic surface indicates the sun and the prosperity of the Caribbean island.[14] The background is a cerulean blue, like the tropical sky and sea surrounding the island. But the dress is of foreign make; it is a product of colonization: "but that dress // had an empire's tag on it, mistress to slave" (*Omeros*, 64). The characteristics of the complex and hybrid culture of Saint Lucia emerge, including the appropriation of the culture and language of the colonizers.[15]

The geometric cut of the yellow frock is visually represented by the sequence of mimetic typographic characters, such as the three acute angles formed by the graphic symbols of *v* and *w* plus an imaginary closing segment (the *v* in "V" and in "velvet" alternating with the *w* in "yellow," "wings," "wife," and "shallow"). On the acoustic plane, the movement of the air is heard in the alternating sibilant and rustling sounds, the frock moving with Helen contrasts with the sound produced by the plastic slippers dangling from her hand. Finally, the movement of the water is evoked by the many liquid consonants ("ye*ll*ow-pane*ll*ed," "be*l*onged," "b*l*ack," "ve*l*vet b*l*ack," "sha*ll*ows") that insist on the presence of the surrounding sea.

The dress is connected to the movement of the body, the human body is related to the animal body; the animal to space; space to ethnic group, culture, and language; language to landscape; landscape to identity, in a continual cross-referencing governed by the direction and rhythm of the lines. The dynamics of the body moving through space are animated by poetry.

THE SEA'S NEEDLEPOINT LACE

The first four chapters, designed like a mosaic, introduce the lives of the characters (from Philoctete to Achilles to Hector to Ma Kilman to Seven Seas) and conclude with the figure of a Greek girl associated to the mythical Antigone, who followed her father into exile as a young girl and buried her brother in obedience to divine law and against the king's orders. Antigone bears the name of a bird, a crane, whose flocks in autumn migrate all the way from Europe and Asia to Africa. She is not the outcome of a purely mimetic literary process, but a character existing independently of her epic model: she is a contemporary Greek girl in a foreign country, and she intends to return to her homeland. She is called to justify the title of the poem: "'O-meros,' she laughed. 'That's what we call him in Greek'" (*Omeros*, 14). Later, the narrator analyzes the title, dissecting its component parts into the many marine objects found in the Caribbean: the sound-invocation of the seashell through its spiral curves, the linguistic overlapping of the terms "sea" and "mother" in the local patois (*mer* and *mère*), the three-dimensional embroidery suggested by the skeletons, all that is left of those who lost their lives at sea: "I said, 'Omeros,' // and O was the conch shell's invocation, *mer* was / both mother and sea in our Antillean patois, / *os*, a grey bone" (*Omeros*, 14).

The sea is a wide cloak with lapels decorated by the lacy patterns made by waves breaking on the beach, the contour of the island. "Lace" recurs in *Omeros* to describe not only the foam of the sea but also Helen's clothes: her underwear, hidden by her frock, an erotic promise of desire, and the exposed petticoats, part of the national costume declaring openly her identity and belonging. Lace is a textual structure used to offset, with its complicated circumvolutions, the straightforward seam of plain sewing, adding the elusive dimension of a labyrinthine intricacy. Products of female handiwork, embroidery and lace are created by complicated movements of the hands and of one or more threads (all white because traditionally lace is a bride's dowry). With these movements a pattern is created, going back and forth, through repetitions, knots, and spaces, proceeding on the right or on the wrong side, filling in spaces or making openings, with a variable progress, scalloped with pinking shears, always an expression of both refined elegance and magical enchantment. As the thread turns into lace, so the blue sea wrinkles into improbable white threads of water that interact with air and light to form a continually changing pattern represented in the lacelike carvings on the balcony railings of the oldest houses on the island. It is a figure of collective, ancestral, and hereditary memory.

Just as the interlacing facts contradict the linearity of the traditional epic as scraps of history are cut to size and put together, like the making of a dress, so *Omeros* resists etymological rule. The fragments that compose the word have been cut up and sewn together; they function independently but as a whole to denote the poem: "The name stayed in my mouth. I saw how light was webbed / on her Asian cheeks, defined her eyes with a black / almond's outline, as Antigone turned and said: // 'I'm tired of America' " (*Omeros*, 14). Sound and light are brought to life by the voice of the rhapsodist-bard producing echoes and resonances, suggesting physical variations, as in the echo between "has ebbed" and "was webbed."

Lace marks a metaphoric beach or coast, the chest of a woman where it joins the head, the point at which visual perception is arrested by the embroidered threads around the neck before meeting the logical thread of thought—her breasts. Silk accompanies the clothes enveloping her body down to the ankles, where the nose discerns "the stench from manacled ankles" and the ears perceive the creaking of the slaves' "coffled feet" arriving in the New World from Africa (15). Later in the poem, Maud will appear beside her husband, the officer, dignified and protective, although in her temporary exile she suffers from the distance separating her from a homeland sorely tried by history. The veil Maud lifted for her officer husband under the crossed swords raised the curtain on history and geography: the wars, the victories and defeats, and the high broken cliffs of the coasts of nations to be conquered. Like the lace on Helen's underwear, the lace veil is an ornamental and elegant accessory, but its etymon contains the sense of the rope that binds, "to lace" meaning to lash. The thread that, thanks to busy hands, has become the symbol of a bride's innocence is also the symbol of a noose, a trap, violence, and imposition. This thread, articulated into a delicate decorative fabric with a double meaning, adorns Helen's corset, where purity and past evil intertwine.

THE THEORY OF CLOTHES

The lines on Helen in a yellow frock, and the transition from the arrogance of the housemaid displacing everything in her master's house to her vagrancy as she searches for a home and work, cause Plunkett to meditate on her fate, similar to that of the island that has likewise been exploited, picking from it as from a saucer of olives and spitting the pits: "It was at that moment that he felt a duty // towards her hopelessness, something to *redress* / (he punned relentlessly) that desolate beauty / so like her island's" (*Omeros*, 29–30, emphasis mine). In the word *redress*, a pun on its different meanings of "make amends" and "dress anew," Walcott rewrites the colonial encounter:

Where shall I turn, divided to the vein?
I who have cursed

The drunken officer of British rule, how choose
Between this Africa and the English tongue I love?
Betray them both, or give back what they give?
How can I face such slaughter and be cool?
How can I turn from Africa and live?[16]

Walcott uses Helen's yellow dress to signify not only redemption and royalty but also race and class. Yellow is the mark of belonging to a continually proliferating land of multiple identities, a land that has been conquered and debated, destination for African slaves and cradle to the mixed race and the mulatto; the color reveals the impossible balance between one and the other. In a place in which art is denied and history degenerate, site of colonial encounter and the ensuing postcolonial collapse, yellow is the linguistic mark of inferiority, noninvolvement, ugliness, and backwardness.[17] Since the nineteenth century, those in the United States called the populations they considered alien *yellow belly*, and these—ranging from Mexicans to Irishmen to Chinese—learned that the conqueror attributes *yellowness* to sickness, cowardice, dirt, and decadence.[18] The poet questions postcolonial ideology, insinuating a doubt by switching the point of view. Was the frock stolen from the woman for whom Helen worked as a housemaid, a subaltern, or given to her? The poem's narrator appears to tacitly credit the first hypothesis, but the fact remains that the original owner, Maud Plunkett, had taken up the dress to *alter* it, to adapt it to the *alterity* of the body of another.[19] The alteration, resulting from adapting the frock to the shapeliness of youth, is performed by the woman who, being Irish, is at once symbol and victim of the British Empire. "In the same yellow frock Maud had altered for her": the key to the line is in the verb that urgently poses the question of alterity.

"Clothes have a language of their own." Clothes speak of belonging and exclusion, they reveal affinities and distances, they declare financial standing and social castes, they flood us with information that must be sifted and interpreted depending on their date and geographical origin. Clothes are words in an idiom that must be studied to appreciate their nuances and significance.[20] The complex code of clothing defines relationships and distinctions between individuals and classes. Some episodes, sections of the intricate fresco Walcott is composing ("I sometimes drafted the chapters in a line and then needed spaces to connect. It would make a mural, in a sense," he explains in an interview), are devoted to garments and their meanings.[21] In the image of Helen, dressed to represent the nation, the perfect circle of beauty is inscribed. By the poem's end, Helen, a chambermaid and waitress in a local hotel, appears

> at the Halcyon. She is dressed
> in the national costume: white, low-cut bodice,
> with frilled lace at the collar, just a cleft of a breast
>
> for the customers when she places their orders
> on the shields of the tables. They can guess the rest
> under the madras skirt with golden borders
>
> and the flirtatious knot of the madras head-tie.

Her outfit causes the men to exclaim, "What a fine local woman!" (*Omeros*, 322). It is worn purely for the benefit of the foreign tourists to Saint Lucia. Walcott declares: "In a large poem, though, the writing is like a novel, and as in a novel, everything is in there—geographic description, the weather, the characters, and the action, and so on."[22] And so on, including the costume.

Gayatri Spivak's "Can the Subaltern Speak?" encourages contemporary intellectuals to comprehend and reveal the speech of the Other not only through an aesthetic (or sensitive) imagination but also an ethical-political one based on moral and civic foundations, and to access a cultural horizon founded on speech, an act that produces a representation of the self (including the ability to represent oneself through what one wears).[23] What must be written is her story, as opposed to history; Helen's war, not theirs (the war waged with arms). Helen appears wearing a dress, not the uniform of a soldier; her arms are not weapons. While Plunkett works away at his word archives, Walcott entrusts to Maud the task of writing with needle and thread (a typically feminine activity) the history of

Nature. She is a skilled seamstress, her creations answer his compositions: "her needles swift as his pen" (*Omeros*, 65).

Her wonderful, splendid, immense, and unfinished quilt is the fabric on which ancient history is written—all that came before the present country, the outcome of the century-old dispute.[24] The female counterpart of the rhapsodist (both intent on sewing), Maud is the woman whose imminent death by cancer signals the end of British influence on the island of Saint Lucia, and at the same time she evokes not only several centuries of British dominion over Ireland but also the Greek attack on Troy. The quilt is Nature and Memory: among its patches are samples of "Bond's *Ornithology*"— "Needlepoint constellations / on a clear night had prompted this intricate thing," that come from far away, like the captured slaves, "their bright spurs braceleted with Greek and Latin tags, / to pin themselves to the silk" (*Omeros*, 88).

Spivak criticizes the way in which the history of thought and of dominant cultures is built around certain figures and follows determined perspectives (that is, from the conqueror's point of view) and thus she advocates a wider range of interpretations of events. In *Omeros*, the Maud–Helen relationship is gradually transformed so that feelings predominate over knowledge, a change beginning with the transfer of the dress from one woman to the other (whether by theft or as gift), continuing through the termination of their unequal relationship (with the inevitable consequence that the latter must search for a job), and culminating in Helen's demands. When she discovers she is pregnant as well as out of work, she asks for a sum of money from her ex-boss (unsuccessful, because she cannot guarantee to repay it), so she can only take refuge in silence and leave, still proceeding "stern high" as if to flaunt her distinctive pride.

The process of "*altering*" oneself, becoming another, of representing oneself to the Other remains incomplete. The deadlock is revealed in the greeting: "'Morning,' Helen said. // Morning. No 'Madam.' No 'Good.'" (*Omeros*, 124). Even though she is irritated, Maud asks: "So, how are you, Helen?" and receives the answer: "I dere, Madam." Maud translates it ironically into proper English: "At last. You dere. Of course you dare" (*Omeros*, 124). There you have it: Maud, subaltern to her husband, becomes seamstress and the intermediary for the unspoken record of the island's history by means of her quilt, to which the birds flock, pecking her fingers.[25] Helen, for her part, displays her naked skin in public to attract male desire, only to frustrate it. Walcott locates, on a purely feminine level, the imaginative-creative function of hybridization in an element of clothing, an accessory preserved in the casket of memory (and thus filed away) that can be associated with Spivak's concept of agency. It is a performance, the "staging," of the "representation (as *Darstellung*) by a subject that is simultaneously agent, actor, and instrument."[26]

THE STOLEN BRACELET

In the second Book, Plunkett struggles with a mesh of dates and numbers in the material he has collected in the library and is struck by coincidences (only coincidences, not prophecies!) between them and the fictional facts of Homer's epic:

> when he came into the bedroom from the pig-farm
> to pick up his cheque book, he was fixed by her glance
>
> in the armoire's full-length mirror, where, one long arm,
> its fist closed like a snake's head, slipped through a bracelet
> from Maud's jewel-box, and, with eyes calm as Circe,
>
> simply continued, and her smile said, "You will let
> me try this," which he did. He stood at the mercy
> of that beaked, black arm, which with serpentine leisure
>
> replaced the bangle. When she passed him at the door
> he had closed his eyes at her closeness, a pleasure
> in that passing scent which was both natural odour
>
> and pharmacy perfume. (*Omeros*, 96)

This is not the only occasion in which a round jewel (a ring, a chain, an earring, as well as the bracelet) appears as a symbol of the limitation of man's freedom or dignity and obsessively references the slave trade. Here Helen tries on a bracelet she has taken from Maud's jewelry box in the presence of Maud's husband, who in his astonishment submits passively to her gaze.

The bracelet belonging to the Irishwoman Maud, an object kept in its appropriate personal jewel box, reminds us of the torque with which the Celts (called Gauls by the Romans) used to adorn themselves, and for whom the necklace and bracelet of a particular winding shape (from which the name is derived) was a mystical object connecting men to the gods and offering protection. The Gauls, according to Julius Caesar's *De Bello Gallico*, fought their battles naked, with only a torque around their necks, sufficient clothing for warriors.[27] A symbol of power and an important indicator of a man's standing, it became the emblem of the tribe; the bracelet and armlet, mostly worn by women, was an accessory decorated with the heads of wild beasts believed to be of divine nature.[28]

The bracelet as a symbol of power becomes the manacles of the captured and deported slaves. Related in particular to the term *manilla*, derived from the Latin *manus*, it is in turn connected to *monilia*, the plural form of *monile*, meaning necklace or, later, bracelet and more generally jewelry. Excavations have unearthed different types of *manilla* (usually made of various metals by European craftsmen) that from the sixteenth century spread throughout Africa, especially to West Africa, where they were used as payment for the slaves sent to the Antilles and the American South.[29] The slave trade was a business, and the commerce of less expensive commodities soon developed along with it. Another kind of bracelet, made of cowrie shells, generally imported from Melanesia, was also used by European traders.

Cowrie shells are regular in shape, smooth and shiny, similar to the natural beads Helen sells to tourists when she can't find a job as a housemaid. They are a symbol of femininity and fertility in West African cultures. Because of their resemblance to eyes, they were applied to mummies and decorated the prows of sailing vessels as a talisman of vitality.[30] Because they were used as money, they became a sign of wealth and were put in the mouths of dead noblemen (this mostly in China) or were used to decorate African masks or to designate a member of the royal family. Thus the oceanic diaspora from Africa (the circle of seashells), that of the Celtic tribes conquered by the Romans (the metal *torchon*), the exploitation by Western finance of the land, labor, and industry of colonized peoples—with its final transformation into the aberration of slavery as an actual right of *dominium* over human beings considered as patrimonial assets—are all strung together by the bracelet.

During the "theft," Plunkett passively meets Helen's eyes in the mirror, transforming Plunkett, as Ulysses's companions were transformed by Circe, into the prey of lechery. Representing the precarious border between an original identity and an otherness resulting from centuries of being subjugated by one dominant culture after another, the mirror is topos of a faithful reproduction of reality and at the same time of a modification of reality in which existence (as Narcissus discovers) coincides with nonexistence. At this moment, Helen states her right to try on, to own that jewel, which, like a work of art, exists both as material substance and as the history of its metamorphoses. Contaminated by the shape of Helen's closed fist resembling a serpent's head, at the end of the "long . . . beaked, black arm," the bracelet is replaced by her in its box while Plunkett is immobilized by her gaze; Plunkett reveals his blindness in his culpable incapacity to recognize the bracelet as evidence of guilt.[31]

A symbol of rebirth and regeneration in Celtic culture, the serpent represents the cycle of life in the shape of the *ouroboros* that holds its tail in its teeth. Thus the bracelet is akin to the forbidden fruit that tempted Eve, stressing Helen's spiritual communion with the absolute ideal of knowledge.[32] As Plunkett draws near the jewel, it begins to coil around itself and hiss: "The bracelet coiled like a snake. He heard it hissing: / Her housebound slavery could be your salvation" (*Omeros*, 96). The serpent in Genesis is linked to deceit through its forked tongue, the tips pointing in different directions, the cause of labor, sin, and death in mankind. Helen's attempted theft is used by Plunkett to appease his own feeling of guilt for dominating his housemaid, taking upon himself the right to forgive. The European man builds up both his image of himself as offering wisdom, help, and deliverance, and his image of the indigenous woman as an object of compassion.[33] Helen counters this attitude with her arrogance and her power to seduce Plunkett who, like the biblical elders observing Susanna's nakedness, insists on his innocence: "No. My thoughts are pure. / They're meant to help her people, ignorant and poor" (*Omeros*, 97). But the bracelet contradicts him: "But these, smiled the bracelet, are the vows of empire" (*Omeros*, 97). This is a warning.[34] In the apparent nakedness of both her body and her reflection due to the optical illusion produced by the position of the sun, Helen is clothed only in her smile: "she wore the same / smile that made a drama out of every passing" (*Omeros*, 97). With this momentary theft Helen closes the gap between herself and him. The yellow frock has been torn, at a certain point in the poem, by her lover Achille in a fit of rage when Helen refuses his offer to help carry the heavy basket full of goods from the market: "she clawed at his good clothes, / so he, in turn, ripped the yellow dress in his rage" (*Omeros*, 39). The basket contains the entire history of the Antilles with all its negotiations, losses, and horrors: "slaves head-down on a hook" (*Omeros*, 37). Maud's bracelet, which Helen surreptitiously tries to steal, is associated not only with bargaining in the slave trade but with her pregnancy, for which Achille accepts the responsibility (although the father is unknown).

In ancient medical lore, the snake could heal or poison, even extend the capacity of the mind; in certain cultures, it is endowed with near-divine powers. Helen (who can be interpreted as Caliban's woman/companion) has the power to bewitch Omeros, a character part serpent part divine seer, the Caribbean bard/poet/narrator who, in his turn, allows her to taste of the fruit of good and evil.[35] This is the spiritual union of Omeros and Helen, the poet having taken the shape of the bracelet, as Zeus does in myth through his metamorphoses to satisfy his lust for mortal women. The yellow frock had been altered by Maud (the Irishwoman is no exception, in her pretense of concern not only for her husband but also for the girl's future from *her* point of view), to fit Helen's figure. The dress may have been Maud's originally, but it expresses Helen's authentic nature, through the line traced by the edge of the cloth and the color of her skin, her ethnic origins as well as the desolate beauty of the island and her own. But the shell bracelet is altered by divine will and becomes the blind poet propagating the "memory of imagination in literature" through this Helen—not the classical one, but the "Helen of the West Indies."[36] So, in *Omeros*, the subject of the bracelet is taken up by the poet when he compares the classical to the Caribbean Helen: "These Helens are different creatures, // one marble, one ebony. One unknots a belt / of yellow cotton slowly from her shelving waist, / one a cord of purple wool, the other one takes // a bracelet of white cowries from a narrow wrist" (*Omeros*, 313). The woman in a yellow sash (proud Helen?), the girl encircled by a purple cord (Liberty in Delacroix's painting?), the woman who "takes // a bracelet of white cowries from a narrow wrist" exist between the two extremes, marble and ebony—women one can meet in Saint Lucia and elsewhere in the world, in the present and the past, among those who wield power and those who are subject to it.

In her ambiguous complexity, Helen emerges as a Caribbean alter ego of the Virgin Mary and a demonical creature (from *daimon*, meaning divine, or a spirit part divine and part human). "The victory was hers," the poet-narrator suggests, turning the bauble suggestive of the slaves' manacles into a symbol of triumph over subordination.[37] And indeed, if the bracelet Helen tries to possess is the poet-serpent, the poet-serpent is, inverting the roles, the bracelet: the bracelet shrieking a summons or a warning; the bracelet coiling around itself; the bracelet used as money to buy goods; the bracelet serving, ultimately, to sing one's story and represent one's helical identity with the he/she and male/female Other, each calling to each from the beginning to the end of the poem, pursuing one another in a deconstructive action in which no one is central and no one is marginal, and nobody is silenced.

NOTES

1. Derek Walcott, *Omeros* (London: Faber and Faber, 1990). References in the text.

2. Roberto Capucci in a public statement declared: "Nature is my mentor. My garden, as I quietly look at it with a childlike sense of fantasy, has helped to instill in me a sense of balance and a constant search for perfection, proportion, harmony, and colour." "Capucci Not Gucci," Celebration

Anniversary Gym blog, April 8, 2009, http://celebration-anniversary-gym.blogspot.com/2009/04/capucci-not-gucci.html. The relationship between Capucci's creations and geometry is examined by Isabeau Birindelli, "Superfici di seta: la geometria negli abiti di Roberto Capucci" (Silken surfaces: Geometry in Roberto Capucci's clothes), in *Matematica e Cultura 2010*, ed. Michele Emmer (Milan: Springer, 2010), 67–78. On the Italian designer's philosophy and art, see Cristina Giorcelli's interview with Roberto Capucci, "Lo sfarzo della forma: un indice di civiltà," in *Abito e Identità: Ricerche di storia letteraria e culturale*, ed. Cristina Giorcelli (Rome: Ila Palma, 2010), 10:19–28.

3. Derek Walcott, *The Arkansas Testament* (New York: Farrar, Straus and Giroux, 1987), 24.

4. Ibid., 48.

5. James A. Francis, "Metal Maidens, Achilles's Shield, and Pandora: The Beginnings of 'Ekphrasis,'" *American Journal of Philology* 130, no. 1 (Spring 2009): 1–23.

6. "Sub oculos subiectio," writes Quintilian in *Institutionis Oratoriae Libri XII*, 9.2.40, in *Rhetorica Movet: Studies in Historical and Modern Rhetoric in Honor of Heinrich F. Plett*, ed. Peter Lothar Oesterreich and Thomas O. Sloane (Leiden: Brill, 1999), 17.

7. Ibid., 20–23.

8. See Cristina Giorcelli, "Earrings in American Literature: A Showcase," chapter 4 in this volume.

9. The reference is to *La Liberté guidant le peuple* (1830) by Eugène Delacroix at the Louvre.

10. Walcott, *The Arkansas Testament*, 48.

11. Ville de Paris was the name of the fleet sunk by the British in 1782, winning from France its dominion over Saint Lucia.

12. *Creole* means "created"; *patois* derives from French "du pays." This modern Caribbean beauty dressed in a golden frock shares characteristics with the Nigerian deity Ochùn, who wore sun-colored clothes, golden or brass-colored necklaces and bracelets, and lived in rivers; see Yves Bonnefoy, *American, African, and Old European Mythologies* (Chicago: University of Chicago Press, 1993), 146. As Marina Warner recalls in "Did She Go Willingly?" Helen wears "a dress whose colour recalls the golden robes worn by the divine Helen of Troy, woven for her by her mother, Leda" (*London Review of Books* 32, no. 19 [October 2009]: 24). Derived from the African diaspora, so that her cult migrated to Cuba and other American countries of Afro-Catholic religion, this kind of black Aphrodite has, like Helen, incredible powers of seduction, which she shares with other deities; see Irina Bajinihas on the cult of Ochùn in Cuba in "Molto donna e un po' Madonna: sulle tracce di Ochùn nella let-

teratura cubana," in *Narrative femminili cubane tra mito e realtà* (Venice: Università Ca' Foscari, Comitato per le pari opportunità, 2003), 69–80. Vodoun Erzulie is a voluptuous deity, elegantly and richly dressed, French-speaking, both virgin and Venus, insatiable man-eater—a proliferation of multiple identities. Like Erzulie, Helen is the missing character in Shakespeare's *Tempest*; she is the female of Caliban's species, she who possesses the divine capacity of creation: "Caliban's Woman is no longer looked at as just a Muse . . . but rather creativity itself, especially creativity of the mind." Julie A. Minkler, "Helen's Calibans: A Study of Gender Hierarchy in Derek Walcott's *Omeros*," *World Literature Today* 67, no. 2 (1993): 274.

13. Paula Burnett, in *Derek Walcott: Politics and Poetics* (Gainesville: University Press of Florida, 2000), 172, explains that Walcott recalls his friendship with St. Omer (*tanist* or *twin*) in *Another Life*. Born in 1927, St. Omer painted the interior of the Immaculate Conception cathedral, tinged with soft yellow light, next to Derek Walcott Square at Castries, the poet's hometown. Burnett, remembering the use of a yellow frock to dress the androgynous Achilles for the Jon Kunnu dance with Philoctete to celebrate the healing of his wound, interprets the frock stolen from Maud in the nationalistic terms of the flag.

14. Susan S. Lanser discusses the color yellow in "*The Yellow Wallpaper* and the Politics of Color in America," *Feminist Studies* 15, no. 3 (Autumn 1989): 415–41.

15. Louis Fernando Restrepo, "Closure and Disclosure of the Caribbean Body: Gabriel García Márquez and Derek Walcott," in *A History of Literature in the Caribbean*, vol. 3, *Cross-Cultural Studies*, ed. Albert James Arnold (Amsterdam: John Benjamins, 1997), 262.

16. Derek Walcott, "A Far Cry from Africa," in *In a Green Night: Poems, 1948–1960* (London: Jonathan Cape, 1962), 19.

17. Roger Daniels and Harry K. Kitano, *American Racism: Exploration of the Nature of Prejudice* (Englewood Cliffs, N.J.: Prentice-Hall, 1970), 44.

18. See entry "yellow" in *Dictionary of American Slang*, ed. Harold Wentworth and Stuart Berg Flexner (New York: Thomas Y. Crowell, 1960).

19. Italics are used to stress the original nucleus of the word, the Latin word *alter*.

20. Publisher's tagline for *Il Vestito dell'Altro: Semiotica, arti, costume*, ed. Giovanna Franci and Maria Giuseppina Muzzarelli (Milan: Lupetti, 2005), http://www.lupetti.com/il-vestito-dell-altro .html (my translation; accessed March 2, 2014).

21. Rebekah Presson, "The Man Who Keeps the English Language Alive: An Interview with

Derek Walcott," in *Conversations with Derek Walcott*, ed. William Baer (Jackson: University Press of Mississippi, 1996), 191.

22. Ibid., 190.

23. Gayatri Chakravorty Spivak, "Can the Subaltern Speak?" [1988], in *Colonial Discourse and Post-Colonial Theory: A Reader*, ed. Patrick Williams and Laura Chrisman (Hemel Hempstead: Harvester Wheatsheaf, 1993), 66–111.

24. The woman's name recalls Maud Gonne, whom Yeats likened to a second Helen.

25. The Latin verb *sarcire*, meaning "to patch," extended its meaning to the person who cuts and sews clothes; the semantic value of *sarta* (seamstress) plays on that of "redress" (*risarcire*). Patchwork is a more appropriate definition of Maud's sewing, made up of scraps and remnants.

26. *Agency* means the production of subjectivity vis-à-vis to power. See Spivak, "Can the Subaltern Speak?," 72–73.

27. *The Dying Gaul* in Rome's Capitoline Museum portrays a Celtic warrior; he is naked and wears only a torque around his neck. For Gallic customs and traditions, see Erik Abranson, *Roman Legionaries at the Time of Julius Caesar* (London: Macdonald Educational, 1979).

28. Many commercial replicas of Celtic jewelry can be found on sale in museum shops or on Internet sites; see, for instance, "Crafty Celts: Fine Handcrafted Jewelry," which states: "The Torc (also spelled Torque), or neck ring, was an important piece of Celtic jewelry, and was worn before 1200 BC to as late as 600 AD. It was a powerful symbol, perhaps representing the wearer's freeborn status, and was often complemented with additional rings worn about the arms and wrists. Torcs were made from copper, bronze, silver, and gold. They were worn by both men and women, and are depicted as such in both Classical and Celtic sculptures. Zoomorphics, or animal forms, were very popular with the Celts. They were used to represent deities, natural and supernatural forces, and personal qualities. The animal heads are placed on the torques so they appear upright when worn." Reproductions inspired by the original torques and more or less faithfully copied from specimens in museums have become popular, in more recent times, with the Irish of the Diaspora. "Crafty Celts: Fine Handcrafted Jewelry," http://www.craftycelts.com/Style/Torcs.html (accessed April 24, 2011).

29. Scott Semans, "Manilla: Money of the Slave Trade," http://coincoin.com/I024.htm (accessed March 21, 2011).

30. Thomas Charles, "What Is the Meaning of Cowrie Shells?," http://www.ehow.com/about _6625137_meaning-cowry-shells_.html#ixzz0yLrElqTQ (accessed June 14, 2010).

31. In these verses there could be a reference to James Joyce's "Araby" ([1914; Harmondsworth: Penguin Books, 1964], 29), one of the stories in *Dubliners*, where an adolescent boy is blind to evidence and sees only what he wants to see. "While she spoke she turned a silver bracelet round and round her wrist," Joyce writes about the girl (the sister of his friend) to whom the boy is attracted; references to angelic qualities and to the attributes of a prostitute emerge from the mention of a religious retreat and of the girl's coquettish playing with her bracelet; these contribute to the boy's blindness and confusion.

32. Minkler, "Helen's Calibans," 275.

33. Spivak, "Can the Subaltern Speak?," 102.

34. Ibid., 87–89.

35. Minkler, "Helen's Calibans," 275.

36. Derek Walcott, "The Muse of History: An Essay," in *Is Massa Day Dead? Black Moods in the Caribbean*, ed. Orde Coombs (Garden City, N.Y.: Anchor-Doubleday, 1974), 25.

37. Spivak, "Can the Subaltern Speak?," 91.

9

KAHLO AND O'KEEFFE
PORTRAIT OF THE ARTIST AS FASHION ICON

Paula Rabinowitz

> *I'm the Frida Kahlo of both personal adverts and*
> *sandwich artistry. Woman, 48. Mad as a balloon.*
> PERSONALS SECTION,
> *London Review of Books*, April 8, 2010

In 1939, following her appearances in exhibitions of surrealist art organized by André Breton, Frida Kahlo traveled to Paris where she was celebrated both as a painter and as Diego Rivera's wife: Wassily Kandinsky kissed her; Picasso was fascinated. As was Parisian couture, which modeled a collection on her Tehuana style: "Schiaparelli introduced La Robe Madame Rivera. . . . And the most widely-read high-fashion magazine appeared on the stands with a cover photograph of Frida's right hand, together with an elegant jewel box containing four of her favorite gems."[1] Painter and wife, two seemingly incompatible positions for the modernist woman artist, actually provided the standards across which Frida Kahlo and Georgia O'Keeffe strung the thread of their complex identities.[2] Like the clothesline looping across the border in Kahlo's 1933 painting *My Dress*

Hangs There, these two poles held in tension dialectical outfits: clothing the modernist artist meant staking out a costume and a style that was as easily recognizable as the women's canvases; while working within the orbit of an older and successful man meant conforming to his aesthetic ideals, including his fashion sense. Their situations—and influences—are matched, unlikely twins whose fashioning continues long after death.

Dressing the part was a requirement of the female modernist artist whose body was as much a signifier of her originality as her work. These women artists have, since the 1970s and 1980s, traveled in and out of fashion themselves as museums, feminists, popular culture, and the art market reassess their stock in trade—revaluing their work, their style, and their names, mention of which, if we are to believe the personal ad, is enough to snare a lover. Hillel Schwartz affectionately calls our world, our time, "the culture of the copy." Celeste Olalquiaga claims that, since the nineteenth century, those in the West have dwelled in "the artificial kingdom," a world in which multiplying kitschy objects serve to stave off the inevitable sense of loss and displacement attendant upon modernity.[3] Modern identities are achieved in part through forms of design—reproducible, serialized, trademarked, fashioned. For each artist, then, dress in its widest sense—that which identifies, decorates, and surrounds the body—is an essential element in her self-portrayal as an exemplary modernist woman: as an artist, a woman at work.

Sixty years after Schiaparelli's designs, in 1999, one could click onto a Frida Kahlo website and find a virtual cut-out doll wardrobe in various color combinations to play dress up, changing Frida's blouse, rebozo, and hair ribbons from purple to red, orange to black. As Oriana Baddeley commented about the emerging interest in all things Kahlo that was signaled by the 1990 *Vogue* and 1989 *Elle* spreads claiming Kahlo as style:

In the case of Kahlo the popular image is of the artist herself, the characteristic brows, the elaborate hair, the Mexican costume. It is primarily her appearance not the formal language of her art, that has graced the pages of *Elle* and *Vogue* magazines. The *Elle* feature transposed the "Kahlo style" to Kahlo lookalikes in contemporary clothing balanced around segments of [Hayden] Herrera's biography of the artist. In the later *Vogue* piece only the style remained as the far more overtly sexual, Kahloesque models lounged and pouted in their "Mexican" interiors.[4]

Dressing extends beyond clothing to the accoutrements of interior decorating as the living space pushes the limits of the body into the spaces it inhabits. This is especially true for an artist, whose studio becomes the zone in which life and work—and for these modern women, body—commingle: house and dress stand, like the work itself, as signatures.

One can test one's knowledge of Frida trivia,[5] among other Internet pastimes such as purchasing clothing from Frida Fashions, whose website boasts "My Dress Hangs Here, Frida," and continues:

> In keeping with the spirit of Frida, we strive to be different! In fact, we strive to be daring! Our entire clothesline is a progression of revolutionary zeal for free expression. With every new design, Frida Fashions works to bring out the creative resistance that distinguished Frida from all other artists, not only of her time, but of all times![6]

Surfing the Internet, one might also find old pictures of Madonna, with her hair dyed black and eyebrows heavily penciled, dressed in a sheer black dress and smoking a thick cigar with David Letterman, dating from the early 1990s excitement after Madonna (a Kahlo collector like another star, Edward G. Robinson, before her) commissioned a biopic screenplay about Kahlo's life as a vehicle for her Hollywood stardom. (This role ultimately went to Mexican-Lebanese actress Salma Hayek; Madonna got to play Evita instead.)[7] Or one can read poems denouncing Frida look-alikes, for instance Marisela Norte's "976 LOCA":

> but from where I am standing I can see
> a whole army of Frida vendidas
> stranded along Wilshire Boulevard

trying to look more Mexxican [*sic*] than me
you know if you really love Frida
you'll let your mustache grow baby.[8]

And the same for Georgia O'Keeffe: there are websites devoted to O'Keeffe's genealogy or genitalia or the paintings by fifth graders imitating O'Keeffe's flowers. Moving across the bodies, homes, and paintings—and of the reproductions of these—of these icons of modernist national feminism the contours of representation in the portrait of the woman as modernist artist emerge; it's difficult to separate clothing from paintings from furnishings from their appropriations as they form a total image. This pastiche of history, identity, artwork, and commodity is, according to Fredric Jameson, the hallmark of postmodernism; however, these women's canny ability to link these visually suggests that it began with modernism.

FRIDAMANIA

At the turn of the millenium, Kahlo reappeared in the clothing of Jean-Paul Gaultier and others. For Gaultier, the "Frida Kahlo look" gets layered with "a contemporary veneer" of other "icons," according to *New York Times* fashion critic Amy Spindler. "This time," she notes,

> it was Marilyn Manson—the creepy Gothic Alice Cooper update who has been serving as the latest evidence that youth are scum—married to Frida Kahlo, a wedding that would have made her real one to Diego Rivera seem easy.... Crowns of thorns were made from braids twisted on the head. A teardrop of blood was painted on faces, eyelids and lips, strengthened with a slash of red, faces whitened. One long eyebrow, like one of Kahlo's stretched across foreheads. The stage set in front of the vast murals of the Musée des Arts d'Afrique et d'Oceanie was a re-creation of a Kahlo painting, given depth with giant leaves of jungle plants and baskets of fruits, vegetables and flowers, which editors stuffed in their Prada bags when leaving.[9]

In an alternative reading of Kahlo's legacy, the Cutler Salon in New York declared that its "*Off-Set* collection was inspired by Frida Kahlo, the controversial Mexican artist . . . and continued to grow beyond Frida to other women who shared a peasant look and life-style."[10] Thus at the millennium, Kahlo stood for both "goth" and "hippie" styles.

As the creative force behind Madonna's bustiers, Gaultier had also been interested in Kahlo's orthopedic corsets. Designer Tom Ford for Gucci and fashion photographer Helmut Lang picked up on the eroticism of Kahlo's self-presentation as a bound, even bondaged, woman. Both presented bustiers and strapped tank tops in black or white in 2001 that nodded at Kahlo's most intensely self-lacerating portrait, *The Broken Column* (1944), in which a tearful Frida displays her naked torso splayed open to reveal her spine as a scaffold of broken Doric columns held together by white leather straps buckled tightly across her chest, belly, and shoulders with partially hammered nails piercing her skin. Her figure drifts in a barren landscape; cracked and broken caverns and crevasses mar the ground on which no one could walk.

After Julie Taymor's movie *Frida*, the "fashionistas are especially proprietary toward Kahlo," noted Ruth La Ferla, citing a number of young designers, editors, and boutique owners who modeled their collections on Kahlo's style. For example, Mexican-born New York artist Sandra Paez opened a boutique in Brooklyn, "Frida's Closet," both to sell her Kahlo/Mexican-inflected peasant blouses and skirts and "to tell Frida's story" in part through a shrine to the artist.[11] More than seventy years have passed since Kahlo's impact on Parisian fashion, but her signature style continues in earrings, home decor, accessories, pendants, dresses, and handbags bearing her image; so when a forty-eight-year-old London woman declares herself the Frida Kahlo of personals and sandwiches, we know exactly what she means, or think we do: beautiful, intricate, self-referential; or bedridden, ill, betrayed—but always dressed for and as a work of art, a work of art that made art herself, an artist to the second power who fashioned her modern wardrobe as a series, as a replicable set of objects and signs. "Kahlo style," as Baddeley calls it, seems to be based on a rendering of the artist's persona, as "passionate," "flamboyant," and full of "emotional and physical pain," a reading of "her life story," through her appearance, that "allows access to her art."[12] A seamlessness between life and art, body and work, persona and environment, visible through style, is precisely what defined the modernist woman as artist; her dress needed to hang somewhere—and her body (which, for Kahlo, mangled as it was from her girlhood polio and terrible accident, was modestly covered by her flowing skirts and blouses) was where it did hang; it became a mobile studio on public display.

Hanging one's clothes as one might hang one's paintings was essential for the modernist woman artist if she were to make her mark visually and achieve recognition. In this, she was not too different from many of her male counterparts: Oscar Wilde's dandified poses; Alfred Stieglitz's cape; the Warner Brothers' cartoon caricature of the French artist, Pepé Le Pew's beret. But a woman's dress hangs less playfully. Its position is serious business, as Kahlo's work implies.

When Kahlo accompanied Diego Rivera on his trips throughout the United States during the 1930s and 1940s, newspapers often commented on her unique fashion sense. She set the tone by appearing in public outfitted as a *Tehuana,* but years before, she was already posing for the camera; she was the daughter of a photographer. One can see her dressed in drag, hair slicked back, in a three-piece suit posing amid her sisters in a family portrait. The modern woman sported "slacks," as Franchot Tone's fiancée Margaret Lindsay reminds him when he says he's going to take her golfing and "beat the pants off her" in the 1935 Bette Davis film *Dangerous.* Many 1930s Hollywood stars, like Marlene Dietrich singing in her tuxedo in *Morocco* (1930) or Katharine Hepburn dressed as a boy in *Sylvia Scarlett* (1936), declared their gender-bending sexuality by wearing pants. Kahlo had assumed that stance a decade before; but, after the 1930s and her marriage to Rivera, Kahlo fashioned a retro peasant look, which like a good many bohemian artists of her time (from Isadora Duncan to Laura Riding to Mabel Dodge Luhan), was based on retooling indigenous artifacts and attire.[13] She extended her dress beyond her body onto her canvases as well as for those taking her photographs and into her Coyoacán home; thus her artistry moved from bodily decoration to its image back to her own representation of this doubling procedure. Like Maya Deren a decade later, whose high-waisted trousers multiplied across the many different Mayas populating her film's domestic interior and signaling her complex sexuality in her 1943 *Meshes of the Afternoon*, Kahlo's paintings often feature varying meditations on fashion and the body. This nexus of clothing, body, and space and their contradictory meanings in modernist women's lives became signifiers of nationalism, art history, politics, and cosmology.

It took hours to plait her hair each day, but she insisted on it even as she lay dying. Her body, no less than her clothing, required the careful hands of women workers. While little has been said about who created Kahlo's clothing, one must assume it was made by traditional artisans, who two generations later were working in sweatshops and maquiladoras in New York and Los Angeles and along the Mexican/United States border. Hanging her dress amid various landscapes—her body, her garden, her idealized memory of a Mexican past, her family, her nurse, her vision of "Gringolandia," as she called the United States—Kahlo disembodied clothing only to redesign its significance. In some paintings (most notably in *My Dress Hangs There*), she lets her dress float above and within an imagined space pulling and pushing between past and present, between U.S. popular culture and its accumulating material products and Mexico's revolutionary history and indigenous peoples and desert landscape.[14] This seesaw between a lush or barren Mexico and a mechanized and violent New York figures precisely her own dressed self; she vivifies a borderland depicted quite literally. As curator John Zarobell notes, her dress and necklace (which she clearly owned) in the 1932 *Self-Portrait on the Borderline between Mexico and the United States* were replicas of Mexican painter José María Estrada's 1845 *Portrait of a Young Woman with a Coral Necklace and Pink Dress*.[15] Here she stands erect (with cigarette and Mexican flag as signs of her identification with modernism and its revolutionary state even as she wears a dress from the colonial period, a century before), though more often she obsessively depicted her own disfigured body as seated or reclining, incapable of standing on her own two feet. These two images of her dress holding center stage of the pictures' frames, among her most significant political paintings, place clothing as a crucial index of understanding nationalist, cultural, and economic conflicts between the United States and Mexico, vectored through women's wear, either

FIGURE 9.1 Frida Kahlo (1907–54), *Self-Portrait on the Borderline between Mexico and the United States*, 1932. María Rodríguez de Reyero Collection, New York. Private collection, New York. Photograph: Erich Lessing / Art Resource, NY. Copyright 2014 Banco de México Diego Rivera Frida Kahlo Museums Trust, Mexico, D.F. / Artists Rights Society (ARS), New York.

the antiquated dress (the one a peasant huipil, the other a colonial gown) or the (invisible) body of the painter. The modern woman as artist is in a sense retrofitted as a national icon through her attachment to an earlier mode of dress, one that, just as much as Katharine Hepburn's trousers, signifies a refusal of contemporary attire, with its girdles, garter belts, stockings, and sheathes.

In *My Dress*, her dress is detached from her body, suspended on a wire hanger, clearly a costume to be put on and taken off, part of a public performance; in *Borderline*, a younger version of the artist stands in stark contrast to the mess of structures, objects, and landscapes surrounding her. Kahlo's body, and her stunning face, were often on display in her many self-portraits; but her attention to how the body was dressed (and in *My Dress Hangs There* its substitution and erasure by the empty dress) gestures toward her engagement with the semiotics of fashion as an aesthetic and political response to modernism. In rapid variation, Kahlo's attire might be traditional Mexican peasant huipils, elaborate colonial-era, floor-length, bustled dresses, or the medical braces and plaster casts she wore, often decorated with her own private frescoes; she might also morph into part infant, plant, or animal.[16]

Kahlo's many photographic images suggest a further degree of performance, as she stages herself before the camera, hair and clothing carefully arranged, sitting beside one of her paintings. Her mouth is always closed in an enigmatic half-smile; usually she smokes. Frida lived her life surrounded by the photographic apparatus: her father Wilhelm/Guillermo's equipment was part of her girlhood; her stormy marriage to Diego Rivera was documented by Lucienne Bloch, Nicholas Muray, and others. She learned to play for and with the camera—to seduce it, as the title of one volume of photographs of her suggests—by dressing up, by looking head-on into the lens, by clamping her lips shut to cover her missing and rotten, blackened teeth. Dressed for public display, a stunning master at self-presentation, Kahlo was a fascinating subject: "With an innate sense of what she wanted to look like [Frida] molded her expression and positioned her body, angling her head and using her eyes to conjure a presence . . . [she] encouraged the transformation of her face into an icon."[17] More than the "anecdotal and tragic details of Kahlo's admittedly fascinating life," in Baddeley's words, were at work here; Kahlo framed herself as she would the images in her iconic paintings—front and center—in the contradictory pose of a knowing naïf.[18]

Historian Caroline Steedman, commenting on her mother's "politics of envy" that had animated her desire for a "New Look" coat in postwar London, notes that for modern women, clothing serves as a vehicle for class mobility.[19] Donning a nice suit and good shoes allows working-class women in the West, at least those who are white, access anywhere as class markers dissolve with an expensive cut. Thus Kahlo's choice to pose as "Miss Mexico" was a bold political statement on a par with Rivera and her collection of pre-Columbian art; it recognized the place race and colonialism played within Mexican history, looking backward to claim a distinctive non-European identity. Her self-fashioning, like his design and construction of the museum based on Mayan, Aztec, and Olmec patterns where they housed their collection of art, produced a revolutionary pronationalist identification with indigenous peasants, one he developed in part from his time in Italy, studying Giotto's work. Her Casa Azul garden in the shady Mexico City suburb of Coyoacán, in which she often was photographed and which served as background for some of her self-portraits, domesticated an idealized Mexican landscape, refashioning her natal home into a pastoral jungle in much the same way as she fashioned her dinner table with Pueblo pottery, her hair with local flowers and ribbons, her fingers with silver rings, her body with woven shawls, her neck with stone pendants or her monkey's arm. In each case, presence mingles with memorialized past. Many of her paintings feature the double-sidedness of clothing, revealing and concealing her duality: European and Mestiza; beauty and cripple; wife and artist; modern and tradition-bound. From body to apparel to home furnishings to garden, each step of self-presentation worked to recast the modern woman as a medium.

PORTRAIT OF GEORGIA

Georgia O'Keeffe's photographic *Portrait* by Alfred Stieglitz also works as an uncanny fashion statement; it might be titled "Portrait of the Artist as Modern Woman." In many of the prints, O'Keeffe appears in black, sometimes sporting derby and man-tailored suit, hair severely pulled in a bun. Or she is barely cloaked in a diaphanous white robe opened to reveal breasts, pubis, torso, flanked by her long flowing hair. Or her hands or neck or breasts are isolated against her paintings. Like Kahlo, her dark eyebrows and mustache accentuate her high cheekbones: the mustached lady at the circus so fascinating to Edgar Degas and Henri de Toulouse-Lautrec, whose body exudes femininity but whose facial hair speaks of a sensuous masculinity trapezed from low sideshow acts into high art. There is at once a play of deep eroticism and serious stoic business in these pictures: a dialectics of gender and labor. She is slender, even bony; yet her breasts are full. Her armpits and crotch are richly hairy. Many have remarked at her self-composure; how comfortable she appears to be in her skin, especially in the photographs of her body positioned in front of her paintings. She and Stieglitz wanted to foreground the work itself, not necessarily the woman who made it; yet, of course, *she* is the center of the picture— her work its background. That was another project achieved with his camera, that signal device of reproduction he turned endlessly on her lovely skeletal face and figure. The photographs were meant to train her audience to see her flowers, her bones, her rocks, her cliffs as her signature, as herself.

In 1922, the first diet book, *Diet and Health* by Lulu Hunt Peters, reached the bestseller list in the United States—to remain there for five years; since then no year has passed without some advice on self-improvement appearing on a bestseller list. A lithe athletic body was the hallmark of the New Woman, who, like Babe Dietrichson in golf or the fictional professional athlete Jordan Baker in F. Scott Fitzgerald's *Great Gatsby*, was an emblem of freedom, self-contained sexuality, and uncomplicated desire.[20] This was a distinctly WASP/Anglo ideal of modern femininity, however, one that exuded a cool streamlined look over Victorian clutter and messiness. An early 1930s diet leaflet offered by Kellogg's to advertise its new cereal, All-Bran, celebrated "the Modern Figure" of the "Modern American Girl" as a distinctive "rounded slimness," a "new sort of good looks" attained by eating "roughage," drinking water, sleeping eight hours, and exercising to wear the new styles: "flowy, clinging, revealing, graceful and alluring!"[21] Exactly the gowns worn by Margaret Lindsay in contrast to the bedraggled tailored suit barely covering the dissipated actress played by Bette Davis in *Dangerous*; later, once she takes up lodging in Franchot Tone's country home, she replaces her mannish out-of-fashion suit with his oversized shirt and dungarees, as she takes on a rustic wild-child look that along with her talents of impersonation seduces him. O'Keeffe's long body exemplified this new look. Kahlo's clothing, by contrast, was designed, in part, to hide her disfigured body; she was not a lithe athlete flowing freely but someone restricted to her bed and chair where she would work lying or sitting down. Yet her fashion sense also emphasized exoticism and the erotic aura of a mysterious primitive. In this she, too, was creating a modernist sensibility not unlike the interest in primitivism among cubists or the naughty boyishness of Bette Davis's histrionic washed-up Broadway star. Their ubiquitous cigarettes announced female sexual freedom and modernity, according to Richard Klein in *Cigarettes Are Sublime*. In her full regalia, Frida is Carmen.[22] But O'Keeffe was something altogether different.

In the 1920s, no newspaper article on Georgia O'Keeffe could resist commenting on her attire and visage: schoolmarm hairstyle, prim outfits, plain colors. O'Keeffe as pioneer: the New Woman artist living and working in a New York skyscraper who was still dressing as the small-town Midwestern school teacher she had been. Later, after her relocation to New Mexico, O'Keeffe's rugged features—her deep-lined face set off against her tightly pulled salt-and-pepper bun that matched her black-and-white frocks—seem at one with the rippled hills of the Southwest. Bones, skulls, arroyos, all worn into a stark smoothness by sun and wind, appear as objects in the paintings—and often in the photographs of her tooling around on a motorcycle or in her car—and are mirrored in her dress and hair, which according to one of her housekeepers she insisted be meticulously brushed and braided twice a day with a precise stroke.[23]

She, too, was resurrected as a fashion icon, first by 1970s feminists embracing her severe and serious refusal of fashion and then as a source of Americana, a Western gal at one with the harsh New Mexico terrain. Her refusal of fashion—and O'Keeffe's black capes and long skirts and white shirtwaists suggest her resistance to the ever-changing dynamics of the fashionable—itself becomes a style, militantly so in O'Keeffe's case. It is a style of the modernist woman artist that children's book author/illustrator Jeanette Winter depicts as a nun's habit, as an old-fashioned schoolmarm. In one image, she is poised to walk through a doorway, leaving school for the wider world, clutching her carpetbag in one hand and her paintbox and palette in another—hat and coat mirroring

Mary Poppins (in fact, the next image has her dancing with arms lifted to the sky through the clouds of the prairie, like another Julie Andrews character in *The Sound of Music*). This image of the single woman suited up and carrying her valise—ready to take off, "traveling light"—was first popularized by Nellie Bly and resuscitated in the Walt Disney film version of the Mary Poppins series.[24] Winter's inspirational children's book published in 1998 followed the second explosion of O'Keeffe's career in the 1990s; at the very moment Madonna was pursuing her Blonde Ambition, young girls could also imagine themselves dour artists, dressed perpetually in long black skirts, working "from dawn to dusk every day / for weeks and months" so that, like the great painter, her "hair turned from black to gray / to white as white as the bones."[25]

In Manhattan's Fall 1999 fashion shows, American designers scandalously catwalked men's and women's wear together. These shows, premiering before those in Europe, were viewed as "more uncensored" by John Bartlett, whose new line was featured in a "stellar show, an odyssey inspired by the marriage of Georgia O'Keeffe and Alfred Stieglitz."[26] The pieces "played against a backdrop as warmly evocative as an O'Keeffe painting. Strength and womanliness combined in a milky leather sheath with a matching tool-like apron slung around the waist. . . . True to O'Keeffe's love of New Mexico, Mr. Bartlett adorned the models with turquoise and silver jewelry."[27] According to Bartlett, O'Keeffe and Stieglitz were "a couple who embodied the pioneering spirit of the century, the cultural link between an urban setting like New York and the unknown, as in the Southwest." For him, "America isn't about avant-garde—it's about being a pioneer, which is the legacy of our culture." Accordingly, the creative director of the high-end department store Barney's commented that "the clothes were strong the way an artistic woman is strong, like Georgia O'Keeffe. It was the antithesis to the tarty early 90's."[28] These images of strong artistic women, "like O'Keeffe and Millicent Rogers, the Standard Oil heiress who made the Southwest fashionable in the 1940's," offer a model for escaping the city's rat race, claims the stylist, even as they remembered O'Keeffe's New York years.[29] Her 1920s New York paintings of the city's canyons, such as *A Street* (1926), anticipate those she found in the New Mexico landscape. Each place presents two looming walls and a sliver of an opening letting in light—a vaginal space, akin to her giant clamshells and calla lilies. The angular walls mirror her own bone structure.

Reporting on the collection, Amy Spindler remarked on the "need to offer meaning that seemed to pervade the season, which was less about fashion than about America itself. And as a permanent record of the event, the designers whose clothes are featured here [in the *New York Times Magazine* spread] have agreed to donate them to the Metropolitan Museum of Art's Costume Institute, and Barney's New York (the sponsor of the institute's current exhibit, 'Our New Clothes') will be displaying them in its windows until July 28." Even at this pre-9/11 moment, American fashion, art museums, department stores, national mythology, and its iconic woman artist become available as mutually sustaining systems of desire, aesthetics, ideology, and commerce. America, according to its designers, is freer than Europe, and the millennium offered possibilities for mining the past like no other moment. Both Kahlo and O'Keeffe served as icons for a variety of constituencies. The process of recognition entailed closely linking their clothed bodies to their paintings so that image and biography merge: Kahlo's investigations of the self-portrait made this inevitable, but O'Keeffe's serialized works also became a form of signature.[30]

HANGING A DRESS, WEARING A CANVAS

It is not easy to think of O'Keeffe following an aesthetic trajectory more typical of either Marcel Duchamp's "readymades" or Andy Warhol's silk screens, but her work can be seen not only as a conscious effort to control but also to comment on her style. Critic Grace Glueck notes of Duchamp: "Turned off by the growing practice of artists repeating their motifs to create a lucrative 'signature' style, he gradually reached the paradoxical decision that the way to avoid getting stuck in that groove was to keep to the images he had already made, replicating them literally . . . challenging the importance of originality in an era of mechanical reproduction." O'Keeffe was clearly one of those artists cultivating a "signature style," so recognizable and so inclusive of her own appearance, even though

FIGURE 9.2. Georgia O'Keeffe (1887–1986), *A Street*, 1926. Oil on canvas, 48⅛ × 29⅞ inches. The Georgia O'Keeffe Museum, Santa Fe, New Mexico, 1997.06.22. Gift of the Burnett Foundation. Photograph: Malcolm Varon, 2001. Photograph copyright 2014 Georgia O'Keeffe Museum, Santa Fe / Art Resource, NY / Artists Rights Society (ARS), New York.

unseen, that she resisted signing her paintings. They were that obvious. Was she one of those painters Duchamp mocked or was she, like Duchamp, trading on her reproducibility? Stieglitz made a photograph in 1917 of the urinal, Duchamp's most notorious readymade signed by "R. Mutt." His insistence that O'Keeffe not sign her work suggested a sly nod to Dadaism. At any rate, her style opens her to endless reproduction. In a 1999 exhibition of four artists influenced by Duchamp at Curt Marcus Gallery, Mike Bildo presented some of his *Not Duchamp* pieces along with "his knockoff of Georgia O'Keeffe's painting *Red Canna* of 1924, here retitled *Not O'Keeffe*."[31] An O'Keeffe became and remains recognizably hers. Her paintings wore her traces. She had produced a trademark of her own reproductions, repeating color, subject matter, and line by herself.[32]

If Frida's body was like a that of a doll's, like the miniature bride who lurks through many of her paintings, replicable, then it was O'Keeffe's colors and lines, especially her collectible objects—shells, fruit, flowers, bones—even her recognizable landscapes of skyscrapers, hills, sky, canyons, that had become reproducible and available, like the glass paperweights Theodor Adorno refers to in "Art-object," for interior decorating.[33] By 1947, mystery writer Dorothy B. Hughes set the tone of her genteel detective's "comfortable" home by outlining the contours of *In a Lonely Place*'s Brub Nicolai's living room: "The room was a good one, only the chair was gaudy, the couch was like green grass and another couch the yellow of sunlight. There was a pale matting on the polished floor; there was a big green chair and heavy white drapes across the Venetian blinds. Good prints, O'Keeffe and Rivera."[34] An O'Keeffe was a "good print" to hang because it fit tastefully into a bungalow. This was by design; inspired by a lecturer's comment that art "as decoration . . . consisted in putting the right thing in the right place," O'Keeffe composed her canvases with an eye to interior decorating.[35] So intimate were the portraits of O'Keeffe in the media and so powerful the reproductions of her work in magazines and posters and postcards that countless people wrote to O'Keeffe offering her thanks and poems but also sending requests to have her enter their homes. One, having been "stunned by the stark essences" he saw in a 1940s *Time* magazine spread, requested a print of *Antelope* for his apartment when he returned to "grad school, golden academia, after serving [his] country," thanking her for any "help" she might offer "towards better interior decoration."[36] He understood that the best he could hope from "Miss O'Keefe," as he misspelled her name (a hazard of not signing one's canvas), would be a copy of her work to hang on his walls; however, another man wrote to her from Ecuador asking for the real thing: "May I have a sketch of yours? Something that you don't want, so I can hang it in my empty living-room, which is not a wonderful emptiness [as she had described New Mexico]. Please."[37]

Part of both artists' appeal rested in consistency; though each canvas was clearly different, even if of the same subject—say Frida's face, or O'Keeffe's Jack-in-the-Pulpits—they could be recognized immediately. They had style. In her artist's statement for her 1923 show, "Alfred Stieglitz Presents One Hundred Pictures: Oils, Water-colors, Pastels, Drawings, by Georgia O'Keeffe, American," she demurred about her ambitions, concluding by contradicting her earlier assertion that she would have preferred not to show her work:

> I say that I do not want to have this exhibition because, among other reasons, there are so many exhibitions that it seems ridiculous for me to add to the mess, but I guess I'm lying. I probably do want to see my things hang on a wall as other things hang so as to be able to place them in my mind in relation to other things I have seen done. And I presume, if I must be honest, that I am also interested in what anybody else has to say about them and also in what they don't say because that means something to me too.

In this brief comment, in which the repetition of personal pronouns, I, me, my, appears thirteen times, the artist admits to a desire to be recognized. She wants her work seen within a history of others she has seen hanging on gallery and museum walls and the criticism (or silence) that it might accrue. She is Georgia O'Keeffe, American, and part of that assertion comes from boldly asserting herself as the "I," who effaces herself, demurring to have her name on her canvases or her photograph available, only her pictures. On the back cover of her brochure, written in bold face and capitals: "THERE IS NO CATALOGUE. THE PICTURES HAVE NO TITLES, BUT ARE NUMBERED AND DATED.

Even by this time, only four years after arriving in New York, her imagery was meant to be her signature, so that artist and art (e)merged as one. Pared even more, she is "O'Keeffe." Her work is new, so pure it is unmarred by naming; it merely hangs.

The staging of O'Keeffe's refusal to sign her works anticipated Jacques Derrida's concept of the stable mutability of the signature as citation: "in order to be legible, a signature must have a repeatable, iterable, imitable form; it must be able to detach itself from the present and singular intention of its production."[39] O'Keeffe's mark was the surface of her canvas, recognizable, "iterable" by her, but also by the camera; it was "imitable," not dependent upon the writing of her name. Her images and her antifashion sartorial style were signature enough. Replacing language with a readily remembered visual image—a trademark—is something O'Keeffe learned, like Andy Warhol would a generation later, doing advertising work. As a commercial artist in Chicago, she was "just making pictures of alarm clocks and tomato cans," but she was also "working herself out."[40]

In Kahlo's provocative painting *The Bride Frightened at Seeing Life Opened* (1943), a small doll, iterable and reproducible, dressed in a white bridal gown, peers over a freshly cut watermelon and beholds a grasshopper and an owl perched among coconut, banana, pineapple, avocado, and an orange-fleshed papaya, its black seeds cutting across the canvas. "Fruits are like flowers," she told her step-daughter, "they speak to us in a provocative language and teach us things that are hidden."[41] The 1938 still life *Pitahayas*, which had so captivated André Breton, evokes a Boschian landscape of volcanic basalt and bruised red fruit all overseen by a playful skeleton wielding a hooked reaper. Some of the fruits are cut open to reveal their gray flesh and black seeds, others remained sealed, yet their scaly skin seems dangerous and horrific. Flowers and fruits, so essential to Kahlo's table settings, evoked life, but they also shrouded decay.

O'Keeffe had become fascinated by the scaly alligator skin of the avocado during her years in the Shelton Hotel. She painted them lying along her windowsill, as if these, then quite exotic, fruits could break through the pane of glass separating her from her river view, from the dead nature of the East River, its east bank lined with factories, smokestacks belching gray ash into the wan sky. The alligator pear coalesces a vista much as the streetlamp in deep focus rivets the towering buildings on either side of *A Street*, so that landscape or still life become embodied. Her still-life paintings exhibited in 1925 at the Andersen Gallery in a show billed by Stieglitz as offering "159 Paintings, Photographs & Things, Recent & Never Before Publicly Shown," elicited Edmund Wilson's meditation on the gendering of still life: "women seem to charge the objects they represent with so immediate a personal emotion that they absorb the subject into themselves instead of incorporating themselves into the subject . . . women artists have a way of appearing to wear their most brilliant productions—however objective in form—like those other artistic expression, their clothes."[42] Thus women's work becomes a form of clothing; dress and canvas (and the objects they represent) are interchangeable so that to hang a painting on a wall is like hanging an artist's dress—even the artist herself—in the collector's closet.

In many of Kahlo's paintings, background landscapes encircle her portrait filling the canvas with mythic renderings of Mexico's volcanic terrain, its leafy jungles, so that they appear to drape her body. In them, her face or body is posed so still it becomes its own still life. This is especially clear in *What the Water Gave Me* (1938), which condenses the entire vocabulary of Kahlo's canvases: figures, costumes, volcanoes, flowers, shells, dead birds, skeleton, parents' faces, tentacled hair, vein-like roots, her own mangled body (only her feet appear, the right foot deformed); the Empire State Building explodes from Mexico's volcano Popocatepetl into a surreal still life in which these miniature objects float like ominous toy ducks in her bath. The layout of the scene, a suicide perhaps—truly *nature morte*—or a hydrotherapy to heal her postoperative incisions, repeats the composition of the still lifes and of her birth/miscarriage paintings of 1932 with a double horizon: the table and plate of the traditional still life objects are formed by the tub and the water level. It is a table set with memories. Her step-daughter Lupe remarks "for Frida setting the table was a ritual" culminating in "the act of placing the flower vase in the center. . . . Into the vase went a bouquet that Frida had cut in the garden. It mimicked the flowers she wore in her hair."[43] Landscape into still life into self-portrait into self.

Isolated, gigantic objects, defying gravity, hanging in suspension, had by this time become signatures of O'Keeffe's work. Close-ups of hollyhocks, irises, calla lilies, Jack-in-the-pulpits, petunias, and clamshells dominated her canvases, perhaps inspired by cinema, certainly influenced by art photography and advertising. These series overlapped with her New York paintings, which often featured foreshortened views of skyscrapers, but included a number of industrial landscapes (of water towers, smoke stacks, elevators, and storage tanks) viewed across the East River from her studio at the Shelton Hotel. Living in New York with Rivera at the same time O'Keeffe and Stieglitz occupied the thirtieth floor of their East Side residence, Kahlo was certainly aware of O'Keeffe's bones and flowers.[44] Frida wrote O'Keeffe that she could "never forget your wonderful hands.... If you [sic] still in the Hospital [sic] when I come back I will bring you flowers, but it is so difficult to find the ones I would like for you!"[45] Flowers, too, were signatures for both women.

These iconic totems, the flowers and fruits, spaces and places, associated with each artist, dress their canvases with accessories that foreground a ready identification: viewers know immediately both what they see and whose vision it is. Their signature bodily features—dark heavy brow, high cheekbones, deeply-creviced clavicles, exposed pelvic bones—reappearing in photographs and (Kahlo's) paintings, strangely connect their work and their bodies to their self-invention as photogenic talismans. Each, with her Hungarian grandparent, forged a distinctive erotic look from her bone structure, which also played with New Woman androgyny and cross-dressing. And, from bones, each forged an erotic canvas that spoke of sexual desire. Blanche Matthias declares that after reading the endless paeans to O'Keeffe she "hungers for her bone structure," in both her body and her paintings.[46]

DESIGNING WALLS

For these modernist women artists, dress extended beyond their bodies to the prosthesis of their meticulously curated homes and studios, which became a kind of external costume. Poet Andrei Codrescu—in *The Posthuman Dada Guide*—asks readers to consider how we live entwined with the external world as a form of what Marshall McLuhan called "extensions," how "the city, the house, the car, the iPhone, the laptop, the iPod, the pillbox, the nonflesh surround" form a complex matrix covering daily life.[47] These modernist women artists recognized their inherently eccentric position within their worlds—circled within families they often sought to escape for an art world itself encapsulated within a "group" (O'Keeffe's alliance with Stieglitz's 291 Group, Kahlo's connection to the muralistas). As uncanny group members—not quite at home as artists, but making homes for art nevertheless—they developed complex second skins: clothing bodies and decorating houses as armature, as armor.

O'Keeffe left a house filled with sisters to pursue her education, becoming a teacher in Texas, before journeying to New York after Stieglitz selected some of her drawings for an exhibit at his gallery, 291. She stayed on in New York living in Stieglitz's niece's fifth-floor studio loaned to her for a year, painting naked and posing for his camera in the great city light of an upper-story apartment. Abandoning her late-Victorian childhood, O'Keeffe fled the dull prairies of Wisconsin for her remembered images of the sea where her family of sisters had lived when she was young. Kahlo remained connected to her large family of sisters, so connected that one, Cristina, became Diego's lover, precipitating the Riveras' divorce in 1939. When Frida first met Rivera, she lived with his children, even occasionally with his ex-wife, enmeshed in a web of art and domesticity in the San Angel double studios designed for them by Juan O'Gorman.[48] O'Keeffe found herself embedded in a large wealthy German-Jewish family overseen by Stieglitz's mother at Oaklawn, their summer spread on Lake George, New York, including sisters, daughters, nieces, and an array of cousins (and occasionally his wife) who welcomed her, but from whom she kept a cagey distance, restoring an outbuilding into her studio, then ultimately relocating to New Mexico following Stieglitz's affair with Dorothy Norman.

Artist studios—say Jackson Pollock's Amagansett barn re-created in the Museum of Modern Art retrospective or Mark Rothko's firehouse on the East Side where he constructed the black paintings for the Houston chapel that was restored as the set for the

2010 Broadway production *Red*—insist on their antidomesticity. Empty, rough—industrial loft spaces in cities, abandoned barns in the country—they are refuges from the feminized, bourgeois home, allowing movement, mess, and scale. They are zones cordoned off from middle-class living rooms; yet they often become living spaces as artists fashion a bedroom and kitchenette in one tiny corner of these garrets in low-rent districts (see *La Bohème* or its incarnation *Rent*) and then become fashionable quarters as moneyed collectors and models and lawyers follow, driving out the artists (see Greenwich Village, Soho, Lower East Side, Tribeca, Williamsburg, Astoria in rapid succession from the 1950s to 2000s). But these spaces are where men produce; women often turn a room or corner of their domicile into a studio space.

O'Keeffe's Lake George barn paintings—boxy red and blue and violet outbuildings—convey emptiness, desertion; these four walls no longer contain even cows, perhaps not even bales of hay, much less human life. Her New York skyscrapers also suggest an eerie evacuation as well; the tilting towers closing in on the center of the canvas cast menacing yellow and black shadows. The streetlight coiled between the buildings flickers like a snake's tongue. Bram Dijkstra argues that O'Keeffe's 1919 painting of *Fifty-ninth Street Studio*, this, her first dedicated studio, expresses a kind of liberating joy at her newfound work space.[49] Its canted doorways, leading from a pale gray room through a series of angled frames first white, then obliquely bisected by red, to darkness of a blackened room with a rust-colored window, limn a story of finally coming home to a place that invites because it dislocates.[50] She had moved into her lover's niece's apartment, where she and Stieglitz jointly created their *Portrait* of her as a free and somewhat ironic new woman who could pose as a defiant nude, then buttoned down in men's attire or as a reined-in spinster. This work led directly to her vision of vaginal city streets. When she fled back to the Southwest, after the break with Stieglitz in the late 1920s, she found a more appropriate landscape of wonderful emptiness that became her subject. Simple, stark, black-and-white—this was her outfit, created on her canvases and in her home—her dress abstracted in two and three dimensions.

As self-portraits, Kahlo's work features an intimacy gleaned from the often domestic settings quoted within them; her garden, her dogs, her monkey, her dresses, her jewels show up as background (sometimes as foreground) props, stressing location as an element of her outfit. Her dress hangs amid the detritus of her idealized Mexico and its counterpart, a demonized Gringolandia. The houses she and Rivera occupied—their two dwellings in Coyoacán, and the joint studios in San Angel, his museum in Anahuacalli—were essential to a cultural implantation of *Mexicanidad* within their works and through their reputations. Home for Kahlo is the interior—psychic and literal—detailed as an indigenous landscape and a cared-for domestic space. Each artist's house is now a museum of her respective personal taste. Kahlo's easel, with the unfinished portrait of Stalin as Mexican peasant, occupies a small corner of her bedroom. Upon her death, Rivera deeded the Casa Azul (and upon his, their museum of pre-Columbian art) to the state to become a national museum; he retained the right to access a corner of Frida's room for himself, however.[51] O'Keeffe's home, Abiquiu, is kept sacrosanct. These intimate museums conflate art and life.

Where does an artist imagine her work, rather than her dress, will hang? How is this negativity, the walls surrounding the canvas, considered? Kahlo's paintings were part of her passion to decorate by filling her canvases and decking out her body and walls with Mexicana. O'Keeffe reworked nature and the city to become at once eerie and inviting. Her paintings inevitably incite the sexualized readings of their images that she so despised—the mysteries of the vulva and vagina, the ultimate uncanny, female genitalia: first home and final tomb. Perhaps each painting, like a dress, stark and powerful, was meant to hang individually in a home, or studio, or gallery, because the cumulative effect of seeing retrospectives of their work is to reduce each canvas. One Georgia O'Keeffe will jump out in a room of modern American art. That is why it is a major news event when one appears in a collection; but dozens of them, like the mediocre ones hanging in her Santa Fe Museum, seem ridiculous.[52] One cannot take in the multitude of Fridas to be seen in a retrospective. She is reduced when amassed.

On the brink of the Second World War, Paris became enamored with a beautiful exotic woman. Couture in 1939 followed Kahlo's reinvention of *Mexicanidad*, refashioning it into a Parisian fashion form. In late 1990s America, Spindler noted the return of interest in Westerns and folk music. "A woman with an artistic bohemian air, more likely to wear a serape than a power suit" signals the style of fin-de-millennium.[53] For these artists—and perceptions of them—a deep visual iconography connecting their bodies, their fashionings and furnishings, and their paintings to indigenous peoples and their lands, even as they inhabited cities, served to announce their female modernity.[54] Paradoxically, by putting the Mestiza into circulation as a valuable aesthetic presence, Kahlo outlined a new political fashion aesthetic. Similarly, by re-creating pioneer Western plainness, O'Keeffe emphasized her disregard of fads by fashioning them into an exaggerated version of a hick. As careful creators of their own images, groomed and marketed throughout the world through photography and human-interest news reports, they inaugurated the connection among fashion, decor, personality, and painting. Both asserted the artist as a different form of womanhood, another type of modern woman at once freer and more stylized . . . a self curated.

NOTES

1. Diego Rivera, with Gladys March, *My Art, My Life: An Autobiography* (1949; repr. New York: Dover, 1991), 138.

2. The bibliography on each artist is gigantic; the definitive comparative study of the two painters also includes their Canadian contemporary Emily Carr: Sharyn Rohlfsen Udall, *Carr, O'Keeffe, Kahlo: Places of Their Own* (New Haven: Yale University Press, 2000), which examines landscapes, literal and imaginative, of each. See also various essays of mine exploring their investments in and purchase on feminism, nationalism, and modernism, especially "Great Lady Painters, Inc.: Feminism, Modernism, Nationalism and Painting," in *Modernism, Inc.: Body, Memory, Capital,* ed. Jani Scandura and Michael Thurston (New York: New York University Press, 2001), 193–218.

3. Hillel Schwartz, *The Culture of the Copy: Striking Likenesses, Unreasonable Facsimiles* (Cambridge, Mass.: MIT Press, 1996); Celeste Olalquiaga, *The Artificial Kingdom: A Treasury of the Kitsch Experience* (1998; repr. Minneapolis: University of Minnesota Press, 2002).

4. Oriana Baddeley, "Her Dress Hangs Here: De-Frocking the Kahlo Cult," *Oxford Art Journal* 14, no. 1 (1991): 11–12.

5. "How Much Do You Know About Frida's Art . . . ?," http://www.fridakahlofans.com/kahlo test.html (accessed July 15, 2013).

6. "Revolutionary Fashions," accessed July 15, 2013, http://www.fridafashions.com/pages/my _dress_hangs_here_frida.html.

7. See Maria Claudia Andre, "Frida and Evita," in *Latin American Fashion Reader: Dress, Body, Culture,* ed. Regina A. Root (Oxford: Berg, 2005).

8. Marisela Norte, "976 LOCA," in *Recent Chicano Poetry/Neuste Chicano-Lyrik,* ed. Heiner Bus and Ana Castillo (Bamberg: Universtätbibliothek Bamberg, 1994), 106–7.

9. Amy M. Spindler, "Dressing Them Like Artists," *New York Times,* October 21, 1997, A22.

10. Patrick McIvor, "Two Sides of a Coin," *HairColor & Design,* 1997, 13.

11. Ruth La Ferla, "Front Row," *New York Times,* October 29, 2002, A28.

12. Baddeley, "Her Dress Hangs Here," 11.

13. See Becky Peterson, "Precious Objects: Laura Riding, Her Tiara, and the Petrarchan Muse," in *Accessorizing the Body: Habits of Being 1,* ed. Cristina Giorcelli and Paula Rabinowitz (Minneapolis: University of Minnesota Press, 2011), 108–25, and "Experimentation, Identification, Ornamentation: Avant-garde Women Artists and Modernism's Exceptional Objects" (PhD diss., University of Minnesota, 2010).

14. The variations on this title—in both Spanish and English—are fascinating and suggest diverging investments (so to speak) by critics about which side of this painting she identifies: *Alla Cuelga Mi Vestido, Mi Vestido Cuelga Ahi, My Dress Hangs Here, My Dress Hangs There.* Sometimes noted as *Her Dress Hangs Here,* or *There,* also. "Here" or "there" may indicate the critics' position more than Kahlo's, but also points to the imprecision of spatial locations. For an assessment of the critical fervor for all things Kahlo in the 1980s following the publication of Hayden Herrera's biography, *Frida: A Biography of Frida Kahlo* (New York: HarperCollins, 1983), and the 1983 film accompanying the exhibition *Frida Kahlo & Tina Modotti* by Laura Mulvey and Peter Wollen, see Baddeley, "Her Dress Hangs Here." Over the subsequent decades, the "cult" has continued to expand.

15. John Zarobell, "The Hybrid Sources of Frida Kahlo," *Berkeley Review of Latin American Studies,* Fall 2008, 23–24.

16. One feature of the ephemeral nature of fashion, and thus its significance for modernity, ac-

cording to Gilles Lipovetsky, is its protean and mutable aspect, ever foraging what has been and converting it into something new, as well as its paradoxical linkage of feminine seductiveness to women's freedom. "Through dress and makeup, women play at being vamps, stars, tuned-in trendsetters, 'women's women.' They reappropriate styles, airs, myths, and epochs at will; seduction has a good time and enjoys its own spectacle without taking itself too seriously." Gilles Lipovetsky, *The Empire of Fashion: Dressing Modern Democracy*, trans. Catherine Porter (Princeton, N.J.: Princeton University Press, 1994), 113. While Kahlo and O'Keeffe certainly appropriated an eclectic array of "styles, airs, myths, and epochs," each creating a seductive spectacle of herself as modern/artist/woman, both were very serious about their work and identities.

17. Carla Stellweg, ed., *Frida Kahlo: The Camera Seduced* (San Francisco: Chronicle Books, 1992), 105. For an evocative fictional "memoir" about Kahlo and the camera, see Elena Poniatowska, "Diego: I Am Not Alone, Frida Kahlo," in Stellweg, *Frida Kahlo*, 15–20.

18. Baddeley, "Her Dress Hangs Here," 11.

19. See Carolyn Steedman, *Landscape for a Good Woman: A Portrait of Two Lives* (New Brunswick, N.J.: Rutgers University Press, 1986) for a discussion of the political economy of one postwar British woman's leveraging clothes into security.

20. See Martha Banta, "Coco, Zelda, Sara, Daisy, and Nicole: Accessories for New Ways of Being a Woman," in Giorcelli and Rabinowitz, *Accessorizing the Body*, 82–107.

21. *The Modern Figure*, n.d., n.p. Diet book produced by Kellogg's in author's possession.

22. Richard Klein, *Cigarettes Are Sublime* (Durham, N.C.: Duke University Press, 1995) argues that Carmen represents a fitting emblem of the modern woman—single, a worker, sexually alive, who smokes.

23. Christine Taylor Patten and Alvaro Cardona-Hine, *Miss O'Keeffe* (Albuquerque: University of New Mexico Press, 1992), 20. Patten details an obsessive and controlling woman, directing her assistant to save every hair from her brush "so that ringlets could be made for future collectors" (150) or insisting that the closet door be kept closed "so when dressing her, I'd be opening and closing that door a number of times. Such things bothered her; everything had to be in its place" (71). Like the many profiles done about her in the 1920s, Patten repeats that for O'Keeffe, "there were no contradictions" (23), emphasizing how "deliberate," "precise," "exact," "particular" was "her relentless insistence on simplicity" (49), her "repeated motions," her "gestures as her own" (119, 19, 72, 37).

24. See Cristina Scatamacchia, "Traveling Light: Nellie Bly's Travelling Bag," in *Exchanging Clothes: Habits of Being 2*, ed. Cristina Giorcelli and Paula Rabinowitz (Minneapolis: University of Minnesota Press, 2012), 97–119.

25. Jeanette Winter, *My Name Is Georgia* (San Diego: Harcourt Brace, 1998), 43, 40. As evidence of the seriousness of all things O'Keeffe, this children's book, an imagined autobiographical poem, even contains an extensive bibliography, going back to the 1940s for its sources.

26. Quoted in Amy M. Spindler, "The New Frontier: A Pioneering Spirit Pervades the American Fall Collections," *New York Times Magazine*, July 25, 1999, 48. Four years later, John Bartlett closed his business. See Cathy Horyn, "Young Stars of U.S. Fashion Can't Seem to Find Right Fit," *New York Times*, December 7, 2002, http://www.nytimes.com/2002/12/07/fashion/07DESI.html.

27. Constance C. R. White, "The Underdressed-for-Success Look," *New York Times*, February 15, 1999, A19.

28. Quoted in Spindler, "New Frontier," 48.

29. Ibid., 48.

30. See Anne Middleton Wagner, *Three Artists (Three Women): Modernism and the Art of Hesse, Krasner and O'Keeffe* (Berkeley: University of California Press, 1996) for an analysis of how O'Keeffe's series develop a form of autobiography.

31. Grace Glueck, "Duchamp's Replications. Duchamp's Replications," *New York Times*, October 22, 1999, B39.

32. These became easily repeated in *Life* magazine in the 1930s, then during the 1940s in *Time*, in the 1960s on PBS, in the 1970s in her large-format Viking Press book, and after that in the endlessly proliferating posters and calendars hanging in the reception rooms of the Breast Center in Minneapolis or the American Cultural Attaché in Rome and many more places between.

33. Theodor Adorno, "Art-object," in *Minima Moralia*, trans. E. F. N. Jephcott (London: Verso, 1974), 225.

34. Dorothy B. Hughes, *In a Lonely Place* (New York: Duell, Sloan and Pearce, 1947), 9.

35. "I Can't Sing, So I Paint! Says Ultra Realistic Artist; Art Is Not Photography—It Is Expression of Inner Life!: Miss Georgia O'Keeffe Explains Subjective Aspect of Her Work," *New York Sun*, December 5, 1922, 22. For extensive sources on O'Keeffe's critical reception, see Barbara Buhler Lynes, ed., *O'Keeffe, Stieglitz and the Critics, 1916–1929* (Ann Arbor: UMI Research Press, 1989).

36. Letter from Pvt. Don McClelland dated October 12, 1960, Box 223/Folder 3983, YCAL MSS

85, Alfred Stieglitz/Georgia O'Keeffe Collection, Beinecke Rare Book and Manuscript Library, Yale University.

37. Letter from Claudio Delgado, Guayaquil, Ecuador, n.d., Box 223/Folder 3983, YCAL MSS 85, Stieglitz/O'Keeffe Collection.

38. "Catalogue for Anderson Galleries, Jan 29–Feb 10 (extended to Feb 27), 1923 exhibition," YCAL 89, Box 4, Folder 94, Flora Stieglitz Strauss Collection, Beinecke Rare Book and Manuscript Library, Yale University.

39. Jacques Derrida, "Signature, Event, Context," in *Margins of Philosophy*, trans. Alan Bass (Chicago: University of Chicago Press, 1982), 328–29.

40. Frances O'Brien, "Americans We Like: Georgia O'Keeffe," *The Nation* 125 (October 12, 1927): 361. Her "I" and her refusal to sign link her to Walt Whitman's pose in *Leaves of Grass*.

41. Guadalupe Rivera and Marie-Pierre Colle, *Frida's Fiestas: Recipes and Reminiscences of Life with Frida Kahlo* (New York: Clarkson N. Potter, 1994), 188.

42. Edmund Wilson, "The Stieglitz Exhibit," *New Republic*, March 18, 1925, 97.

43. Rivera and Colle, *Frida's Feistas*, 24.

44. See Paula Rabinowitz, "Mogul and Star: Georgia O'Keeffe and Alfred Stieglitz on the Thirtieth Floor," in *Public Space, Private Lives: Race, Gender, Class and Citzenship in New York, 1890–1920*, ed. William Boelhower and Anna Scacchi (Amsterdam: VU University Press, 2004), 153–67.

45. Frieda Kahlo, Letter to Georgia O'Keeffe, March 1, 1933, Box 197/Folder 3383, YCAL MSS 85, Stieglitz/O'Keeffe Collection. This short letter Kahlo sent O'Keeffe from Detroit charts a complicated connection among four artists. Kahlo insists O'Keeffe get her husband Stieglitz to answer her letter if she is too weak to write and comments on her own husband Rivera's joy at his work on the Detroit murals. This commission would lead O'Keeffe to enter into the Museum of Modern Art's contest for a mural design to Americanize the new Radio City Music Hall after complaints surfaced about why Rivera, a Mexican, had received the RCA commission over an American artist. O'Keeffe's entering and winning this contest infuriated Stieglitz, who objected to both the commercialism of a music hall and the museum and who detested murals calling them "that Mexican disease" (quoted in Benita Eisler, *O'Keeffe and Stieglitz: An American Romance* [New York: Doubleday, 1991], 430). Moreover, Stieglitz was in the midst of his affair with Dorothy Norman, which would eventually drive O'Keeffe to permanently move to New Mexico, while Kahlo and Rivera were soon to separate because of Rivera's affair with Frida's sister Cristina Kahlo.

46. Blanche C. Matthias, "Georgia O'Keeffe and the Intimate Gallery: Stieglitz Showing Seven Americans," *Chicago Evening Post Magazine of the Art World*, March 2, 1926, 1, 14.

47. Andrei Codrescu, *The Posthuman Dada Guide: Tzara & Lenin Play Chess* (Princeton: Princeton University Press, 2009), 2.

48. These have been restored. See Joseph Giovannini, "In Painters' Poetic Homes, the Soul of a Nation," *New York Times*, March 4, 1999, B14. He describes the couple's house and its setting: "A biographical neighborhood of rare character and radical political sensibility, this Mexican Bloomsbury offers a view into the painters' relationships and the country's cultural history. Beyond being the backdrop for a couple with the ideals of cultural revolutionaries and the mating habits of scorpions, the restoration of the San Angel studios, along with the other house-museums [Casa Azul and Anahuacalli], reveals a second history . . . the operatic birth of modern architecture in Mexico."

49. Bram Dijkstra, "Introduction: American and Georgia O'Keeffe," in *Georgia O'Keeffe: The New York Years*, ed. Doris Bry and Nicholas Callaway (New York: Alfred Knopf, 1991), 105–29.

50. Bram Dijkstra, *Georgia O'Keeffe and the Eros of Place* (Princeton: Princeton University Press, 1998).

51. Martha K. Baker, "Writers' Homes That Speak Volumes," *New York Times*, September 5, 1999, Travel Section, 17, describes her mission to visit the homes of obscure and eccentric women writers whom she has read to "stand and breathe in the same spaces where the writer had been . . . becoming a pentimento on our own experiences rather than the author's."

52. "Museum's First" discloses that "O'Keeffe's 'Skunk Cabbage' has taken root at the Montclair Art Museum," thanks to a Clifton, New Jersey, man's donation of the 1922 work. *New York Times*, December 24, 1998, E1.

53. Spindler, "New Frontier," 48.

54. For more on the artist as a model, see Karen Karbo, *How Georgia Became O'Keeffe: Lessons on the Art of Living* (Guilford, Conn.: Globe Pequot Press, 2012).

10

STRAYS

Tarrah Krajnak

Between 1975 and 1995, a group of elderly German nuns living in Lima, Peru, acted as the intermediaries for the adoptions of dozens of impoverished, illegitimate, or unwanted children, finding them homes across Europe and the United States. They maintained contact with the children from afar, exchanging photographs and letters. In 1979, I was one of them. In 2011, I returned to Lima after thirty-two years to meet these remarkable centenarian nuns who still live and work within the confines of the small convent. A year later my images transformed into a metaphorical reflection on the meaning of motherhood, death, family, and home. My photographs do not reveal the faces of the nuns but rather the fleeting details of their collective identities. When I think of them now they are like ghosts wandering the convent halls in their traditional white habits; they are the memory of a hand or the folds in polyester fabric.

FIGURE 10.1 [FOLLOWING, LEFT]
Tarrah Krajnak, *Untitled* (from *Strays*), 2012. Pigment print, 6 × 9 inches.
FIGURE 10.2 [FOLLOWING, RIGHT]
Tarrah Krajnak, *Rosary in Hand* (from *Strays*), 2012. Pigment print, 6 × 9 inches.

11

THE EROTIC PLAY OF THE VEIL

TAPADAS *IN LIMA*

Camilla Cattarulla

The German painter Johann Moritz Rugendas lived in South America from 1821 to 1847, spending eleven years in Mexico and Chile, and often traveling to Brazil, Bolivia, Uruguay, and Peru. During this time, he produced most of his art (about six thousand drawings, watercolors, oil paintings, and lithographs), in a style melding the Romantic with the "Costumbrista," covering a wide range of subjects—landscapes, plants, animals, people, everyday life, and historical subjects. In particular, during his visits to Lima, he painted some oils of women wearing a long dress (the *saya*) and a black veil (the *manto*), which covered half their faces, leaving only one eye visible (usually the left one), and was tied around the shoulders in such a way as to emphasize bosom, waist, and hips. These women were called *tapadas* ("the covered ones"). The tradition of the *tapadas* was first described in reports from sixteenth-century colonial Peru, and the custom continued into the mid-nineteenth century.[1]

Rugendas was not the only one to document this enduring tradition. Julian Mellet, a Frenchman who traveled around Peru in the first half of the nineteenth century, also described the *tapadas*. Writing in 1815, Mellet noted the similarities between the *tapadas*' costumes and those worn by Lima's nuns, mentioning that even husbands were unable to recognize their wives when wearing the *saya y manto*:

The *saya* and *manto*, as they are called in this country, which together seem almost like a religious dress, hide all their deficiencies and prevent others from distinguishing any of their features: the manto hides the entire body and shows only the eyes; often husbands can only recognize their wives by their manner of walking, though women often masquerade it.[2]

In his novel *La novia del hereje o la Inquisición de Lima* (The heretic's bride, or Lima's inquisition, 1854), set in the latter half of the sixteenth century, Vicente F. López describes a *tapada* in great detail:

a shape brushed against his arm; from certain outside traits it seemed like a human being. The way in which it walked around all covered up or, in other words, its dress, was the most extraordinary thing. You could no longer see the lineaments of the face, nor discern any form other than that of the head, the back part of the body and the feet. It was, in short, a body stuck in a tight cowl and wrapped up in such a way that of all the face you could only see one dark eye glimmering with the energy and vivacity of the basilisk. Its steps were short and light; its movements were mischievous showing that it understood what it saw and knew the people it met. It was, in short, one of the many tapadas who walked the streets and promenades of Lima.[3]

The tradition of the *tapadas* could be found in practically all colonial cities of the Andean area.[4] Nevertheless, because of the importance of Lima, capital of one of the Spanish viceroyalties since 1542, this custom became associated with the city, a crossroad of social, cultural, political, and religious encounters and contrasts, in which the *tapadas* played a significant role.

Various theories have been advanced on the origin of this costume. The most likely one seems to be that it was brought to Spanish America by Spanish women (many of them of Muslim origin and of low social status) who came along with the conquistadors and missionaries, in most cases illegally, because it was forbidden for young women to immigrate to the colonies. The Hispano-Arab origin of the *saya y manto* seems confirmed by its presence in southern Spain, culturally more influenced by Arab occupation, and especially in the areas of Jaén, Baeza, Andújar, and Ubeda, where women used the veil on certain religious festivities, such as the day of St. Sebastian or St. Blaise, during Lent, or at nuptial processions.[5]

There are other theories. Antonio de León Pinelo, author of the 1641 book *Velos antiguos y modernos en los rostros de las mujeres: sus consecuencias y daños* (Old and new veils on the faces of women: consequences and damages), perhaps the most useful juridical-sociological text on the condition of women in Spain in the seventeenth century, cites a work by Juan de la Puente, who suggests a Christian origin for the veil used to cover one eye.[6] According to him, "Spanish women have taken from Arab ones the habit, praised by Tertullian, of hiding one of their eyes. If this were the case, it was not a Christian tradition, as argued by Saint Paul."[7] León Pinelo, while not excluding a Christian origin of the veil, considered the *tapadas* as a leftover of Arab domination.

Instead, an Inca origin of the *manta* is hypothesized in William Elroy Curtis's *Capitals of Spanish America* (1888), above all because of its black color:

The custom of wearing the manta originated among the Incas, but they wore colors until the assassination of Atahualpa, their king, by the Spaniards under Pizarro. Then every woman in the great empire . . . abandoned colors and put on a black manta, and it is since been worn as a perpetual mourning for "the last of the Incas."[8]

Spanish-American literature of the nineteenth century also dealt with the origin of the *tapadas*. Ricardo Palma, for one of his *Tradiciones peruanas* (stories illustrating local costumes, meant to encourage a sense of Peruvian national identity against its colonial past), browsed through many ancient documents in the hope of identifying the origin of the *manto*, without being able to satisfy his curiosity.[9] Vicente F. López considered *tapadas* of native origin, a consequence of the imposition of Catholicism by the Spaniards:

Though we do not know for certain the origin of this singular tradition, there are ancient chroniclers (among them archdeacon Barco de Centenera) who state that it comes from Peruvian natives, who, when forced to abandon idolatry, had had to let their vestals out of their cloisters; who, not wanting to bare themselves and show themselves to the world, adopted a personal habit that made them just as invisible as the high walls of their convents.[10]

Contrary to López's claim, Martín del Barco Centenera, author of the epic poem *Argentina y Conquista del Río de la Plata* (1602), does not argue for a pre-Hispanic origin of the *tapadas*, although he does call the veil "rebozo," the word used for the mantle or shawl worn by Indians (the verb *rebozar* meaning "to hide" or "to conceal"). Yet López may have considered this term to indicate the origin of the costume worn by the women of Lima.[11] Whatever the case, describing the source of the *tapadas*, López suggests a connection between these and the *beatas*, who, first in Spain and later in colonial Peru, dedicated themselves to the cult of the Virgin Mary as ideal woman.

FIGURE 11.1
Miguel Angel Giglio,
Tapadas limeñas, 2013.
Ink on paper, 21 × 30 cm.
Courtesy of the artist.

Along with the cult of the Virgin Mary, two other cultural currents predominated in Spanish society between the fifteenth and seventeenth centuries that had an impact on the image of women: Don Juanism and the tradition of courtly love. Don Juan Tenorio, a character who first appeared in a play by Tirso de Molina, became the archetype of the shameless, audacious, lucky, deceitful, and boastful lover. Disregarding social niceties, Don Juan takes pleasure in seducing women, though, in turn, he often falls for strong and domineering women. The myth of Don Juan became pervasive in the mentality of a culture in which women were completely subject to the will of fathers, husbands, or brothers. A second cultural current comes from the Arab-Andalusian lyrical tradition, which celebrated the perfection of women through daring metaphors. This idealized image of woman continued from the Middle Ages into modern Spain and was archetypically embodied in Don Quixote's Dulcinea. All three currents contributed to the condition of Spanish women, colluding to define their proper moral conduct.[12]

In the Americas, however, this cultural construct underwent a transformation of which the *tapadas* are the most evident example: underneath the veil, the women of Lima could escape their traditional role as angels in the house or the church and entice and seduce men, like female Don Juans. This tradition continued for at least three centuries and is described by Rugendas who, in his *Tapadas en la alameda,* represents them sitting with bare arms (and, in one case, a bare ankle), perhaps waiting to be approached by men. Words such as "coqueta" and "coquetar" often recur in the literature on *tapadas.*[13] José Luis Romero defines the "veiled lady" of Lima as an archetype of "courtly coquetry."[14]

Among those who first testified to the continuation of this phenomenon into the nineteenth century was Flora Tristán, a French woman of Peruvian descent who, in noting (like Mellet, before her) the inability of husbands to recognize their wives, celebrated the *saya y manto* as an instrument of women's freedom, allowing the women of Lima to go where they pleased and behave as they wished without fear of discovery:

In Lima, a woman may have breakfast with her husband in the morning (French-style dressing-gown, hair made up precisely like our Paris women), then, if she feels like going out, she'll put on the saya without a corset . . . let her hair down; she'll tapa, that is, she'll hide her face with the manto and will go out where she pleases. . . . In the street, she might chance to meet her husband who will not recognize her, she'll tease him with her eye, she'll flirt, she'll deliberately provoke him, start a conversation, make him buy her ice cream, fruit and sweets, make an appointment with him then leave, to start all over again with a passing officer. She can carry on with this game as much as she wants, without ever dropping the manto; then she might visit her women friends, go for a walk, and finally go home for supper. Her husband won't even ask her where she's been because he'll know perfectly well that if she wants to hide the truth from him she'll have no problem lying and, since he can't stop her, he'll choose the wisest course, which is not to worry about it. And so it is that women go alone to the theater, corridas, public assemblies, balls, for walks, to church, to pay visits.[15]

The *tapadas* both look and allow themselves to be looked at. They do so in an urban setting—streets, public places—as if to defy the stereotype of the flaneur as a quintessentially male figure that excludes, even linguistically, the possibility of a *flâneuse*.[16] The veil does not imprison the *tapadas* or separate them from the world: on the contrary, it allows them to penetrate it. In other words, the women of Lima, as early as the sixteenth century, appropriated the city for themselves. Although they did this through a disguise, they became both actors and spectators on the urban stage. The *tapadas* are an urban and public phenomenon: disguised, women take the upper hand; they move at will, meet men where they want, address them, provoke them. The *tapadas* undermine the division between masculine and feminine worlds; they invert traditional gender roles.[17] Relegated to the margins by colonial society and Spanish tradition, women, through their disguise, could regain the center: paradoxically, the invisibility offered by the *tapada* made them visible and mobile, free to move and speak. Moreover, Flora Tristán observed that *tapadas* could lie: husbands could not chastise their wives for going to the wrong places, because the *tapada* hid the truth. They allowed wives to maintain their traditional role at home, while defying it when they went out. The veil authorized deceit. As Francesca

Denegri notes, it created a clandestine channel through which the women of Lima reconciled social control and freedom and simultaneously established continuity and discontinuity with Spanish customs and culture.[18]

Hidden by the *manto*, the *tapadas* in public adopted a coquettish behavior that caught the attention of foreigners, as Flora Tristán notes:

> More than one foreigner has described to me the magic effect that Lima women seem to have on their imagination. Having been driven to face innumerable dangers by their desire for adventure in the firm belief that fortune awaited them on these distant shores, they perceive these women as the priestesses of the land or, perhaps, expecting Mahomet's paradise, they believe that God has brought them to a fairy land to repay them for the terrible sufferings of the voyage and to reward their courage.
>
> These flights of fantasy do not seem impossible when one considers the absurdities to which foreigners are driven by the beautiful women of Lima and the way their senses are caught in the whirlwind of passion. The desire to gaze on those faces that the women hide so carefully leads the men to follow them with the utmost curiosity.[19]

Seduction is exercised through that which is hidden: precisely because it covers, the veil stimulates the desire to uncover and unmask the woman. Lima women took to the extreme the principle of visual dissimulation that characterized (and still characterizes) Arab women's codes of dress. But Lima women appropriated an item of clothing used in Arab culture to control women and turned it into an instrument for avoiding control.

This transformation of the veil by Lima women was noted by another French traveler, Maximilien René Radiguet, who lived in Lima between 1841 and 1845:

> The *saya y manto* dress, which originally was meant to foster ideas of chastity and devotion, on account of one of those contradictions, has now come to the point of shielding completely opposite behaviors; its widespread use makes the city an immense salon of affairs and ingenious stratagems that make fun of the vigilance of the most ardent Othellos.[20]

The semantics of the veil, in other words, were reframed and became a means of seduction, a source of sexual attraction, allowing women to adopt behaviors traditionally
reserved for men. In this way, noted Flora Tristán, the veil served as a tool of sexual liberation, as if the *tapadas* anticipated a feminist alternative discourse on gender.[21] The
veil provided Peruvian women with social visibility by affording them protection while
allowing them to affirm their feminine identity within a male-dominated society. The
manto permitted women to emerge from anonymity. As a sign—almost a uniform—it
marked their distance from or even rebellion against certain social and cultural norms.
León Pinelo remarked on the difference between "*cubrirse*" (to "cover oneself") and
"*taparse*": the first corresponds to the original, "honest," and authorized use of the veil;
the second is a form of travesty and concealment.

Hiding the face is a simple act, which requires only the adoption of a simple loose veil,
without any affectation or care other than that of covering an image to prevent it from
being seen. The word taparse does not seem to refer to the veil, but rather to the way,
to the carefulness and artifice with which one tries to cover and hide the face in an in-
genuous and inexpressive fashion. And thus to cover oneself means to place the manto
on one's face, loosely and without any trick or artifice. Taparse is to hide oneself . . . fold-
ing, wrapping, and pinning the manto so that it leaves one eye uncovered, which is always the left one, while the rest of the face remains even more hidden and masked than
if it were entirely covered.[22]

That the veil served to hide the woman's identity is suggested also by its everyday usage:
a *tapada* is a woman who covers herself with a shawl or a veil in order not to be recognized.[23] The conflation of shawl and veil, a single piece of material, is related to its dual
function: a shawl is used simply as a cover-up, but a veil conceals the identity of the
woman while allowing her to engage in the art of seduction through the single visible
eye. Ferdinando Dogana calls the *manto* "an object whose characteristics summarize and
synthesize the personality of the individual or some dominant aspect or need."[24] The

veil can be seen as the concretization of erotic fantasies for the *tapadas,* or as the "place of realized expectations" for men.[25]

Because of this, the veil received much attention from civil and religious authorities both in Spain and in its American viceroyalties, who early on perceived the *tapadas* as violators of female moral codes of behavior and as threats to traditional society.[26] In an effort to rein women in, a series of legislative measures were passed over the centuries to try to put an end to this tradition. In Peru, these measures began with ecclesiastical laws. At the Third Council of Lima in 1583, Peruvian bishops harshly criticized the *tapadas* because their behavior was contrary to the cult of the Virgin Mary:

> No women should walk the street or be seen at their window with their faces covered. The decree should be kept and observed by all women in such a way that their frivolity will not distract the people from the cult of God. Women should rather show their faith and piety with a modest countenance and a religious dress.[27]

This decree is cited by Martín del Barco Centenera in his poem *Argentina y Conquista del Río de la Plata,* which recounts how the Council of Lima forbade "*tapadas*" during public festivities. Barco Centenera took it for granted that the *tapadas* were upper-class women who would reluctantly comply with the bishops' imposition. But the veil erased all distinctions of class or race. Under the *manto,* there might be white women, but also Indians, Blacks, *mestizas,* who might be slaves, servants, or aristocrats.[28] The *manto* lied. It even lied about gender, because men could wear it to pass as women. Marjorie Garber notes in reference to sumptuary laws (which were passed in Spain, and also in the colonies where, however, they were not applied): "The ideal scenario—from the point of view of the regulators—was one in which a person's social station, social role, gender and other indicators of identity in the world could be read, without ambiguity or uncertainty. The threat to this legibility was 'confusion.'"[29] The veil could shift from an instrument of travesty to an instrument of transvestism. For this reason the veil signals the impossibility of a univocal signification, even though the *tapadas* were culturally connoted as feminine and became a symbol of female sexual freedom in Peruvian colonial society.

Men masked as *tapadas* in order to commit crimes were mentioned in a petition sent by the Cortes of Castilla to Philip II in 1586, which led to the decree of June 9, 1590, valid for Spain but implicitly extending to the American viceroyalties:

The custom of women to go "tapadas" has come to such an extreme as to cause great offense to God and considerable damage to the Republic, because in this way the father does not recognize the daughter, nor the husband the wife, nor the brother the sister, and [women] have all the freedom, time, and space they want, and they make it possible for men to equally make passes at the daughter or wife of a gentleman as at those of the most lowly and humble people, which would not happen if they would go around bared, because light shows the difference between the one and the other. . . . Futhermore, one would avoid the evil deeds and sacrileges that men—dressed as women and "tapados" in such a way as to make it impossible for them to be recognized—have committed and commit.[30]

And it concluded:

We order that no woman found in our Reigns, of whatever state, quality or condition, may have permission to walk, or go around, with her face covered in any way, but must bare it, under the penalty of three-thousand maravedi for every occasion on which she does the contrary . . . and we order our judiciary administration to ensure through its efforts (even in the absence of complaints) the observance and the adherence to what is above mentioned in full awareness that if they do not to do it they will be charged in the proper seats for whatever negligence they may have been guilty of and for this they shall be punished.[31]

This decree was followed by a second one in 1593, a third in 1600, and yet another in 1634, bearing witness to the difficulty of eradicating the tradition in Spain.[32] Similar efforts were made by the viceroys of Peru. The dispositions of the bishops at the Third Council of Lima were followed by ordinances from viceroys Juan de Mendoza y Luna, marquis of Montesclaros (1609), and Diego Fernández de Córdoba, marquis of Guadalcázar (1624). Harsh laws on the *tapadas* were passed in Spain and in the colonies, with penalties including fines and incarceration, depending on the social condition and race of the *tapadas* and also punished men who talked to *tapadas*.[33] Ricardo Palma cites other viceroyal decrees passed by Diego López de Zuñiga, count of Nieva (1561), Luis Gerónimo de Cabrera y Bobadilla (viceroy from 1629 to 1639), and Pedro de Castro, count of Lemos (viceroy from 1667 to 1672).[34] All these laws were systematically ignored by the women of Lima, and *tapadas* continued to walk the streets alone or in groups, during the daytime and at night, going to religious functions and processions, public festivals and corridas. They were helped by the fact that the *manto* was a very simple costume and easy to re-arrange according to circumstances, turning it from a veil into a shawl and back.

Contemporary Peruvian literature responded immediately: under viceroy marquis of Guadalcázar (before 1639), Juan Mogrovejo de la Cerda wrote the short story "La endia-blada,"[35] satirizing seventeenth-century Peruvian society through a dialogue of two dev-ils: Asmodeo, newly arrived in Lima from Europe, and Amonio, a long-time resident of Peru. Asmodeo cites the *tapadas* as his efficient assistants and laments the fact that an auto-da-fé has contributed to their disappearance. Amonio says that he too has been dam-aged by the viceroy's act because he has lost many souls:

Forever gone is the velvet of the hands, the glittering of the feet, the freedom of the body, the vivacity of the walk, the confidence of the speech, and the sensuality of the movements. This is the time of disappointment. One-eyed women have ceased to make you fall in love; veils have ceased to be the false witnesses of faces; those faces, which adorned with veils seemed sacred relics, now confess that they are indeed bones, though not of saints; . . . And, finally, gestures tell the truth and the age speaks truly.[36]

For Amonio, the mystery of the veil has vanished and, along with it, the whole game of seduction: the invisibility offered by the *manto* coupled with the possibility of looking at and being looked at gave free rein to the imagination. Without the veil, age, class, and gender are unveiled and lose their mystery. Covering is seductive.

A century later, Concolocorvo (the pseudonym of writer Alonso Carrió de la Vandera) in *Lazarillo de ciegos caminantes* (Blind man's guide, 1773) attributed the sex appeal of Lima women not only to the veil, but to their habit of leaving one foot or part of the leg bare (which was indeed typical of *tapadas*):

> Lima women ... and I say the same of plebeians, with the exceptions of Indians and black savages, follow an order that is the opposite of that of European, Mexican, or Buenos Aires women; I mean that while these make greater show of the area from the neck to the breasts ... , Lima women hide this splendor with a completely nontransparent veil during the warm season, and in the cold one they cover themselves to the waist with a double veil, which is actually quite extravagant. All their originality is located in the area from the waist to the tip of their feet. ... The more formal and honest women in this country bare half of their shin. The more original or fashionable ones pull up part of the veil to uncover the beginning of the calf, while those that the public views as scandalous ... pull their gowns half-way up like imperial tents.[37]

References to the *tapadas* are also found in the many *cancionerillos* of the seventeenth century.[38] Juan del Valle Caviedes (ca. 1625–98) wrote biting lines on the corruption of Lima society, noting the presence of *tapadas* in the procession of the Corpus Domini. He attacked them as shameless women who used the veil to adopt scandalous behaviors bordering on heresy.[39]

The pervasive impact of *tapadas* on Peruvian culture continued into the twentieth century in ballets and zarzuelas, such as compositions by Reynaldo La Rosa (*Las tapadas,* 1916) and Luis Pacheco de Céspedes (*Umbral de tapada,* 1948). The lyrics for Reynaldo La Rosa's music were written by Julio de la Paz along with José Carlos Mariátegui (author, in 1928, of *Siete ensayos de interpretación de la realidad peruana,* a foundational analysis of Peruvian literature). *Las tapadas* premiered at the Teatro Colón of Lima on January 12, 1916.[40] Taking inspiration from the "veiled ladies," it tells a love story set in the colonial period. The theme and the setting, influenced by Ricardo Palma, to whom the work is dedicated, were meant to bring to life the atmosphere of the *Tradiciones peruanas.* The work, however, was a critical failure, viewed as a poor imitation of classic Spanish theater based on faulty historical reconstructions.[41]

The tradition of the *tapadas* outlived the viceroyalty and continued into the second half of the nineteenth century.[42] Following independence from Spain, when Peru was in the throes of civil wars, the *saya y manto* was named after the successive governors ruling after Bolívar's regime (1826): *gamarrina* (after Agustín Gamarra), *orbegosina* (after Luis José Orbegoso), and *salaverrina* (after Felipe Santiago Salaverry), showing political support for the caudillo of the moment as a symbol of national identity.[43] Ultimately, what the laws of the viceroys and religious authorities failed to enforce was achieved by the commercial, industrial, and cultural influence of Europe on Peru. In particular, French fashion had a decisive impact: when men and women began to wear Paris-style clothes, the *tapadas* rapidly went out of fashion.[44] This sudden disappearance highlights the paradox of the *tapadas* who, despite the fact that they were active and free subjects, were unable to produce their own discourse. On an ideological, moral, artistic, and po-litical level, they were always the object of the discourse of others. Visible in their invis-ibility, they were mere phantoms of erotic encounters. By the mid-nineteenth century, at most, they served as symbols of a golden era that resisted Europeanization: "The colony—it was once said—was a paradise. Let us save what is left of it and revere what has disappeared because of our faults. The colonial woman, the tapada of devotion and stratagems, was angelical. Let us preserve it as such."[45]

The static nature of colonial society allowed the custom of the *tapadas* to endure. With independence, the achievement, albeit difficult, of internal political stability accelerated modernization. In Georg Simmel's terminology, Peruvian society became "nervous," and as clothes were used to mark not only class divisions but also a break with the past and tradition, *tapadas* lost their original function.[46] Having lost their veil of anonymity, Peruvian women became visible and identifiable. At the same time, they acquired the right to speak in public, to develop their own cultural discourses, and to actively enter the exclusively masculine intellectual sphere, which the *tapadas* had never been able to do: in short, they became modern.

1. On *tapadas* in nineteenth-century iconography, see Keith McElroy, "La Tapada Limeña: The Iconology of the Veiled Woman in 19th Century Peru," *History of Photography* 5, no. 2 (1981): 133–49.

2. "La saya y el manto, así nombrados en el país, y cuyo conjunto parece formar un hábito de religiosa, ocultan todos sus defectos e impiden distinguir ninguna de sus facciones: el manto oculta toda la figura y no deja ver más que los ojos; a menudo los maridos no reconocen a sus mujeres más que en el modo de andar, aún cuando muchas veces lo disfrazan." Julian Mellet, *Voyages dans l'intérieur de l'Amérique méridionale* (Paris: Masson et fils, 1824); my translation from *Viaje por el interior de la América Meridional* (Santiago di Chile: Editorial del Pacifico, 1959), 121, passim. On Julian Mellet's travels, see Roberto Páez Constella, "Lima, Guayaquil y La Serena colonial: Bebidas y seducción en la literatura de viajes de Julian Mellet (1808–1820)," *Logos: Revista de Lingüística, Filosofía y Literatura* 8 (1998): 151–63. On the persistence of the tradition of the *tapadas* in the nineteenth century, see also Manuel Atanasio Fuentes, *Lima: Apuntes históricos* (París: Didot, 1867).

3. "pasó raspando su brazo un bulto; que á juzgar por ciertas exterioridades, no podía menos que ser un ente humano. El modo con que iba cubierto, más bien diré, su traje, era lo más extraordinario que se podía ver. Del rostro que lo llevaba no se veía más facción ni sobresalían otras formas, que la cabeza, la esfera posterior del cuerpo y los pies. Era, pues, un bulto metido en un saco angosto y envuelto de tal modo, que apenas se podía ver en su cara un ojo negro que brillaba con la energía y la viveza del basilisco. Sus pasos eran cortos y ligeros; sus movimientos maliciosos iban dando á entender que comprendía cuanto veía, y que conocía á cuantas personas encontraba. Era, en fin, una tapada de las muchas que ya entonces cruzaban las calles y paseos de Lima." Vicente F. López, *La novia del hereje o la Inquisición* (1854; repr. Buenos Aires: A.V. López editor, n.d.), 39–40. This and all other translations are my own. A *tapada* is also the protagonist of the story by the Chilean writer Alberto Blest Gana *La venganza*, published in March 1862 in *La Voz de Chile* and set in Lima in 1763.

4. On *tapadas* in Santiago, Chile, see Rolando Mellafe, *Las Tapadas y los Tapados*, in *Formas de sociabilidad en Chile* (Santiago de Chile: Ed. Vivaria, 1992). Among foreign travelers who, in the first half of the eighteenth century, noted the presence of *tapadas* in Lima, see John Byron *The narrative of John Byron containing an account of the great distresses suffered on the Coast of Patagonia. With a description of St. Jago de Chili* (London: S. Baker and Leigh, 1778).

5. The *tapadas* are one of the most common characters in the theater and poetry of the Spanish

Siglo de Oro. On the tradition in Spain and South America, see María Elena de Arizmendi-Amiel, "Las tapadas," *Revista de Dialectología y Tradiciones Populares* 43 (1988): 53–58; Laura R. Bass and Amanda Wunder, "The Veiled Ladies of the Early Modern Spanish World: Seduction and Scandal in Seville, Madrid and Lima," *Hispanic Review* 77, no. 1 (Winter 2009): 97–146; Marco Antonio and León León, "Entre lo público y lo privado: Acercamiento a las *tapadas* y *cubiertas* en España, Hispanoamérica y Chile," *Boletín de la Academia Chilena de la Historia* 60 (1993): 273–311.

6. On the life and work of Antonio de León Pinelo and, in particular, on Spanish legislation on the veil of the *tapadas*, see Antonio Muro Orejón, "Las Pragmáticas contra las 'tapadas' y otros pecados públicos en España y en las Indias hispanas," in *Homenaje a la profesora Lourdes Díaz-Trechuelo: Catedrática de historia de América de la Universidad de Córdoba* (Córdoba: Monte de Piedad y Caja de Ahorros de Córdoba, 1991), 77–92.

7. "De las árabes tomaron las mujeres españolas el taparse de medio ojo, de lo cual alaba Teruliano. Si todo fuera como esto, constumbres eran cristianas, pues lo aconseja S. Pablo." In Antonio de León Pinelo, *Velos antiguos y modernos en los rostros de las mujeres: Sus consecuencias y daños. Ilustración de la Real Premática de las Tapadas* (1641; repr. Santiago de Chile: Editorial Universitaria, 1966), Book I, 171.

8. William Elroy Curtis, *The Capitals of Spanish America* (New York: Harper & Brothers, 1888); Curtis cites as his source Mrs. Admiral Dahlgren's *South Sea Sketches*.

9. See Ricardo Palma, *La conspiración de la saya y manto* [1877], in *Tradiciones peruanas*, ed. Julio Ortega (Paris: Archivos, 1993), 183 and passim.

10. "Aunque no se sabe á punto fijo el origen de esta costumbre singular, hay cronsits antiguos (el arcediano Barco de Centenera, entre ellos) que dicen, que habiendo sido obligados los indígenas de Perú á abandoner la idolatría, tuvieron que salir de los claustros sus vestals; que resistiendo ellas al principio andar descubiertas, ydejarse ver del mundo, adoptaron un claustro personal que las hiciera tan invisibles detrás de él como las altas murallas de sus convents": López, *La novia del hereje o las Inquisición*, 40. "During the Inca empire, there were women who played important roles in the religious structure, the so-called *acllas* or sun virgins who led a secluded life dedicated to the cult of the sun, the main god of the Incas" ("En el imperio incaico hubo mujeres que tuvieron un papel destacado en la organización religiosa, eran las llamadas *acllas* o vírgenes del sol que llevaban una vida recluida consagrada por completo al culto de dicho astro, deidad principal de los incas"): Magdalena Chocano Mena, *La América colonial (1492–1763): Cultura y vida cotidiana* (Madrid: Editorial Síntesis, 2000), 65.

11. One may note that the word "veil" (*vélum* in Latin), in its original Latin meaning, does not refer so much to the actual textile, which can be tightly woven and completely nontransparent, as to its function of hiding face and shoulders; see *Vocabolario della lingua italiana* (Milan: Istituto dell'Enciclopedia Italiana, 1994).

12. On the cult of the Virgin Mary, Don Juanism, and courtly love, see Luis Martín, *Daughters of the Conquistadors: Women of the Viceroyalty of Peru* (Dallas: Southern Methodist University Press, 1983).

13. "Coqueta: from fr. coquette, fem. de coquet, de coqueter, presumir un hombre entre las mujeres, de coq, gallo. 1) Se aplica a la mujer presumida que se preocupa mucho de su arreglo personal o de gustar a los hombres. También, a la que toma el amor como una diversión y procura enamorar a distintos hombres" (Coqueta: from the French *coquette*, feminine of *coquet*, from *coqueter*, a man who shows off among women, from *coq*, cock. 1) Women who are particularly concerned with their looks or with being attractive to men. Women who see love as a pastime and try to make more than one man fall in love). María Moliner, *Diccionario del uso del español* (Madrid: Gredos, 1997).

14. José Luis Romero, *Latin America: Its Cities and Ideas* (1976; repr. Washington, D.C.: Organization of American States, 1999), 76.

15. "A Lima capita che una donna fa colazione con il marito al mattino (vestaglietta alla francese, capelli tirati su proprio come le nostre parigine), poi se ha voglia di uscire mette la saya senza corsetto . . . , si scioglie i capelli, si tapa, cioè nasconde il viso col manto ed esce per andare dove le pare. . . . Per strada incontra suo marito che non la riconosce, lo stuzzica con l'occhio, fa la smorfiosa, lo provoca di proposito, si mette a conversare, si fa offrire gelati, frutta e dolci, gli dà un appuntamento e alla fine lo lascia, per ricominciare con un ufficiale di passaggio. Può portare avanti il gioco quanto vuole, senza mai lasciare il manto; va poi a far visita alle amiche, fa un giro e rientra all'ora di cena. Il marito non chiede neanche dove sia andata, poiché sa benissimo che se vorrà nascondergli la verità, ella saprà mentire e, siccome non è in grado di impedirglielo, prende la decisione più saggia, che è quella di non preoccuparsene. Così vanno da sole allo spettacolo, alle corride, alle pubbliche assemblee, ai balli, a passeggio, in chiesa, a far visita." Flora Tristán, *Pérégrinations d'une paria* (Paris: Arthus Bertrand, 1838). My translation from the Italian, *Peregrinazioni di una paria*, trans. and ed. Giovanna Festa (Napoli: La città del Sole, 1998), 288. In 1986, an English-language translation was published in London by Virago, *Peregrinations of a Pariah*.

16. On this subject, see Anna Scacchi, "Visibilità e sguardo femminile sulle strade vittoriane," in *Passaggi: Letterature comparate al femminile*, ed. Liana Borghi (Urbino: QuattroVenti, 2001), 135–51.

17. "With their face covered with the veil, with no one being able to recognize them, they do those things that in France are done by men" ("Cubierto el rostro por el rebozo, sin que nadie pueda conocerlas, ellas hacen los menesteres que en Francia realizan los hombres"). Amédée F. Frézier, *Relation du voyage de la mer du sud aux cotes du Chili et du Perou* (Paris: Chez Nyon, 1732); repr. in *El Perú visto por viajeros,*vol. 1, *La costa,* ed. Estuardo Nuñez (Lima: Ediciones Peisa, 1973), 16. Frézier was in Lima in 1713.

18. See Francesca Denegri, *El abanico y la cigarrera: La primera generación de mujeres ilustradas en el Perú, 1860–1895* (Lima: Flora Tristán Centro de la Mujer Peruana, 1996), 56 and passim.

19. "Parecchi stranieri mi hanno raccontato che le limegne provocavano un effetto magico sull'immaginazione di molti di loro. Spinti ad affrontare mille pericoli da un desiderio di avventure, nella ferma convinzione che la fortuna li attendesse su quelle rive lontane, queste donne apparivano loro come le sacerdotesse del luogo, o forse, immaginando il paradiso di Maometto, credevano che Dio li avesse fatti approdare in un paese incantato per ripagarli delle terribili sofferenze della traversata e ricompensarli del coraggio avuto.

"Questi voli di fantasia non sembrano più impossibili quando si vedono le stranezze che le belle donne di Lima fanno fare agli stranieri, i cui sensi sembrano trascinati dal turbine della passione. Il desiderio di scorgere quel viso che esse nascondono con cura li spinge a seguirle con grande curiosi." Tristán, *Peregrinazioni di una paria,* 287.

20. "El traje de saya y manto, que en su origen estuvo destinado a servir ideas de castidad y celos, ha llegado por una de esas contradicciones, a proteger costumbres diametralmente opuestas; su uniformidad hace de la ciudad un vasto salón de intrigas o de ingeniosas maniobras que burlan la vigilancia de los mas fieros Otelos." Maximilien René Radiguet, *Souvenirs de l'Amérique Espagnole* (Paris: Michel Levy Fréres, 1856); my translation from the special edition limited to the sections on Peru, *Lima y la sociedad peruana* (Lima: Biblioteca Nacional del Perú, 1971), 34.

21. As Ferdinando Dogana, writes, "[clothing] can serve to hide; it can be in the service of modesty or of exhibitionism, it can be a tool for social adaptation and conformism or of originality and differentiation." ("[Il vestito] può avere la funzione di celare; può essere al servizio della modestia oppure dell'esibizionismo, strumento di adeguamento e conformismo sociale oppure di originalità e differenziazione"). Ferdinando Dogana, *Psicopatologia dei costumi quotidiani* (Milan: F. Angeli, 1993), 87. On the role of women in Peru from the pre-Hispanic period to independence, see Sara Beatriz Guardia, *Mujeres peruanas: El otro lado de la historia* (Lima: Editorial Minerva, 2002).

22. "El cubrirse el rostro es un acto sencillo que sólo requiere echarse en él un velo simple y

suelto, sin más afectación ni cuidado que encubrir una imagen, para que no sea vista. El taparse, no parece que se refiere al velo, sino al modo, a la cautela y artificio con que se procura esconder y ocultar el rostro engañosa y pálidamente. Y así el cubrirse, es echarse el manto sobre el rostro todo suelto y sin invención ni arte. Y el taparse, es embozarse, . . . doblando, torciendo y prendiendo el manto, de suerte, que descubriendo uno de los ojos, que siempre es el izquierdo, quede lo restante del rostro, aun más oculto y disfrazado que si fuera cubierto todo." León Pinelo, *Velos antiguos y modernos en los rostros de las mujeres,* Book II, 328–29.

23. Martín, *Daughters of the Conquistadors.* He goes on to note that a woman might "handle her shawl with the same artful and teasing skills the bullfighter used to entice the bull with his cape" (282).

24. "Un oggetto che riassume e sintetizza in qualche sua caratteristica la personalità dell'individuo o qualche aspetto o bisogno dominante." Dogana, *Psicopatologia dei consumi quotidiani,* 111.

25. In the Gothic novel, instead, the veil is seen as "the place of all failed expectations." See Eve Kosofsky Sedgwick, "The Character in the Veil: Imagery of the Surface in the Gothic Novel," *PMLA* 96, no. 4 (1981): 258.

26. As Francesca Denegri notes, regardless of its origin, the *tapada* is a result of women's need to escape the control of civil and religious institutions. See Denegri, *El abanico y la cigarrera,* 56.

27. Quoted in Martín, *Daughters of the Conquistadors,* 302. The dispositions of the Third Council of Lima were followed, in 1585, by those in Mexico forbidding wearing the veil during the procession of the Corpus Domini.

28. See Canto XXIII, vv. 8953–54. Advice on how to identify a *tapada* was offered by Maximilien R. Radiguet: "One must never fear being excessively harsh in judging the *manto,* especially when, in contrast with the habit of Lima women of showing their arms, a long sleeve is adjusted over the glove, so that one cannot see anywhere the color of the skin. Have no doubts: the traitorous mantle hides an African woman, as black as the night" ("Nunca debe desconfiarse bastante del exceso de severidad en el recogimiento del manto, sobre todo si, en oposición a la costumbre de las limeñas de llevar los brazos desnudos, una manga larga viene a ajustarse sobre el guante, de modo que no se pueda ver por parte alguna el color de la piel. No dudeis: la manta traidora esconde entonces a una africana, negra como la noche"). Radiguet, *Lima y la sociedad peruana,* 34.

29. Marjorie Garber, *Vested Interests: Cross-dressing and Cultural Anxiety* (New York: Routledge, 1992), 26.

30. "Ha venido a tal extremo el uso de andar 'tapadas' las mujeres que de ello han resultado

grandes ofensas a Dios y notable daño a la República, a causa de que en aquella forma no conoce el padre a la hija, ni el marido a la mujer, ni el hemano a la hermana, y tienen la libertad, tiempo y lugar a su voluntad, y dan ocasión a que los hombres se atrevan a la hija o mujer del más principal como a la del más vil y bajo, lo que no sería si diesen lugar yendo descubiertas, a que la luz discierne las unas de las otras. . . . Además de lo cual se excusarían grandes maldades y sacrilegios que los hombres vestidos como las mujeres y tapados sin poder ser conocidos han hecho y hacen." In Muro Orejón, *Las Pragmáticas contra las "tapadas" y otros pecados públicos en España y en las Indias hispanas*, 84.

31. "Mandamos que ninguna mujer, de cualquier estado, calidad y condición que sea en todos nuestros Reinos, pueda ir, andar, ni ande, tapado el rostro, en manera alguna, sino llevándolo descubierto, so pena de tres mil maravedis por cada vez que lo contrario hiciere, . . . y mandamos a las nuestras justicias que de su oficio (aunque no proceda denunciación) procedan a la observancia y cumplimiento de lo suso contenido con apercibimiento que no lo haciendo se les hará cargo en las residencias que se les tomaren de cualquier negligencia que en ello hayan tenido y serán castigados por ella." Ibid., 85.

32. León Pinelo writes that on seven occasions in Spain (and in the viceroyalties) measures were passed in the effort to forbid the veil. See *Velos antiguos y modernos en los rostros de las mujeres*, chap. 25.

33. See ibid., chap. 25 (on the decree of the marquis of Montesclaros); Manuel de Mendiburu, *Diccionario histórico-biográfico del Peru* (Lima: Imprenta de J. Francisco Solis, 1878), Book III, 242–44, cites the law passed by the marquis of Guadalcázar.

34. Palma, *La conspiración de la saya y manto*, 184. In 1788, Chilean governor Ambrosio O'Higgins also condemned this custom: "As serious as they are common are the inconveniences caused by the masking, mostly of the face, by veils and hidden faces, with which certain people at night go to public or private events, as well as in the streets, in groups on horses, and with bells during carnival" ("Son tan graves como comunes los inconvenientes que se originan de los disfraces, más caras, embozos y tapados de cara, con que suelen concurrir algunas gentes de noche á funciones públicas ó á las de particulares en sus casas, y también por las calles, en cuadrillas á caballo, con cencerros en tiempo de carnavales"). Quoted in José Toribio Medina, *Cosas de la colonia: Apuntes para la crónica del siglo XVIII en Chile* (Santiago de Chile: Imprenta Ercilla, 1889), 141.

35. The date of the work is uncertain, but its references to the *tapadas* suggest it appeared between 1624 and 1639, the last date of the manuscripts found in the volume that includes the text

by Mogrovejo. See Raquel Chang-Rodríguez, *El discurso disidente: Ensayos de Literatura Colonial Peruana* (Lima: Pontificia Universidad Católica del Perú, 1991), 144, and see also 153–67 for "La endiablada."

36. "Ya se acabó lo terso de las manos, lo brillante de los pies, lo airoso del cuerpo, lo vivo del andar, lo despejado del decir y lo lascivo del hacer. Este es el tiempo del desengaño. Ya las mujeres no enamoran tuertas; ya los mantos no son testigos falsos de las caras; ya unos rostros que con el velo parecían reliquias, confiesan que aunque no de santos, son huesos; . . . Y, en fin, ya dicen la verdad los gestos y hablan claro las edades." Ibid., 165.

37. "Las señoras limeñas . . . , y lo mismo digo de la gente plebeya, a excepción de las Indians y negras bozales, siguen opuesto orden a las europeas, mejicanas y porteñas; quiero decir, que así como éstas fundan su lucimiento mayor desde el cuello hasta el pecho, . . . las limeñas ocultan este esplendor con un velo nada transparente en tiempo de calores, y en el de fríos se tapan hasta la cintura con doble embozo, que en realidad es muy extravagante. Toda su bizarría la fundan en los bajos, desde la liga a la planta del pie. . . . Las señoras más formales y honestas en este país descubren la mitad de la caña de su pierna. Las bizarras o chamberíes toman una andana de rizos hasta descubrir el principio de la pantorilla, y las que el público tiene por escandalosas . . . elevan sus faldellines a media porta, como cortinas imperiales." Concolocorvo, *Lazarillo de ciegos caminantes desde Buenos Aires hasta Lima* (1773; repr. Madrid: Ediciones Atlas, 1943), 168. The Spaniard Felipe Bauzá, who was in Peru in 1790, also discusses the way *tapadas* uncover their legs. See Felipe Bauzá, *Carácter, genio y costumbres de los limeños*, in Nuñez, *El Perú visto por viajeros,*1:38.

38. See Raquel Chang-Rodríguez, "Tapadas limeñas en un cancionerillo peruano del siglo XVII," *Revista interamericana de Bibliografia* 28 (1978): 57–62.

39. See *Coloquio entre la vieja y periquillo sobre una procesión celebrada en Lima*, in *Obras de Don Juan del Valle y Caviedes*, ed. Rubén Vargas Ugarte (Lima: Tip. Peruana S. A. Rávago e hijos, 1947), 86.

40. See José Carlos Mariátegui, *Escritos juveniles (La edad de Piedra)*, ed. Alberto Tauro (Lima: Biblioteca Amauta, 1987), 1:221–56.

41. On the reception of *Las tapadas*, see Eugenio Chang-Rodríguez, "El joven José Carlos Mariátegui," *Cuadernos americanos* 41, no. 4 (July–August 1982): 139–80.

42. Among the last to register their existence (and decadence) was the French traveler Ernest Grandidier in his *Voyage dans l'Amerique du Sud, Perou et Bolivie* (1859).

43. On these early dictators, see Curtis A. Wilgus, ed., *South American Dictators during the First*

Century of the Independence (Washington, D.C.: George Washington University Press, 1937). In the concept of the veil as a symbol of tradition and resistance to colonialism, some have seen a parallel with the role of women and the use of the veil in twentieth-century nationalist discourses in Turkey and Algeria. See Meyda Yegĕnoğlu, *Colonial Fantasies: Towards a Feminist Reading of Orientalism* (Cambridge: Cambridge University Press, 1998), especially chap. 5, "The battle of the veil."

44. On the end of the custom of the *tapadas* in the nineteenth century, see Denegri, *El abanico y la cigarrera*, 54–64. Denegri quotes from the newspaper *El Comercio*, reporting in 1860: "The procession of Santa Rosa was lively and crowded. But two things were missing: the memory of what has already passed and the memory of what is passing and that will possibly soon have passed for ever. We are referring to the Indians and the *tapadas*. The *tapadas* could barely be seen. The *saya* and the *manto*. Why bother. Our young women have abandoned their inimitable dress" ("La procesión de Santa Rosa estuvo animada, concurrida. Pero faltaban dos cosas: un recuerdo de lo que ya pasó y otro de lo que va pasando, y tal vez muy pronto no exista. Queremos hablar de las Indians y de las tapadas. Las tapadas apenas se veían. La saya y el manto. Para qué hablar de eso. Nuestras señoritas han abandonado su inimitable traje"). Ibid., 64–65. On women in republican Peru, see Alicia del Aguila, *Los velos y las pieles: Cuerpo, género y reordenamiento social en el Perú republicano (Lima, 1822–1872)* (Lima: IEP Ediciones, 2003).

45. "La colonia—se dijo—fue un edén. Sálvemos lo que de ella nos queda y reverenciemos lo que desapareció por nuestra culpa. La mujer colonial, la tapada de devociones y astucias, fue angelical. Conservémosla como tal, copiando el paradigma de antaño." Sebastian Salazar Bondy, *Lima la horrible* (Lima: Peisa, 1974), 89.

46. Georg Simmel, "The Philosophy of Fashion" [1905], in *Simmel on Culture*, ed. David Frisby and Mike Featherstone (London: Sage Publications, 2000), 192 and passim.

12

CLAD IN THE BLOODY LIVERY

FASHION AND COLOR DURING ARGENTINA'S CIVIL WAR

Amanda Salvioni

Buenos Aires is, as you know, a very elegant city. Rosas had won by this point.

D. F. SARMIENTO, *Campaña en el ejército grande*

In 1832, the Argentine dictator Juan Manuel de Rosas promulgated a decree stating that all public officials—officers and clerks, soldiers, doctors, lawyers, teachers, and even priests—should wear a stripe of bright red material on their breasts, over their hearts, on pain of being banned from public office. The ribbon, a symbol of loyalty to the cause of the federal system upheld by the dictator, was commonly called *cinta colorada* or *divisa punzó*, from the French *ponceau*, indicating poppy red. The *divisa punzó* rapidly spread to all social ranks, through subsequent decrees and through public support. Although the ribbon typically bore the phrase "¡Viva la Confederación Argentina! ¡Mueran los salvajes Unitarios!," the real significance was clearly communicated more by the color than by the verbal message. Both the sentence and the color were signs of the same political language, but the latter carried special meaning and effect. The color red soon passed from the ribbon to other items of clothing, decorating part, and sometimes the whole, of military and school uniforms, the emblematic men's vest—called *chaleco federal*—

and women's headgear and outfits in various shades of scarlet. Subsequently it extended from clothing to furniture, upholstery, walls, home and workplace furnishings, funeral biers, horses' plumes and harnesses, even book bindings, invading in equal proportion private and public spaces. The fashion dictated by the regime blurred the distinction between taste and coercion and gave individuals and their habitats the uniform brand of a political standard.

With the 1832 decree, coming three years after the assumption of extraordinary powers that sanctioned the authoritarian character of his regime, Rosas consolidated a practice that was a legacy of the revolutionary insurrections of the preceding century, one fated to continue in the history of all totalitarian regimes everywhere. This consisted of an intense and induced semiotization of social behavior through stylized dress. Through the use of a marked chromatic symbolism, the political party in power, in this case the Partido Federal, built its discursive monopoly by using an extremely eloquent signal: the color red served as a powerful means of homologation. It strengthened the cohesion of the masses and their identification with a national political project and evoked a system of values, disciplined social life, laid bare opposition, and conformed the public and private spheres, exercising an unprecedented form of control.[1]

Yet this process of producing signs was not limited to the monologues of power. Argentina's visual awareness had already been developed when opposing political factions were expressed through the use of colors. The dispute between the Federal and the Unitarian parties, flaring up immediately after independence from Spain and taking root during the years of dictatorship, was manifested through an open color war: as the Federals tended to red even before the Rosas decree, Unitarians identified instead with sky blue (one of the two colors of the national flag, the other being white). Each was displayed over the heart with ribbons and rosettes. With no developed icons to represent its identity and without a unifying political project, the young nation used color as a sign of identification. But chromatic symbolism was not confined to the abstraction of flag waving; it also involved bodies themselves and their immediate and daily fields of action, investing colors with a marked physicality.

Red and sky blue did not exhaust the contrasting symbolism created and fueled by political confrontation and expressed in individual personal attire. Associated with articles of clothing, accessories, and gestures, each color recalled distinct ethnographic heritages identifying the social groups sustaining the two contending parties: the Federal party, rooted in the inland rural provinces; and the Unitarian party, linked to European liberal traditions and the elegant social life of the elite in the cities. So the reds of the Federación wore the native poncho and gaucho pants—the *chiripá*—and followed the ways of a rural culture, while the sky blue Unitarians were at their ease in coattails, white gloves, and urban bon ton.[2]

Within the nation's complex mythology, colors, clothes, and gestures followed the same antonymic system of irreconcilable values—political, ideological, aesthetic, and cultural—that had pushed independent Argentina into a civil war. In this context, the body was invested with the double materiality of an "ideological sign": it was both the representation of an idea and directly involved in actual struggle.[3] Dressed in accordance with one party or the other, individuals became vehicles for a message, representing something other than themselves, and at the same time, they were material parties in a social-historical actuality, living flesh exposed to the horrors of battle.

So it is not by chance that fashion, if read as carrying a political message, became a practical and theoretical preoccupation for both Rosas and his opponents, and occupied a textual space dedicated to themes seemingly far removed from those of clothing and taste, such as political journalism, literary criticism, and even military bulletins. Argentine rhetoric and even the syntactic structure of the language used within the different national projects between the 1830s and 1850s revealed how the protagonists themselves defined fashion: a combination of visual and behavioral codes loaded with meaning, as central to the preoccupations of the intellectual elite as the theoretical elucidation of their politics.

In 1837, a crucial year in Argentina's cultural history, a group of young people, affected by European Romanticism and persuaded of the necessity to found an independent culture and aesthetics for their young country, met near a Buenos Aires bookshop to create an agenda for the future awaiting them as the literary elite of the nation. The birth of the Salón Literario forged Hispanic-American Romanticism, a literary coterie meant to break up and till the arid soil of a late and exhausted neoclassicism. In strictly political terms, its young participants fancied themselves as the ideal upholders of the revolutionary spirit of May, cutting loose from both the "happy experience" of Bernardino Rivadavia's Liberalism, which had failed ten years earlier, and Federalism. They advocated liberal democracy in order to overcome the conflict between Federals and Unitarians, though they were decidedly nearer Unitarian ideas. When Rosas closed the Salón in 1838 and this repression sent them underground, its members founded Joven Argentina, an association following Giuseppe Mazzini's principles. Branded as the Generation of '37, or the Banished Generation, they were all forced to take refuge abroad.

Among the '37 group, Juan Bautista Alberdi was convinced that he might still negotiate with the regime to steer a different course for national politics. This was a delicate and risky move. Toward the end of 1837, when threats of repression began to inhibit the Salón's activities, Alberdi founded *La Moda,* a journal designed to circulate the objectives of the political-literary coterie by exploring the possibilities of mediation between a liberal reformism and Rosas's paternalistic authoritarianism. There appear to be two reasons for choosing the title: first, in this way, Alberdi, practically the only editor on the board, averted the government's suspicions by assuming an apolitical and inoffensive appearance; and second, the title attracted female readers, the only section of the public capable of assuring a sufficient number of subscriptions because they had the money and the time for reading.[4]

But the political dissimulation did not save the journal from Rosas. In the preceding years, a similar experiment—from which Alberdi probably got his idea—had been attempted in France: *La Mode,* a journal founded in Paris by Émile de Girardin in 1829, featuring among its authors Honoré de Balzac, Charles Nodier, Alphonse de Lamartine, and Eugène Sue, had faced considerable hostility because of its politics and was closed by the authoritarian government in 1854. Alberdi's *La Moda* was short-lived; under pressure from the regime, it folded in April 1838 after only one year and twenty-three published issues.

The first issue of *La Moda* opened with a "Prospecto" that listed the contents and sections planned for the journal, a blueprint of what the editors meant by the word "fashion." It included attention to European styles of clothing—for men and women—but also of furnishings and even of conversation. Examining contemporary literary and social ideas, through poems and chronicles of daily life, the journal was to be modern, fusing cultural observations and trends in music, art, and literature, as well as fashion.[5] Overall, its educational purpose consisted both in imposing formal codes proper to a "civilized" and "democratic" nation—above all in literature, seen as endowed with an absolute propaedeutic power—and in transmitting a repertory of texts and ideas indispensable for the "modernization" of the country. In reference to clothes, fashion was considered not only a code of communication capable of conveying all the complexities of a political message, but also a code of implementation, because its enunciation coincided with direct political action or at least political rumor.

In the third issue, the article "Moda de señoras" (Women's fashion) explains the principles that govern any judgment on fashion: like language, fashion is both a manifestation of society and an instrument for transforming society. In this sense, fashion is in the same predicament as a nation's society or culture and should aim toward the same objectives: "Among us, fashion participates in the indecision that affects the whole of our society. We don't have dominant fashions in ideas, no style dominates."[6] Alberdi maintained that one of the vulgarities of the nation was the survival, alongside these new social forms and modes of expression, of the traditions and clothing from the rural world of the old Hispanic heritage, reclaimed by Rosas: the poncho and *chiripá,* which Alberdi found barbaric and archaic. The modernization of customs imposed homogeneity, obtained by importing a modern and "democratic" fashion, elegantly simple, with no frills or furbelows. Alexis de Tocqueville's lesson from the United States had been quickly grasped.[7]

According to Alberdi's understanding of Tocqueville, in the United States fashion was an epiphenomenon of democracy; so too in Argentina, it should become the instrument for constitutional reform. This idea inverted the supposedly natural relationship between national identity, state institutions, and customs, giving priority to the latter. Moreover, Alberdi placed this means for reform in women's hands, specifically in those women inspired by Saint-Simonianist ideals, who were also the ostensible readers of the journal. Their acceptance of the aesthetic and formal ideals of the journal amounted to a powerful political action. Alberdi gave a very efficient illustration of the parallels between the country's constitutional assets and its fashions, considered as social expressions, in his dictionary "Album alfabético," published in March 1838. Under the heading "Costumbres" (Customs/costumes), Alberdi drew a clear distinction between the two levels of modernity in a nation: the political and legislative one and that of fashion and customs. "Within the customs of a people is really where its political constitution resides. In this *living code* which until today we ourselves have neglected while we have been busy writing *abstract codes.*"[8] Fashion was the living code still to be written, while politics and literature were the abstract codes that had occupied the national elite; without the life breathed into them by daily life, however, they risked remaining on paper. Alberdi's program consisted of a civilizing social reformism oriented toward the future and aimed at perfecting the social order as the basic condition for a constitutional state.

In this context, fashion emerges as the imitation of an aristocratic model—for instance, the sober elegance of British aristocracy—but it is addressed to the masses in order to exert its democratizing power. By 1839, *El Iniciador* commented: "A people that doesn't participate in fashion is one dead to its moment." The exclusive way in which the journal addressed fashion is apparent in the notion of the "people" or "public" to whom it is directed. Not everybody is capable of appreciating or adopting, much less of affording, the aesthetics proposed; only the educated classes of the capital city possessed the sensibility, education, and money necessary to strive to conform in the sense Alberdi intended. He outlined an explicit distinction between "pueblo" and "masa," identifying in the first a community concerned with the country's destiny, and in the second the amorphous mass of the rural areas, still bound to the atavistic indifference of colonial subservience:

> For whom do those few who are enlightened and skilled speak? They are not the people.... The crowd is the people: ignorance is their title of sovereignty and infallibility.... Yes, the people is the sacred oracle of a journalist ... but the people, ... the people are not questioned as the masses, not the people of the crowd, the mass of people ... but the representative people, the modern people of Europe and America, the people heard through their intelligent and legitimate organs of science and virtue. The masses are holy, because they are the body of the people.... They should not be consulted directly in high matters, because they lack awareness of their high needs.... A shopkeeper, a wife, a shoemaker, a grocer have no vote in the matter, because they are the masses. One must write for them if they are to have a means to speak.[9]

The distinction between the people and the masses corresponds to Cartesian thought: the public is the representative depositary of rational functions, and the masses are the body, sacred but credulous. In this system of values, the concept of a population of readers acquires an ever more exclusive significance. The aim of *La Moda* wavered constantly between the intent of reforming the population, predominant in the early issues, and the expression of contempt toward those who seem unable to grasp its reforming message. This sense of contempt prevailed near the final months of the journal and found expression in a series of articles excoriating bad taste in clothes and customs, contrasting them with European styles intelligently adapted to their national situations. These articles favored the reintroduction of a Manichaean division of society, distinguishing between the superior people, wearing coattails and redingotes, and the ignorant masses, tied to old customs and fatally condemned to the tasteless poncho or scandalously red vest.

Juan Manuel de Rosas's choice of red recalled the origin of the Federal party: in 1815, the Uruguayan patriot José Artigas, as head of a confederation of states on the Río de la Plata, founded the Liga Federal and convened a congress to extend the federal system to all the provinces recently freed from Spain. After receiving a negative answer from the remaining Provincias Unidas del Río de la Plata, led by Buenos Aires, which supported a unitary and centralized form of government, Artigas modified the white-and-blue national banner, designed by the Argentine Manuel Belgrano in 1812 as the symbol of independence, by adding a wide red stripe. The new flag for Artigas's Liga came to represent the Federal project, which for many years would be in conflict with the Unitarians. Belgrano had taken the colors for his flag from the national rosette, an emblem symbolizing the insurrection for independence in 1810. Spread among the patriots during the May Revolution, the rosette recalled the Bourbonic colors, white and blue, associated with the deposed King Ferdinand VII of Spain, whom some of the Hispanic-American fringes supporting independence initially recognized as the lawful ruler of a still monarchic order.

Hence, the federal red was a spurious element in the original chromatic make-up of the flag, and Unitarians felt that they were the legitimate repositaries of the national sky blue. The war of colors, however, is disputed. Some claim that at the height of the anti-Spanish hostilities, a red ribbon was sometimes added to the white and blue rosette, as a tentative symbol of the Jacobin rebellion. Rosas himself tried to demonstrate that there was indeed a historical problem with sky blue in the flag by substituting it with dark blue, which was more easily distinguishable even from a distance and not to be confused with the hateful Unitarian color. The flag Rosas designed for his confederation consisted of two horizontal dark blue stripes and one white one, in the center, to which he added the golden Incan sun—an example of the syncretism between the ancient Masonic symbol and native iconography—and surrounded it with four red, Phrygian caps. Those caps, the emblem of the 1789 French revolution, had been converted into a Federal symbol, despite Rosas's irrepressible anti-French and anti-Jacobin political stance, to represent the freedom of the nation from both the old (Spanish) and the new (French and European) colonization. When, at the height of the Terror—the period of the most violent persecution of Unitarian conspirators on the part of Rosas's regime—dissenters were forbidden to wear anything at all that was sky blue, opposition was expressed through a substitute color. Green, symbol of hope, was thus adopted by men and women of the Unitarian party, at least up to the moment when Rosas's police, having discovered its symbolic value, were ordered to destroy all green clothes and objects found in the conspirators' homes.

Many years after Rosas's downfall (in 1852), his nephew Lucio V. Mansilla described the staggering scarlet wave provoked by his dictatorship. Red was the color of clothes, soldiers' uniforms, gauchos' *chiripá*; the color of outside and inside walls, doors, ceilings, and houses. Mansilla recalled the alleged physiologic properties of the federal red: "Red incontestably possesses a markedly dynamic power," synesthetically akin to "the smell of gunpowder."[10] Red, like the smell of gunpowder, is seen as both an omen and a detonator of violence because it possesses the tangible power of awakening brutal reactions as well as of representing an ideal passion.

Actually, the idea of giving the color red a symbolic meaning that extended beyond the narrow political Federal symbolism and of ascribing to it a force that brought changes not only on a symbolic level but also to the way of living was borrowed from Rosas's opponents. In Domingo Faustino Sarmiento's *Facundo o Civilización y barbarie* (1843), a question appears suddenly in the text: "Do you know what the color red means? I don't know either, but will gather together some references."[11] Sarmiento's memories aim to show that there is a link between red and barbarism: only barbaric nations flaunt red on their flags; explorers in Africa always remember to carry a red cloth as a gift to rulers, just as the Chilean government gives red blankets and clothes as presents to the fierce Araucanian caciques, "because this color greatly pleases the savages" (132); the cape of Roman emperors was red, like that of the dictator; the barbaric leaders' royal mantle was red; Spain had been the most recent among civilized countries to repudiate red, and the claimant to the throne, the absolutist don Carlos, had hoisted a red flag, a proof of his unworthiness; Genoa's royal code ordained that magistrates should wear a red robe to inspire, "with its grave and decorous presence, terror and fear in evildoers," it was said (133); the executioner was always clothed in red, and Artigas had added a red stripe to the flag; Rosas's army wore red, and his portrait was printed on red paper! Sarmiento's argument turned on the semantics of color: sky blue cries "¡justicia, paz, justicia!"; while red screams "¡terror, sangre, barbarie!"

The chromatic symbolism ends with Rosas and his federal world: it demonstrates the barbaric character of those whose ideals were blazoned in red: "The human species, in all times, has given this meaning to the scarlet, red, purple color. Study the governments of the peoples who brandish this color, and you will find Rosas and Facundo: terror, barbarism, blood flowing everyday" (133). Sarmiento hates red, just as he hates blood, so that in his writings he returns obsessively to the theme of the *divisa punzó*. The all-encompassing use of red in Argentina, like the daily bloodshed, represents the failure of the liberal and romantic project, which he conceives as an intolerable personal failure.

In *Facundo,* Sarmiento offers his version of the origin of the *divisa punzó.*[12] At first the *divisa* was the recognizable emblem of a small number of enthusiastic supporters; then everyone was obliged to wear it to feign popular consent; finally, it was enforced by police brutality. This unanimous agreement with federal principles—wearing the sash to "prove the uniformity" of opinion—is the result of the enforcement of a uniform, a vile camouflage. And the emblematic clothing for this manufactured consensus is the military uniform. If the enforcement of red in civilian clothes is deplorable, what takes place in the army is even worse: "from the depths of its [the army's] bowels, arose the color red, and it became the soldier's uniform, the flag of the army, and ultimately, the national cockade that every Argentine must wear, under pain of death" (132).

In *Campaña en el ejército grande,* Sarmiento, writing battle bulletins from the war between Urquiza's liberating army and Rosas's forces, lingers more than once on the idea of the soldiers' uniforms as an instrument of the country's political transformation. Sarmiento himself obstinately continues to wear a European-style uniform, braving the coarse jokes of Urquiza's soldiers, who comment with surprise and scorn on the elegant accessories of this decidedly eccentric officer. Experience was to prove Sarmiento right; he was to emerge as winner in the symbolic contest.[13] The European-style uniform worn by the soldier Sarmiento is in itself a protest against the gaucho spirit, that is, against barbaric anarchy. While the *chiripá* survives—the civilized voice of the narrator declares—there can be no citizens. Sarmiento sees very clearly the relation between clothing and political systems: "Each civilization expresses itself in its costume, and each costume indicates an entire system of ideas," he writes in *Facundo* (133). Unlike others of his generation who had tried, like Alberdi, to use fashion to negotiate with the regime, Sarmiento, writing from exile when the possibility of a national reconciliation was remote, considered the conformity to the federal red as a sign and instrument of the regime's slavery. It linked Argentina to other brutal regimes from Rome through the Middle Ages, from Turkey to China: "every civilization has had its costume and every change in ideas, every institutional revolution, a change of dress" (133).

MANUELITA AND AMALIA

Rosas's decrees on the use of the *divisa punzó* did not restrict the omnipresence of federal red to the public scene. The transfer from a simple emblem to all clothing and then into the environment led to the breakdown of barriers between the public and the private spheres, a hallmark of any dictatorship.[14] It comprised two similar and contrary impulses, from the inside out and from the outside in: the public exhibition of the private sphere of the dictator—who paraded the sham austerity of his home and lifestyle—and its opposite, the invasion of citizens' private lives by the public sphere, for example through the imposition of red and the ubiquitous Rosas portraits. The female body plays a very prominent role in this mechanism, because it inhabits and governs private space, creating in the domestic sphere the social microcosm on which the public sphere is founded and mirrored: the family. Surrounded by the women of his family, the dictator could count on their function as mediators between power and the people: his wife Encarnación Ezcurra and her sister María Josefa Ezcurra allegedly controlled, unofficially, the intelligence service and its armed wing, the terrible Mazorca squadrons; after her mother's death, his daughter Manuela took over the exclusive post of "primera dama" and scribe, embodying the virtue of goodness and interceding with her father on behalf of civil society. Thanks to these female figures as visible icons of power, Rosas was able to conduct his affairs of state without having to answer for acts of espionage and repression, nor did he need to observe the moral virtues advocated by his own system of values.

Similarly, the Unitarian opposition considered women as formidable agents of resistance, because of their conventional place in the private sphere that protected them from the risk of exposing themselves. Yet they were also capable of subverting the order to which men were constrained, for instance, through a consciously disruptive use of fashion. María Josefa Ezcurra surmised the power of those elegant society dames who refused to wear red, and soon the Mazorca police began punishing those who would not wear the *divisa punzó* in their hair by tarring their heads and gluing on a Federal ribbon. Unitarian liberals saw women as a means to subtly criticize the dictatorship: they turned to their female readers as a way to camouflage their politics through appeals to women's interest in fashion, molding female literary figures to incarnate the Unitarian ideals of democracy and progress; they forged the apparent confinement of women to the private sphere into the fortress of their opposition. Thus for the Unitarians, too, woman was the mediator between the domestic circle and the public sphere, between the opposition and the regime on grounds that were not those of armed combat, but were just as effective.[15]

This use of the female figure in Federación society, in relation to the chromatic symbolism of the regime, was recorded in contemporary paintings and contributed to the formation of the iconography of Rosas's time. The most important painting, for both its artistic quality and its evocative powers, was the last in chronological order. It was painted in 1851, the year before the fall of the dictator, when a committee honoring Rosas's daughter commissioned the portrait from the young painter Prilidiano Pueyrredón.

The painting was then to be reproduced as a lithograph, and copies were to be given to the guests invited to a ball in Manuelita Rosas's honor. A descendant of an old and powerful family that was not very supportive of the regime, Prilidiano Pueyrredón had recently returned from the Polytechnic Institute in Paris, trained in the artistic techniques of the French academy after having completed his studies in engineering. He was to become one of the most successful artists and architects in Argentina in the second half of the nineteenth century. His uncertain federal convictions, now that he was back in his homeland, were to be consolidated by this favor he was to offer to the cause. His was not an easy task: the board of honor had listed a number of conditions on how Manuelita, then thirty-four and well known to the painter since childhood, was to be portrayed. The first was the *punzó* red of her dress. She must also be painted standing up, smiling, as she placed a written plea addressed to her father on a desk, recalling her public role as representative and mediator between the people and the supreme leader; she must transmit an impression of goodness, her principal public virtue.

After mastering the difficult chromatic problem of using red as the predominant color, Pueyrredón asked for permission to insert white frills in the dress, in two horizontal bands, to break the uniformity of the skirt and enhance the flowing velvet, stressing by contrast the majestic stance of the figure, and to play with the alternating red of the dress and whiteness of the skin of arms, shoulders, and face. To complete the emblematic figure, Manuelita wears on her dark chestnut hair, brushed in a severely plain style, the *divisa punzó* and a precious diadem, symbols of the Federación and of her own social rank. The risk of the figure being flattened by the bright red is mitigated by the domestic background, which takes up other shades of red in the curtains, the carpet, the armchair, and in a vase of flowers in which the different tones of red alternate with shades of gold. To complete the successful chromatic balance of the picture, the wall at the back is a very light turquoise, which absorbs the excess of the overabundant red. Manuelita's posture is imperceptibly inclined toward a writing table of marble and gilded wood, only partly visible; her face is partially turned toward a hypothetical person beyond the picture, on whom she rests her placid gaze; she is smiling very slightly.

The position of the Unitarians, by contrast, was represented by a novel of anti-Rosas dissent: *Amalia* by José Mármol. Pueyrredón's Manuelita resembles her literary portrait of that same year by Mármol, exiled in Montevideo, who seemed to cherish a peculiar veneration for Rosas's daughter.[16] In his view, Manuela is not beautiful, but she is pleasing to look at; she is intelligent when she is allowed to use her faculties; her gaze is vague but is firmly fixed on things. This is a sufficient description of an enigmatic figure, like the one portrayed in Pueyrredón's picture. She is not, nor ever can be, like the elegant women of the Unitarian aristocracy, but she is the most human and presentable face of the dictatorship. The central figure of Pueyrredón's painting shows no sign of movement or strength, except in the outstretched right arm, the only gesture breaking the representation of an apparently static female body. The arm, white as marble, extends obliquely from the hand resting on a white sheet of paper, as if it were a continuation of her lily-white fingers. It is an obvious allegory: Rosas does not appear, but Manuelita is his image, his intermediary; through her person we see the emanation of the restorer of the law, evoked by the paper that is linked to the woman's body, a body that is—and could not be otherwise—clad completely in red, a woman whose personality is nullified and overwritten by that overwhelming symbol of the Federación. Her goodness itself is not only an individual virtue but is the expression of a higher order of morality: it is a private virtue used to persuade the public of the rightness of Rosas's project. Similarly, the elegant interior Manuelita inhabits is a container for the redundant symbols of the regime.

In the iconography of the Rosas period, private interiors were not commonly represented, but Cayetano Descalzi, a Genoese painter who had moved to Buenos Aires in the 1820s and became a portrait painter for the *porteña* society, on one occasion painted the intimate world of a woman's toilet. In *Boudoir federal* (1845), the anonymous female figure is depicted in the privacy of her domestic environment, but all the symbols of the political and social life going on outside have invaded this space. In this portrait, the woman's back is turned, but her face is visible in the large mirror she faces, from which she indirectly observes the onlooker. A young woman, not yet completely dressed, caught in the act of combing her hair, she wears a white corset and blouse, and a *punzó* red scarf and skirt. The color of her clothes is not the only indication that we are in a Federal boudoir: there is also a bottle of maté on a ledge and a guitar hanging on the wall, recalling the popular *criollas* traditions that the Federación claimed as its cultural heritage. And just in case this was not enough, a lithographic reproduction of a famous portrait of Rosas by Descalzi himself dominates the scene, evidence of the public sphere invading this most private of domestic interiors. Rosas is present, or rather he looms over a highly erotic scene, and his eyes miss nothing: even the object of desire, the half-clad woman, is part of a world that is permeated and regulated by the same values that regulate the Federal utopia.

An abyss divides the Federal private parlor of the anonymous lady in Descalzi's picture from that described by José Mármol in *Amalia*, in which the heroine is also caught at her toilet. In Amalia's room there is no trace of red, only the harmony and perfection of green and sky blue as in a garden or a landscape painting.[17] Amalia is the ideal woman, a daughter of Argentina possessing all the fine elegance of a French lady, idealized to the point of losing her human features and acquiring divine ones; she has just fallen asleep while her chambermaid combs her hair. She appears as a framed portrait with bare arms and closed eyes, in the magnificent mirror of her wardrobe. She is a Greek goddess, a myth.[18] In this museum of feminine gentility, as Mármol calls it, and its innumerable repetitions in a clever use of reflecting mirrors, the ideal woman finds both a domestic and a mental refuge, so lost in her meditations as to appear to be sleeping. Nothing seems to trouble her; nor does she seem ready to pass through that secret threshold. And yet her precious boudoir, a private oasis of elegance and refinement in a town besieged by Rosas's barbarism, will also be invaded by the red outside world: her cousin Daniel Bello and her future lover Eduardo Belgrano, who has been wounded by the Mazorca militia, arrive seeking sanctuary and smear the beautiful porcelains with blood. "And Daniel . . . passed into the next room, which was his cousin's bedroom, and thence into a small and elegant dressing-room where, going to the toilet-table, he poured some water into a basin, and proceeded to wash his hands, spattering as he did so the china and glass with the blood and clay which covered them" (21).

José Mármol's novel, among the most eminent representatives of Río de la Plata Romanticism, appeared in 1851 in installments in the Montevideo review *La semana*, when the author was in exile there, and was published in book form in 1855. Inspired by Sarmiento's *Facundo*, Mármol's plot is set in Buenos Aires in 1840, the year in which Rosas, threatened on many fronts, both within and outside the confederation, opened the period of Terror. The Unitarian characters—the young widow Amalia and her lover Eduardo Belgrano, hunted by the Mazorca police; her cousin Daniel Bello, who conspires against Rosas by feigning loyalty to the Federal cause so as to cover his espionage activities; and his fiancée Florencia Dupasquier, a beauty of French origin—are all idealized: they have beauty, intelligence, superhuman courage. In contrast, the characters on the Federación side, all real people in history—Rosas himself, a fiendish personage; María Josefa Ezcurra, the essence of vulgarity and cruelty; the whole court in residence at the dictator's Palermo estate (a sad "parody of Versailles")—are part of a cowardly and evil lot, degraded by the barbarism of the regime, the only exception being poor Manuelita herself. The clash between civilization and barbarism described in *Facundo* has become in *Amalia* the battle between good and evil, although the first seeds of a metaphysical axiology were already present in Sarmiento's Manichean antinomy. Here, however, the symbolic value of the color and cut of the clothes is not used only for political and moral definitions, as it records an even deeper level of significance.

The identification between the color red and the blood spilled by Unitarians is apparent from the beginning. The novel opens (and closes) with the massacre of a group of Unitarians caught in the act of trying to escape into exile on the streets leading to the river. Eduardo Belgrano is wounded, and his friend Daniel Bello conducts him to the safety of Amalia's home: "I had no idea of parading you at this hour through the Calle del Cabildo, where there would be twenty watchmen to throw the light of their lanterns on our persons, *clad in the bloody livery of the Federals*" (15, emphasis mine). The regime has discovered the only possible way to clothe the rebels' bodies in red: by covering them with blood. This recurrent metaphor in the Unitarian discourse exemplifies the transition from the metaphorical red of the Federación, a message carried by the *divisa punzó*, to the red of reality, to the objectivity of blood. Unitarians refuse to wear Federal red not only because it would symbolize their acceptance of an antagonistic political faith; they would, in fact, be wearing the metaphor of their own death, as ex-citizens, as nonpersons, as subjects.

In the meantime, those "clad in the bloody livery" cannot freely walk the streets of the city. They are forced to seek refuge in a private place, the antithesis of a public one: a woman's boudoir. Again, through the Unitarian woman, the elegant lady of *porteña* society, the strongest opposition to the government of the regime is revealed. Women are incorrigible, as Rosas is told by one of his men; young women refuse to dress their hair with the red ribbon representing the *divisa punzó*, they hide the ribbons under their bonnets, which provide them with an excellent excuse to conceal the hated symbol. Why not forbid the use of bonnets, then? Why not decree not only what should, but also what should not be worn?[19]

While the two heroes burst into Amalia's secret rooms, smearing them with blood, Florencia Dupasquier, the other heroine complementing the female universe of the Unitarian party, is paying a visit to María Josefa Ezcurra. Her motive is to try to get María to disclose the next moves of the Mazorca, who are still searching for the fugitive Eduardo Belgrano. Florencia is Amalia's angelic alter ego, and for her to enter the house of Rosas's sister-in-law is like crossing the threshold of an infernal pit inhabited by a promiscuous and degraded people. The mistress of the house is depicted as a bony and slovenly woman, wearing on her white hair a "large bow of *blood-colored* ribbon" (97, emphasis added). She explains her theory about why Unitarian women are in "seclusion," as "those idiots have shut themselves up in their houses": "they keep to their houses so that they may not have to wear the badge, as is the law; or have it stuck to them with pitch, which is stupid; what ought to be done . . . is to nail it to their heads so that they couldn't take it off even in their houses" (98). Therefore, the private space in which they take refuge to freely act has become the space of dissidence. The house is no longer woman's environment, but a political space, a public place. This voluntary confinement of elite women, a consequence of their refusal to wear the *divisa punzó*, expresses the desire that their bodies not be used as banners, contaminated by red.

If the walls of the house have now defined a place for resistance, and, consequently, a dangerous place, and if crossing their threshold means having to wear the red ribbon, an intolerable symbol of imposed identity, Unitarian women might still resort to another solution. And this is the one chosen by Florencia: wearing it as a mask. Florencia wears the *divisa* but does so negligently, partly transgressing the rules of Federal fashion: she wears a small *pink* ribbon, shyly peeping from the left brim of her hat. In this way she can go out and cross the public space under the protection of the Federal symbol, but at the same time maintain a marginal space to express her individuality and political convictions. The dialogue of the two women is balanced on the delicate thread of appearances: the accuser knows that Florencia is a Unitarian, and the latter knows that María Josefa knows, but appearances are maintained.

In another scene the device of the mask is explicit and openly acknowledged by a female character. At a Federal ball—an important social event that even the women of the aristocracy are obliged to attend, in part to protect their menfolk from possible retaliation by the regime—Amalia meets an elderly Unitarian woman who expounds her radical political views, based more on social exclusion (Federals seem to her to be parvenus from a lower class) than on the Unitarian constitutional project. The woman talks freely to Amalia; there is no need for the young woman to express her political opinion, since her attitude and her dress have already spoken for her: "Faces like yours, manners like yours, language like yours, dresses like yours, the ladies of the present Federation neither have, nor use, nor wear. You are one of us, even if you did not wish to be so" (163). The opinions expressed by the elderly lady expose José Mármol's text—a *roman a thèse*, a "ficción calculada," "a social study" as the author calls it in the preface (v)—to the same risks the Unitarian party itself was unable to avoid. The identification of the ideals of democracy and progress with the manners and fashions of the *porteña* high society, whose members had studied in Europe, fatally resulted in a classed ideology, incapable of constructing a theory that could unite the entire population. The worst offense of Rosas's government, in the Unitarian opinion, was that of having built its foundations on the approval of the lower classes, who represented the national identity in his political discourse. And the lower classes believed him.

For Amalia's elderly acquaintance, being a Unitarian was a consequence of birth, just as being a Federal seemed to be a genetic condition that neither virtue nor beauty could modify. At the sight of Rosas's younger sister, Augustina, the beautiful mother of Lucio Victorio Mansilla, the old lady becomes positively venomous, pointing out that the young woman's rosy cheeks perfectly match the *punzó* red of the Federación: "she is a beautiful country girl, but still a country girl; that is to say, her complexion is too red, her hands and arms are too large; she is too rustic" (162). Augustina was *only* a "federal beauty," a provincial girl: at once too fleshy, too countrified, and too superficial. Amalia, perhaps involuntarily, provokes the pun: the rosy cheeks are the color of *roses*, that is, the color of *Rosas*.

Before the Terror, the use of masking, the trick of modifying the color or the size of the *divisa punzó*, was so widespread that "two persons meeting knew perfectly well each other's political opinions merely by looking at the button-hole of the coat, if they were men, or at the head, if they were women" (160). Now this code is no longer permissible in the male world, where the subtle play on appearances could prove fatal to those who attempt it. In *Facundo*, Sarmiento describes the risks of using the *cinta colorada* as a mask; he also shows that the situation is mirrored in the Federals' being unable to wear fashionable clothes that distinguish them from the common people:

> In 1840, a group of *mazorqueros* surrounded, in the darkness of night, an individual who wore a frock coat in the streets of Buenos Aires. The knives were two fingers width from his throat. "I am Simón Pereira," he exclaimed. "Señor, a man who goes dressed like this puts himself in danger." "That's just why I dress like this; who but I wears a frock coat? I do it so I can be recognized from far away." This man is a cousin and business partner of Don Juan Manuel Rosas.[20]

Thus, in Mármol's novel, too, Daniel cannot use the same kind of dissimulation as Florencia. He is obliged to feign a loyalty to the federal idea, to the point of having to become a member of the Sociedad Popular Restauradora—the brains of the Mazorca—in order to be able to act safely. At the meeting, the men greet the new member; all are dressed exactly *comme il faut*, following Federal dictates:

> all of them dressed alike . . . all wearing a black hat adorned with a red band four inches in width, a dark blue jacket with a corresponding badge, half a yard in length, a red

waistcoat, and an enormous dagger at the waist. And, like their dress, the faces of these men seemed to be in uniform—a heavy mustache, whiskers ending at the chin, and an expression to be met with only in calamitous times of popular revolutions. (132–33)

Like Augustina Rosas, the men follow the laws of somatic determinism: their faces, like their clothes, are *uniform*, and become federation property, perpetrators of terror.

NOTES

1. See Jorge Myers, *Orden y virtud: El discurso republicano en el régimen rosista* (Buenos Aires: Universidad Nacional de Quilmes, 2002), 29, who mentions the political use of red in Rosas's regime.

2. See Regina Root, *Couture and Consensus: Fashion and Politics in Postcolonial Argentina* (Minneapolis: University of Minnesota Press, 2010). And Victor Goldgel Carballo on fashion as the "experience of Novelty," in "La moda del progreso: El Río de la Plata hacia 1837," *Estudios* 16, no. 32 (July–December 2008): 227–47. See also Susan Hallstead, "Políticas vestimentarias sarmientinas: tempranos ensayos sobre la moda y el buen vestir nacional," *Revista iberoamericana* 70, no. 206 (January–March 2004): 53–69.

3. "Every ideological sign is not only a reflection, a shadow, of reality, but is also itself a material segment of that very reality. Every phenomenon functioning as an ideological sign has some kind of material embodiment, whether in sound, physical mass, color, movements of the body, or the like. In this sense, the reality of the sign is fully objective." Valentin Nikolaevič Vološinov, *Marxism and the Philosophy of Language* (1929; repr. Cambridge, Mass.: Harvard University Press 1986), 11.

4. This is the question posed by José A. Oría in the journal *La Moda: Un periódico representativo, 1837–1838* (Buenos Aires: Guillermo Kraft, 1938).

5. 1. "Noticias continuas del estado y movimiento de la moda (en Europa y entre nosotros) en trajes de hombres y señoras, en géneros, en colores, en peinados, en muebles, en calzados, en puntos de concurrencia pública, en asuntos de conversación general.

Una idea sucinta del valor específico y social, de toda producción inteligente que en adelante apareciere en nuestro país. . . .

Nociones claras y breves, sin metafísica, al alcance de todos, sobre literatura moderna, sobre música, sobre poesía, sobre costumbres. . . . Se declama diariamente sobre la necesidad de cultivar el espíritu de las niñas y de los jóvenes. . . . Valiera mas buscar el remedio y tomarle. Nos parece el mas propio, el de mezclar la literatura a los objetos ligeros que interesan a los jóvenes. . . .

Nociones simples y sanas de una urbanidad democrática y noble en el baile, en la mesa, en las visitas, en los espectáculos. . . .

Poesías nacionales siempre inéditas. . . .

Crónicas pintorescas y frecuentes de los paseos públicos. . . .

Por fin un *Boletín Musical*. . . *.*" *La Moda: Gacetín semanal de Música, de Poesía, de Literatura, de Costumbres,* facsimile edition by José A. Oría (Buenos Aires: Academia Nacional de la Historia, 1938), no. 1 (November 18, 1837): 1–2. Further references are to *La Moda.*

6. "La moda, participa entre nosotros de la indecisión que afecta todas nuestras cosas sociales. No tenemos modas dominantes como no tenemos ideas, ni costumbres dominantes." *La Moda,* no. 3 (December 2, 1837): 3.

7. "M. Tocqueville ha conseguido dar una cuenta fiel de todos los fenómenos sociales que presentan los Estados Unidos. . . . La democracia resalta allí tanto en los vestidos y en las maneras como en la constitución política de los Estados. . . . De modo que una moda, como una costumbre, como una institución cualquiera, será para nosotros tanto más bella, cuanto más democrática sea en su esencia, es decir, cuanto más sobria, más simple, más modesta fuere." Ibid.

8. "En las costumbres de un pueblo es donde verdaderamente reside su constitucion política. Es éste *código vivo* lo que nosotros hemos descuidado hasta hoy mientras nos hemos ocupado de escribir *códigos abstractos,*" *La Moda,* no. 20 (March 31, 1838): 8; emphasis added.

9. "¿Para qué sirven esos pocos que se dicen ilustrados y hábiles? Esos no hacen pueblo. . . . la muchedumbre es el pueblo: la ignorancia es su título de soberanía y de infalibilidad. . . . Sí: el pueblo es el oráculo sagrado del periodista . . . pero el pueblo, . . . el pueblo no interrogado en sus masas, no el pueblo multitud, el pueblo masa . . . sino el pueblo representativo, el pueblo moderno de Europa y América, el pueblo escuchado en sus órganos inteligentes y legítimos la ciencia y la virtud. Las masas son santas, porque son el cuerpo del pueblo. . . . No deben ser consultadas directamente en altas materias, porque carecen de la conciencia de sus altas necesidades. . . . Un tendero, una muger, un zapatero, un pulpero, no tienen voto en la materia, porque son masas. Debe escribirse para ellos sin hacer caso de lo que digan." *La Moda,* no. 18 (March 17, 1838): 5.

10. "Todo el mundo vestido de colorado, con chaleco almenos, cintillo y divisa; el uniforme de la tropa colorado; el chiripá del gaucho colorado . . . ; todo lo externo más o menos pintado de colorado—pínteme usted todavía más colorado, le decía un emigrado, que al fin resolvió pedir indulto y volver, a un pintor que le observaba 'no hay más colorado'; al pobre emigrado todo le parecía poco para contarse seguro, y no era flojo el hombre—colorado todo lo interno, paredes, puertas, a veces el cielo raso, aquellos conciliábulos al resplandor de velas de sebo, tristes como luz sepulcral, en unos cuartos fríos en invierno, mal aireados en verano, teniendo que deliberar a puertas cerradas, y el constante y espasmódico pregonar ¡muera! ¡mueran los salvajes unitarios!

" 'El rojo posee incontestablemente un poder dinamógeno muy marcado.' 'Indudablemente que en aquella atmósfera de los años terribles debía haber algo que incitara a la tragedia, lo mismo que hay en el olor de la pólvora un no se qué que arrebata.' " Lucio Mansilla, *Rozas: Ensayo histórico-psicológico* (Buenos Aires: AZ editora, 1994), 73–74.

11. This and all following quotations are from Domingo Faustino Sarmiento, *Facundo: Civilization and Barbarism*, trans. Kathleen Ross (Berkeley: University of California Press, 2003), 132.

12. Ibid., 134.

13. Domingo Faustino Sarmiento, *Campaña en el ejército grande* (Río de Janeiro: imprenta imp. y const. de J. Villeneuve y c., 1852), 78.

14. In the words of Tulio Halperín Donghi, "The abdication of public functions into private hands leads to a new imprecision in the limits between one sphere and the other" ("La abdicación de funciones públicas en manos privadas conduce a una nueva imprecisión de los límites entre una y otra esfera"), quoted in Fernando Aliata, "Lo privado como público: Palermo de San Benito; un ejercicio," *Revista de Arquitectura* 144 (November 1989): 51–52. Also see Jorge Myers, "Una revolución en las costumbres: las nuevas formas de sociabilidad de la elite porteña, 1800–1860," in *Historia de la vida privada*, vol. 1, *País antiguo. De la colonia a 1870*, ed. F. Devoto and M. Madero (Buenos Aires: Taurus, 1999), 111–45.

15. See Francine Masiello, *Entre civilización y barbarie: Mujeres, Nación y Cultura literaria en la Argentina moderna* (Rosario: Beatriz Viterbo, 1997), 20.

16. Mármol, reacting to the image of Manuela Rosas commonly held in Unitarian circles and adding to it, considered the tyrant's daughter a victim of her father, a shameful example of pure female virtue submitted to barbarism, a prisoner of her devotion to her father. See José Mármol, *Manuela Rosas: Rasgos biográficos* (Montevideo: Imprenta Uruguayana, 1851).

17. "El retrete de vestirse estaba empapelado del mismo modo que la alcoba, y alfombrado de verde. Dos grandes roperos de caoba, cuyas puertas eran de espejos, se veían a un lado y al otro del espléndido tocador, cuyas porcelanas y cristales había desordenado Daniel pocos momentos antes. . . . Seis magníficos cuadros de paisaje y cuatro jilgueros dentro de jaulas de alambre dorado, completaban el retrete de Amalia, en el que la luz del día penetraba por los cristales de una gran ventana que daba a un pequeño jardín en el patio principal, y que era moderada por un juego doble de colgaduras de crespón celeste y de batista." José Mármol, *Amalia* (Buenos Aires: Imprenta Americana, 1855), 117–18. This passage does not appear in the English version, *Amalia* (New York: E. P. Dutton, 1919). Further references in the text. All translations are mine.

18. "En medio de este museo de delicadezas femeniles, donde todo se reproducía al infinito sobre el cristal, sobre el acero, y sobre el oro, Amalia, envuelta en un peinador de batista, estaba sentada sobre un sillón de damasco caña, delante de uno de los magníficos espejos de su guardarropas; su seno casi descubierto, sus brazos desnudos, sus ojos cerrados, y su cabeza reclinada sobre el respaldo del sillón, dejando que su espléndida y ondeada cabellera fuese sostenida por el brazo izquierdo de una niña de diez años, linda y fresca como un jazmín, que en vez de peinar aquellos, parecía deleitarse en pasarlos por su desnudo brazo para sentir sobre su cutis la impresión cariñosa de sus sedosas hebras. En ese momento, Amalia no era una mujer: era una diosa de esas que ideaba la poesía mitológica de los griegos" (247). This passage does not appear in the English edition.

19. "La Universidad y las mujeres son incorregibles. No hay forma de que los estudiantes usen la divisa con letrero; me ven venir por una calle y, casi a mi vista, desatan la cintita que llevan al ojal, y se la guardan en el bolsillo. Tampoco hay medio para que las mujeres usen el moño fuera de la gorra y, aun sin gorra, la mayor parte de las unitarias, especialmente las jóvenes, se presentan en todas partes sin la divisa federal. Yo en lugar de Vuecelencia haría prohibir las gorras en las mujeres" (59). This passage does not appear in the English edition.

20. Sarmiento, *Facundo*, 133.

13

TO FASHION THE WONDERFUL GARMENT

W. E. B. DU BOIS'S THE QUEST OF THE SILVER FLEECE AND NELLA LARSEN'S QUICKSAND

M. Giulia Fabi

Clothes are a crucial, if overlooked, element of the "symbolic structure" that W. E. B. Du Bois deploys to unify his first novel.[1] The clothing and color symbolism of *The Quest of the Silver Fleece* (1911) foregrounds gender ideologies and sexual politics.[2] Du Bois's "spiritual epic of cotton"[3] is not only an "economic study" (as Du Bois would later define it) but chiefly a carefully constructed literary text.[4] If cotton (the raw material) and clothes (the finished product) enable the novelistic intersection of romance and political critique, Du Bois's deep and complex use of clothing and color symbolism unveils the gender politics of his project of uplift and liberation, as well as the relational definition of women's role that underlies his concern with women's "purity," which remains in unresolved conflict with his heroine's strong individuality (*Quest*, 98). This conflict did not pass unnoticed by contemporary black women writers, and certainly not by Nella Larsen, whose first novel is an intertextual revision of *The Quest of the Silver Fleece*.[5] In *Quicksand* (1928), Larsen registers the clothing and color symbolism running through Du Bois's novel to articulate her critique of the gender politics such symbolism enshrines.[6] Exploring this neglected intertextual relationship enables a deeper appreciation and revises traditional scholarly assessments of both novels, foregrounding the political significance of Larsen's fiction and illuminating the critically underestimated complex literariness of *The Quest of the Silver Fleece.*[7]

THE QUEST OF THE SILVER FLEECE

In *The Quest of the Silver Fleece*, the various phases of Zora's *Bildung* are systematically accompanied by changes in the representation of her clothes and body. The heroine's shift from being "half-clothed" to learning how to dress parallels her move from sexual exploitation in her mother's cabin to intellectual training, community leadership, and eventually marriage (16). Clothes constitute, literally, a red thread. The color red is connected from the very first lines of the novel with the "red waters of the swamp" so prominent in the novel (13). The swamp, in turn, is closely connected with the "full-blooded" heroine (125). When we first see this "child of the swamp" in her mother Elspeth's cabin (44), Zora is illuminated by a "crimson light," she is dancing in a "halo of flame," and her "garments twined and flew around the delicate molding of her dark, young, half-naked limbs" (14). Her dance, her body, her "full purple lips apart" and her "half hid bosom panting" are gazed at by several spectators (15): the white men who frequent Elspeth's cabin, Bles the temporary interloper, and the reader, whose spectatorial and voyeuristic position is ensured by the authorial voice that describes the scene in ways at once admiring and objectifying.

Zora's body is highly sexualized in her first meeting with the hero. Despite Bles's brief fascination with "her soul," the hero's gaze follows her "rent gown" through which "her warm, dark flesh peeped furtively" (16). If the scantily dressed Zora is a "vision" for Bles, to help her overcome her "half-naked" condition is a crucial part of his project for her uplift (16, 14). In the first chapter dedicated to Zora, the initial steps of her intellectual transformation (developing a friendship, reading, studying, planning to cultivate the swamp to pay for her education) go hand in hand with the process of covering her body. While she refuses to accept any money from Bles (a refusal of the commercial relations governing her mother's cabin that confirms Zora's intrinsic virtue), she does accept the "vivid red" dress that had "caught his eye" and that he buys for her (50). This "wonderful garment" brings "glad tears" to her eyes (50), but it also makes her the object of differing conjectures about her. On the one hand, Bles is "busy with his plans" and imagines for her a domestic future when she will also learn to decorate a home and "make it beautiful" (51). On the other, the schoolteacher Miss Taylor gazes at "the scarlet gown" that shows too much of Zora's body, "hanging from shoulder to ankle in formless, clinging folds" (53), and draws the conclusion that she "is a bold, godless thing" and that the "simplicity and vividness" of her clothes "is—well—immodest" (67).

Miss Taylor's judgment is clearly informed by her racial bigotry and superficiality, yet her evaluation of Zora is only partly rejected in the novel. However "wonderful" the red garment and her accompanying "black and bare" feet and ankles (53), they are nevertheless part of a transitional phase Zora must outgrow in her process of acculturation and uplift. The utopian island of "virgin and black" soil in the swamp will point the way (78). When Zora takes Bles to see it, she is again the object of Bles's sexualized gaze in noticing once more how "her garments twined and flew in shadowy drapings about the perfect moulding of her young and dark half-naked figure" (76). The description is admiring, but not necessarily approving, and in decorating the nest he prepares for her in the swamp Bles puts "a little picture in blue and gold of Bougereau's Madonna," revealing the redemptive female role model his uplift of Zora intends (97). In the ensuing conversation, prompted by Zora's questions, the model is qualified: "purity" is deracialized as not exclusively synonymous with "just whiteness," and it is relativized as the state of being "as good as a woman knows how" (98). Yet the notion of purity remains a gender-specific requirement for women, and the model retains its prescriptive qualities not only for Bles, as his later rejection of Zora will reveal, but apparently also for Zora herself. While the reader does not have access to the thoughts of "the girl [who] was staring silently at the Madonna," but only to her cautious sounding of Bles's definition of purity (98), at the end of the novel a picture of the Madonna hangs in the room that Zora herself has learned to "make ... beautiful" (51).

Nor is that model disavowed in the course of Zora's transformation. Her uplift takes her to the "tiny bedroom" in Miss Smith's school, a transitional space that, with its "one broad window looking toward the swamp" and its "white curtains . . . and white hangings," mirrors Zora's own in-betweenness (120).[8] There, Zora is initiated to home work (including sewing), cultivates reading habits, and "learn[s] new and unknown ways of living and dressing" (122). The explicitly close relationship between living and dressing is presented as part of the "mighty change from youth to womanhood and manhood . . . wherein a soul . . . comes suddenly to consciousness of body and clothes; when it gropes and tries to adjust one with the other, and through them to give to the inner deeper self, finer and fuller expression." Bles, too, undergoes such a change, but "Alwyn's Sunday suit, vivid neckties, and awkward dress" draw far less authorial attention than Zora's appearance. Her developing "grace and womanliness" is connected with "shy self-poise" and encodes notions of femininity that evoke the never-disavowed Madonna: her hair "began to be subdued . . . and combed until . . . it lay in thick twisted braids . . . like some shadowed *halo*" (123–24, emphasis mine). In contrast to her first red dress, at the student social she dons a white dress; and while her transformation was still "far—very far— from complete," her change reveals she will become a "passionate mother of men" (125).[9] This role is prophesized as part of her future development, but adolescent Zora is already practicing her social destiny with the "new-born" cotton plants in the swamp: "All the latent mother in her brooded over them. . . . They were her dream-children, and she tended them jealously; they were her Hope, and she worshipped them" (125).

At this point, Zora's mothering may be metaphoric, but it is nevertheless already sacrificial, and her looks and manners change accordingly. After she nearly loses her life to save the worshipped crop from torrential rains and she is rescued by Bles who takes her to Miss Smith's, she "looked different; her buxom comeliness was spiritualized," and as "she saw Bles pass" she "drew back timidly when he looked" (156). Purified by her self-immolation and near-death experience, she is temporarily rewarded with Bles's love. That this romantic bliss is granted only a short narrative existence could be interpreted as an indirect critique of the traditionalism on which it is based. This is partly the case.

On the one hand, it is true that Bles's traditionalism is challenged by Zora and shown to be a fatal weakness of the hero, who cannot withstand the prejudiced sexual double standard and the self-interested, racist defamation of Zora voiced by profligate Harry Cresswell.[10] On the other hand, Bles is not the only one harboring gendered notions of female purity. Zora herself entertains a sense of being "not worthy" (170), and while she struggles to see purity as a process rather than a biological property, she is still concerned about how she can "grow pure" (171). Similarly, the traditional textual/sexual politics of Bles's injunction, "You should have *died,*" is undermined by a different narrative fate for his sexually violated heroine (170). That defiance is thematic, as Zora survives and can eventually grow "more than pure" (433), but not symbolic, as the ensuing death and resurrection motif reveals.

Zora slowly recovers from the shock of Bles's rejection. In the process, she witnesses "the rape of the Fleece" (181), speaks in "a dead voice" (186), defends herself, like a "primal tiger" (187), from Harry Cresswell's renewed attempt to molest her, and risks becoming "a peon bound to a master's bidding" (188), reduced to "slavery of soul and body" (219). To this social death, she opposes a "desperate resolve . . . not to fall into the pit opening before her. Somehow, somewhere, lay The Way" (189). As she turns "toward the future" (189), "The Way" initially lies in her identification with the Fleece, "an holy thing which profane hands had stolen" and that "to Zora's mind" will bring "illumination, atonement, and something of the power and the glory" (215). In her relationship with it, she continues to practice the roles she has learned in the process of uplift. On the one hand, she watches the Fleece "like a brooding mother" (215). On the other, when poetic justice miraculously returns the Fleece to her, she "draped her shimmering cloth about her, dragging her hair down in a heavy mass over ears and neck until she seemed herself a bride" (230–31). "And as she stood there," the death and resurrection motifs come together in "the mystical union of a dead love and a living new born self" (231).

This foreshadowing of the marital happy ending is accompanied by an analogous anticipation of her future leadership role signaled in the narrative by a greater focus on her self-perception and point of view. In turn, this greater emphasis on her consciousness, her soul, occurs at the expense of her body. Zora's partly resurrected self warns men "with the cold majesty of her eyes" (216); during her brief relapse into orgiastic dancing, she stands "tip-toed with skirts that curled and turned," but her clothes are not explicitly related to the shape of her body (221). When she enters the home of her past seducer as Mrs. Vanderpool's personal maid, she is set off from the other Cresswell servants, who respectfully call her "Miss Zora," and "the men scarcely saw her and the ladies ran to her for help in all sorts" (226). This move from spiritualized "ghostly beauty" to bodily invisibility continues in the North (156). In the next phase of "The Training of Zora," the heroine is living in New York and Washington with Mrs. Vanderpool (245). There she undergoes another "curious training" in "dress and taste in adornment," but she soon outgrows it: her mistress "now and then found herself learner before the quick suggestiveness of Zora's mind" (247). Mrs. Vanderpool refers to Zora's appearance, imaginatively comparing it to "the dusky magnificence of some bejewelled semi-barbaric queen," and she, too, has plans for Zora's clothes and body (223). Relating them to the racialized sexual economy of marriage, Mrs. Vanderpool contemplates "tak[ing] her to France and marry[ing] her off in the colonies" (249). Zora's body, however, is no longer on display. An earlier sexualizing gaze is replaced by a focus on her "thought-life" of reading and thinking in which "more and more her real living centred" (251).

As Zora's body recedes, Bles's, undergoing some aesthetic uplift of his own, emerges. "The Education of Alwyn" includes crucial lessons in dressing that expose him to the risk of violation (253). His education by the "well-gowned" Miss Wynn includes critical evaluations of his identity, the cynical manipulation of his gifts and ideals for Miss Wynn's personal social advancement, and eventually even a threat to his autonomy, as she plans to write his speech for him (320).[11] As a result, Bles has to learn to defend his integrity and virtue, so to speak, as well as his identity.[12] His eventual refusal to compromise his ideals for money and social position evokes the theme of prostitution that runs through the novel in relation both to the illicit sexuality in Elspeth's cabin and to the socially sanctioned institution of marriage.[13]

Bles survives the real danger of this metaphoric rape of his integrity thanks also to

Zora, who helps him invisibly, from afar, to remain "the master of [his] fate" (318), and "hover[s] over his soul like some dark guardian angel" (294). Yet the narrator's focus on Zora's "thought-life" is not accompanied by the "Vision Splendid" of expanded gender roles (251). Her supportive, self-sacrificial role and continued concern for her "unforgiven [sexual] sin" survive even the shocking news of Bles's engagement to Miss Wynn (433). She imagines Bles's fiancée as "some good and pure woman who would help and uplift and serve him" (293). Her "high ideal" requires that woman "to be handsome, well dressed, earnest and good" (301). Even after she finds "The Way" in church, she continues to privilege Bles's well-being and postpones her own project to return to the South because she intends to study "Settlement-work and reform movements" and also because she wants to help Bles to pursue his political career "without sacrificing his manhood or betraying his people" (298).

Zora's life-changing experience in church is the final resurrection that brings her permanently back from her metaphoric death: "Thus from the grave of youth and love, amid the soft, low singing of dark and bowed worshippers, the Angel of Resurrection rolled away the stone" (296). Her discovery of the "mighty ideal" through which "all things else were possible" makes her decide to go "back South to work for my people" (296–97). In her long, oppressive train ride in a Jim Crow car, Zora's experiences make her sympathize even more with the plight of "my poor people" (331). Her sexual vulnerability becomes metonymic of their oppression. On the train, she confronts the sexual politics of her newborn identity as a black female leader in a Jim Crow nation, including the need for constant self-control to ward off sexual misinterpretations: she rejects the commercial advances of a newsboy and drops out of the window his "book with a picture of a man and half-dressed woman" (331); she is "eyed . . . respectfully" by a gang of colored section hands, and "with one of them she talked a little as he awkwardly fingered his cap" (332); and she disciplines the improper, sexually suggestive physical closeness of a porter.

Zora has ultimately grown into "sumptuous womanhood," and back in Alabama she becomes a "mother of men" (125). Guided by her "love" for her people (355), she is almost overwhelmed by "sorrow," "helplessness," and "suffering" for their condition of oppres-

sion (357), but it is the fear of the sexual danger to which adolescent Emma (the interra-
cial "daughter of shame" born in Elspeth's cabin) is exposed that reveals to her "the paramount mission of her life." Assuming that "the child was too ignorant to protect herself,"
Zora decides:

> She would protect this girl; she would protect all black girls. She would make it possible
> for these poor beasts of burden to be decent in their toil. Out of the protection of wom-
> anhood as the central thought, she must build ramparts against cruelty, poverty, and
> crime.... It was her duty, her heritage. (359)

"Zora's Way" lies in reclaiming and purifying the swamp (355). Her decision to buy
the swamp in order to "have land—our own farm with our own tenants—to be the beginning of a free community" links her own special position to the community (362).
Living at Miss Smith's school, she travels "all through the countryside" investigating the
condition of black people (356). Offering a research methodology and interpretation of
sociological investigation that is different from the superficiality Du Bois satirizes in
white sociologist Mr. Temple Bocombe, Zora sits with and listens to her people "till gradually the black folk came to know her and, in silent deference to some subtle difference,
they gave her the title of white folk, calling her 'Miss' Zora" (356). Even Colonel Cresswell, seeing her from a distance, mistakes her for a white "lady" (364). Zora's looks no
longer partake of "the brilliant attire, half fantastic, half crude" that characterizes much
of "the black population" around Toomsville (368).

However, Zora's difference and special status are not enough to ensure her escape
from confining gender roles. Her charismatic eloquence at a church meeting where she
is trying to recruit volunteers to help clear the swamp incites the jealousy of "greasy"
Preacher Jones (368), but her project of black self-determination is providentially rescued by the intervention of an "old man . . . tall, massive, with tufted gray hair and wrinkled leathery skin, and . . . the eyes of death" who speaks for her and leads the people to
clear the first twenty acres of the swamp (375). The deus ex machina betrays the lack of
a social space for a female leader like Zora. Du Bois focuses on Zora's strategy of nego-

tiation with it and rewards her with renewed access to Bles's company. Zora's successful immersion once she is back in the South is in part due to her attention to and careful manipulation of the strictures of her racialized and gendered societal definition, as when she lets Bles explain in public what she has planned. Zora's leadership is also crucially accompanied by her ability to develop a functional relationship with clothes and with the way in which her looks define and distort her identity. On the one hand, in the utopian community she founds in the swamp, clothes, like cotton, serve an economic function as one of the means of self-support.[14] On the other, clothes become a means of resistance and self-determination. Defying traditional notions of propriety, she throws away her hat and "loosen[s] her dress at the neck" to run and warn Bles about impending danger (385). And it is through such impropriety of dress, stereotypically (and mistakenly) read by Colonel Cresswell in sexual terms, that she is able to save Bles from being lynched.

However instrumentally or strategically used, traditional gender roles do survive even in the communitarian experiment in the swamp, and they do not completely lose their stifling power. Zora's very life project is still informed by them, because she sees "the paramount mission of her life" as a form of "mighty atonement" (359). The founding of the free community sees the destruction of Elspeth's cabin and the building of a new log cabin where Zora will propose to Bles to "work together as good friends" (399). As he accepts "to be [her] co-worker—nay, in a sense to be a follower, for he was ignorant of much," he initiates a process of reeducation to more egalitarian gender roles:

> Yet the sacrifice, the readjustment was hard; he grew to it gradually, inwardly revolting, feeling always a great longing to take this woman and make her nestle in his arms as she used to; catching himself again and again on the point of speaking to her and urging, yet ever again holding himself back and bowing in silent respect to the dignity of her life. (400)

At the same time, however, Zora has decorated her own den in the settlement in ways that foreground the gendered symbolic structure of the novel and enshrine the gender-inflected values of purity and self-sacrificing motherhood. On the walls, she hangs a few pictures that include "a Madonna . . . and some sad baby faces" (399).

The final two chapters bring the novel full circle, recalling and revising two key moments in ways that differentiate the utopian present from the past. In "The Mob," the flames that accompanied the first description of Zora's dancing and illumined her body are now strategically used as a "fence of fire" to save the settlement from a white mob, and while planning this defense Zora's and Bles's love is renewed (423). The lovers' actual reunion in the last chapter, titled "Atonement," evokes, instead, the "mystical union" with the Silver Fleece that initiated the process of Zora's resurrection and purification (231). As she did then, Zora wears the Silver Fleece:

> Searching down in the depths of her trunk, she drew forth that filmy cloud of white— silk-bordered and half finished to a gown. Why were her eyes wet to-day and her mind on the Silver Fleece? It was an anniversary, and perhaps she still remembered that moment, that supreme moment before the mob. She half slipped on, half wound about her, the white cloud of cloth, standing with parted lips, looking into the long mirror and gleaming in the fading day like midnight gowned in mists and stars. (430)

This moment of hopeful self-contemplation, when "the old dream-life . . . had come silently back," has Zora in her own room enjoying the luxury of her "informal attire" without worrying about its possible social misinterpretation; but it is not allowed to last (430). Acting on her new, but still stereotyped, reading of Zora as a sexless leader "not meant for marrying" because "wedded to a great cause" (418), Mrs. Cresswell (née Mary Taylor) tries to convince Zora that "pure" Emma is a more suitable mate for Bles (433). Zora's self-doubts and her never disavowed guilt for her "unforgiven sin" return in full force, bringing back to the surface traditional textual/sexual notions of female identity through the tropes of the self-sacrificial violated woman ready for "atonement" and the noble manly lover who chooses to save her (433).[15]

At one level, this misunderstanding, soon cleared, enhances the romantic quality of the final reunion of the two lovers. However, the costs of such romanticism are high since Zora rethinks her entire life in relational and male-centered terms: "was not all her life simply the want of him?" Zora wonders (432). At the same time, despite his declared sense of unworthiness, Bles utters the final word on Zora's identity. Prompted by his definition of her as "more than pure" and signaling her acceptance of it, Zora's "sobbed" and faltering marriage proposal represents a partial challenge to traditional gender roles (433–34). The limited transgressiveness of this closure emerges also at the level of narrative form. As in traditional fairy tales, the story ends before marriage and therefore does not put Zora and Bles's potentially more egalitarian relationship to the test of family life as biological mother and father.

While the protagonists are returned to the more familiar (in all senses) pleasures of romance, the final paragraph of the novel, *"L'envoi,"* underscores metanarratively the paradigmatic politics of their story, as well as its fictionality.[16] "L'envoi" is italicized and typographically set off from the rest of the text (but also placed before "The End" and therefore still part of the novel). While the story is told in the past tense, "L'envoi" features a series of exhortations in the present imperative that request readers play a more active role in the "world" (434). This final intervention of the authorial voice does not mediate the shift from textual fiction to extratextual fact, but rather widens the gap between romance and history in terms of gender and genre. The sharp contrast of verbal tenses relegates the characters to the realm of "fantasy." As the author "draws aside his fictional veil and speaks *in propria persona,*" he explicitly foregrounds his own controlling role as puppeteer, exposing his characters as fictional pawns.[17] Leaving the female protagonist and her leadership in a timeless past, the authorial voice takes over Zora's mission of working for "my people" and assumes an emphatically exhortative and threatening masculine tone:

Let my people go, Infinite One, lest the world shudder at

THE END. (434)

The textual/sexual politics of the romantic ending of *The Quest of the Silver Fleece* bring full circle the objectifying authorial gaze on the heroine with which the novel opened and stand in contrast to Du Bois's thematic celebration of the uplift and leadership of his "new, honest, young fighting Negro woman."[18]

The gender politics informing the symbolic structure of Du Bois's novel were not lost on an insightful reader and brilliant writer like Nella Larsen.[19] In *Quicksand,* Larsen signifies systematically on Du Bois's clothing and color symbolism in order to challenge thematically, ideologically, and narratively the romantic teleology of the marital happy ending and its textual/sexual politics.[20] In her novel, clothes continue to signal different moments of the heroine's story, but rather than indicate a process of growth, they mark the various confining and objectifying societal scripts of black womanhood imposed on Helga to which she initially tries to adapt, then later rebels against, and eventually seems to succumb to.[21]

Larsen's intertextual revision of *The Quest of the Silver Fleece* starts by endowing her heroine with greater narrative depth and power. She chooses Helga as the central consciousness and substitutes Du Bois's dominating authorial voice with a radical use of the circumscribed point of view, manifesting her deliberate participation in the aesthetic experimentation of "the Europeans and American moderns" that she had already avowed in a 1926 letter to Charles S. Johnson.[22] Helga's point of view dominates the greatest part of the novel, enabling a psychological exploration of her relationship with her body and clothes, with societal readings of them, and with the notions of female identity they enshrine, an exploration from the inside that was largely missing from Du Bois's portrayal of Zora. However, Helga's expanded narrative role as central consciousness does not correspond, at a thematic level, to greater control over her narrative career. On the contrary, not only is Helga, like Zora before her, unable to escape societal definitions and stifling gender roles, but her career actually inverts the progressivist direction of Zora's, bringing Helga from elegant clothes to seminudity, from a teaching career to unpaid domestic work, from "careless health" to sickness (2).[23] Far from clearing any literal or metaphoric swamp, Helga at the end is lost in a "quagmire" (133).

Seeing this intertextual connection illuminates in new ways the significance of the final, critically debated section of *Quicksand.* Taking Helga on a journey to Alabama similar to the one that leads Zora to clear the swamp and eventually to marriage, and following her heroine beyond marriage proposals into married life as the wife of an "adored pastor" (120), Larsen explores the social strictures of female activism (to which Du Bois briefly alluded through the jealousy of the preacher), the limits of female solidarity (that Du Bois eschewed by having Zora organize mostly with men in the swamp), the gendered division of labor (to which Du Bois again alluded only briefly by referring to how Zora plans and Bles speaks), and the bodily entrapment of biological motherhood. Helga's life, when she *literally* becomes a "passionate mother of men," explodes Du Bois's rhetoric, manifesting its underlying, life-threatening dangers for women (*Quest*, 125).[24]

In the last four chapters, Larsen focuses on a few years of Helga Crane's married life, using clothing and color symbolism to paint a scene that evokes and merges the beginning and end of Zora's story, further undermining the progressivist logic of the earlier text. The decoration of Helga's house is patterned on that of Zora's den in the redeemed swamp, both in color (the dominating ones are white and oak) and in the "religious pictures" hanging on the walls (*Quicksand*, 121). These intertextual similarities, however, make the differences between the endings of the two novels even more glaring. Helga's project to uplift the women of the "tiny Alabama town," "tactfully" instructing them "in what she considered more appropriate clothing and in inexpensive ways of improving their homes according to her ideas of beauty" (118–19), parodies Du Bois's description of Bles's plans for adolescent Zora, while the repeated pregnancies that oblige Helga to give up her plans for "the uplifting of other harassed and teeming women" (*Quicksand*, 124) also fill her house with living "baby faces" (*Quest*, 399). "After the first exciting months," the conditions in Helga's house make it increasingly more like Elspeth's cabin (*Quicksand*, 123): it is untidy and invaded by people; it is an "immoral" place of (marital) sexual molestation (134); without books, it is mired in poverty and increasing nakedness.

Clothes and colors reveal the depth of Helga's "oppression and degradation" (135). In the last two chapters, the description of the heroine's looks parallels, but in dramatically dystopian terms, the one in the first chapter. The difference may be gauged from the contrast between the "green and gold negligee" she wears in the opening chapter (2), and her present condition as Mrs. Green married to a "rattish yellow man" (118).[25] When she wears the "filmy *crêpe*" nightgown, a relic from her "prematrimonial days" that barely hides her breasts, she is gazed on in the proprietary, use-oriented terms of her "desirability" by her husband (129). As in the first chapter, and evoking Zora's own search for "The Way," during the closing vigil of painful soul-searching Helga is planning an escape. Contrary to the rashness of her flight from Naxos for which her colleagues initially blame her, Helga's mother-love now compels her to look for "a feasible way out" and to exercise a caution that in the context of her entrapment emphasizes her powerlessness, rather than her reasonableness (135). The ending of the novel ominously insinuates that "Away" (135), her last thought, may no longer be "a way" for her.

The final paragraph brings to brilliant completion Larsen's process of intertextual revision. As in *The Quest of the Silver Fleece,* the last paragraph of *Quicksand* is typographically set off from the rest of the novel, and it signals a shift in narrative voice that distances the reader from the heroine. However, in *The Quest of the Silver Fleece* the first-person voice that takes over seems to be that of the "Author" who signed the opening "Note" and underscored the "truthfulness," but also the status as "tale" of his book. In *Quicksand,* instead, the final paragraph returns to the third-person narrative voice of the novel's opening, offering an inverted mirror-image of the change in point of view that went typographically unmarked at the beginning when the narrator started slipping into Helga's thoughts (2).

These different narrative choices lead to widely diverging results. Larsen maintains the same past tense of narration in the last paragraph, offering no extraliterary way out of Helga's predicament. As the author abruptly relinquishes her privileged focus on Helga's point of view, she leaves her readers to witness Helga's abject condition, shocking them into a greater awareness of how the "rare and intensely personal" workings of Helga's mind shielded them from the crude brutality and the stunting repetitiveness of many of the oppressive situations she encountered (1). Larsen thereby affirms to the end the individuality of her heroine *via negativa,* that is, she emphasizes the previous centrality of Helga's consciousness by withdrawing the readers' narrative access to it. As a result, the final exclusion from Helga's mind does not simply reinforce the sense of Helga's tragic predicament, but also incites a reflection on Helga's story that enhances the circularity of the text, as the reader is brought back to its promising beginning and left to wonder exactly how things could have gone so wrong.²⁶ By contrast, at the end of his novel, Du Bois disempowers his heroine, as the narrative voice takes over Zora's vision, pushing her into the textual past and himself into the extratextual present and future. Similarly, despite its apparent transgressiveness, Zora's marriage offer to Bles signals her acceptance of his redefinition of her purity, and her enclosure within the narrative confines of a marital ending serves to substantiate the feasibility of the author's political analysis and utopian project by promising an ostensibly safe social space for his heroine. Reading intertextually between *Quicksand* and *The Quest of the Silver Fleece* problematizes that illusion of safety, foregrounding how Zora's individuality has been sacrificed to the demands of an inspirational happy ending and reaffirming the centrality of African-American women to the project of communal liberation.

NOTES

1. Arlene A. Elder, "Swamp versus Plantation: Symbolic Structure in W. E. B. Du Bois's *The Quest of the Silver Fleece*," *Phylon* 34, no. 4 (1973): 358–67.

2. W. E. B. Du Bois, *The Quest of the Silver Fleece* (1911; repr. Boston: Northeastern University Press, 1989), 50. Subsequent references are cited parenthetically in the text.

3. William Stanley Braithwaite, "What to Read," in *Critical Essays on W. E. B. Du Bois*, ed. William L. Andrews (Boston: G. K. Hall, 1985), 38.

4. In *Dusk of Dawn* (1940), Du Bois describes *The Quest of the Silver Fleece* as "an economic study of some merit": quoted in Arnold Rampersad, *The Art and Imagination of W. E. B. Du Bois* (Cambridge, Mass.: Harvard University Press, 1976), 132.

5. Du Bois's double-edged glorification of women that Larsen identified and critiqued at the time continues to be debated by scholars today. Critics Susan Kay Gillman and Alys Eve Weinbaum, for instance, have argued that he "simultaneously condemns social injustice and reproduces gender

dominance" in *Next to the Color Line: Gender, Sexuality, and W. E. B. Du Bois* (Minneapolis: University of Minnesota Press, 2007), 73. On Du Bois's textual/sexual politics, see also Joy James, "The Profeminist Politics of W. E. B. Du Bois with Respects to Anna Julia Cooper and Ida B. Wells Barnett," in *W. E. B. Du Bois on Race and Culture: Philosophy, Politics, and Poetics*, ed. Bernard W. Bell, Emily Grosholz, and James B. Stewart (New York: Routledge, 1996), 141–60; and Nellie Y. McKay, "W. E. B. Du Bois: The Black Women in His Writings—Selected Fictional and Autobiographical Portraits," in *Critical Essays on W. E. B. Du Bois*, ed. Andrews, 230–52; and Barbara McCaskill, "Anna Julia Cooper, Pauline Elizabeth Hopkins, and the African American Feminization of Du Bois's Discourse," in *The Souls of Black Folk One Hundred Years Later*, ed. Dolan Hubbard (Columbia: University of Missouri Press, 2003), 70–84.

6. Nella Larsen, *Quicksand* (1928), in *Quicksand and Passing* (London: Serpent's Tail, 2001). Subsequent references are cited parenthetically in the text.

7. Du Bois's long-standing "concern" with fiction has been emphasized by his literary executor, Herbert Aptheker, who also noticed that in "his correspondence . . . there is evidence that Du Bois—and others—had a fairly high regard for *The Quest of the Silver Fleece* not only as a social document but also as a novel"; see the introduction to *The Quest of the Silver Fleece* (Millwood, N.Y.: Kraus-Thompson, 1974), 11, 10. For a more recent analysis of the critical underestimation of Du Bois's fiction and a reevaluation of his "attention to issues of language and form," see Maurice Lee, "Du Bois the Novelist: White Influence, Black Spirit, and *The Quest of the Silver Fleece*," *African American Review* 33, no. 3 (1999): 389.

8. "Verisimilitude and symbolism commingle" in the description of Sarah Smith's school, which "was based on the Calhoun School, where Du Bois had directed research for his 1906 land tenantry study"; see David Levering Lewis, *W. E. B. Du Bois: Biography of a Race, 1868–1919* (New York: Henry Holt, 1993), 446. For an in-depth analysis of how "*Quest* adapted the findings of Du Bois's fieldwork in the rural South," see Maria Farland, "W. E. B. Du Bois, Anthropometric Science, and the Limits of Racial Uplift," *American Quarterly* 58, no. 4 (2006): 1017–45.

9. Du Bois's portrayal of Zora reveals the influence of Pauline E. Hopkins's *Contending Forces: A Romance Illustrative of Negro Life North and South* (1900; repr. New York: Oxford University Press, 1988). Like Zora, Sappho Clark is a sexually violated heroine; she is compared to "the Virgin" (386), and her "ministry" is "to the women of the race"; see Allison Berg, *Mothering the Race: Women's Narratives of Reproduction, 1890–1930* (Champaign: University of Illinois Press, 2002), 50. However, whereas in *Contending Forces* "the reunion of mother and child overshadows that of hero and hero-

ine as the dramatic climax of this matrifocal novel," as Berg has convincingly argued (50), in *The Quest of the Silver Fleece* the lovers' reunion takes center stage and the complex issue of motherhood is more traditionally postponed beyond the happy ending.

10. See, for instance, the exchange on beauty between Zora and Bles (165–66).

11. Miss Wynn's "cynicism" (*Quest*, 263) informs her ambivalent definition of Bles: "That good Miss Smith has gone and grafted a New England conscience on a tropical heart, and—dear me!—but it's a gorgeous misfit" (265). Despite its apparent lightness, Miss Wynn's comment is an "attack" on Bles's identity and ideals (263). Larsen echoes it in Axel Olsen's definition of Helga: "You have the warm impulsive nature of the women of Africa, but . . . you have . . . the soul of a prostitute" (*Quicksand*, 87).

12. Despite his engagement to Miss Wynn, he remains chaste, because he cannot forget Zora. He cannot do more than kiss Miss Wynn's hand (*Quest*, 281), and it is she who kisses him good-bye on the lips when she breaks their engagement to marry Sam Stillings (325). While his faithfulness to Zora indicates some reciprocity in their relationship, there is no questioning of the sexual double standard that makes Bles's chastity a choice and hers a requirement. In her intertextual revision, Larsen continues the story of some of Du Bois's female characters. Helga enters the novel as an older Zora, while elegant Miss Wynn seems a younger, calculating Anne Gray who is shown in the process of orchestrating the first marriage that will make her the wealthy widow of "a husband who had been perhaps not too greatly loved" (*Quicksand*, 74).

13. The racial and sexual economy of bourgeois marriage is spelled out by Miss Wynn with a degree of critical awareness that escapes other characters who have accepted being bought on the marriage market, like Miss Taylor and Helen Cresswell: "Bles Alwyn, the Fool—and the Man. But by grace of the Negro Problem, I cannot afford to marry a man" (*Quest*, 324–25).

14. From chapter 32 to the end of the novel, Du Bois focuses on Zora's utopian project: "a plan of wide scope—a bold regeneration of the land. It was a plan carefully studied out, long thought of and read about" (*Quest*, 400). He outlines what Mark Van Wienen and Julie Kraft have termed the "Afro-centric socialism" and "cooperative economics" ("How the Socialism of W. E. B. Du Bois Still Matters: Black Socialism in *The Quest of the Silver Fleece*—and Beyond," *African American Review* 41, no.1 [2007]: 75) of the free community in the swamp and also the living conditions in Zora's settlement home: "The rooms of the cottage were clean and light, supplied with books and pictures, simple toys, and a phonograph. The yard was one wide green and golden play-ground, and all day the music of children's glad crooning and the singing of girls went echoing and trembling through

the trees, as they played and sewed and washed and worked" (*Quest*, 379–80). On *The Quest of the Silver Fleece* as utopian novel, see Keith Byerman, "Race and Romance: *The Quest of the Silver Fleece* as Utopian Narrative," *American Literary Realism* 24, no. 3 (1992): 58–71; Dohra Ahmad, *Landscapes of Hope: Anti-Colonial Utopianism in America* (New York: Oxford University Press, 2009); and Maria Farland, "W. E. B. Du Bois, Anthropometric Science, and the Limits of Racial Uplift," *American Quarterly* 58, no. 4 (2006): 1017–45.

15. Far from being simply an internalized state of mind, Zora's traumatic past continues to have such a strong hold on the present because her original "sin" remains societally "unforgiven" and its negative consequences are continually reenacted, as evidenced by the last conversation with Mrs. Cresswell (*Quest*, 433). To the end, Zora continues to be haunted by the specter of the illicit sexuality of the swamp, and marriage seems to offer a permanent refuge from it.

16. In relation to the utopian narrative economy of *The Quest of the Silver Fleece* and to Du Bois's dialogue with other speculative fiction writers of his time, it is interesting to note that his decision to close his novel with "*L'envoi*" finds a parallel in H. G. Wells's volume *The Future in America*, which ends with a final chapter titled "The Envoy" (New York: Harper and Brothers, 1906), 254.

17. William W. Cook and James Tatum, *African American Writers and Classical Tradition* (Chicago: University of Chicago Press, 2010), 130.

18. These are the words with which Du Bois described Helga in his review of *Quicksand*, and they may apply to Zora as well. W. E. B. Du Bois, "Two Novels," *Crisis* 35, no. 6 (June 1928): 202.

19. A later novel that also signifies on *The Quest of the Silver Fleece* is Zora Neal Hurston's *Their Eyes Were Watching God* (1937). See Henry L. Gates Jr., *The Signifying Monkey: A Theory of African-American Literary Criticism* (New York: Oxford University Press, 1988), 193.

20. Despite the growing body of fine scholarship on the intertextuality that characterizes Larsen's fiction and more specifically on *Quicksand* as "a book about books," her revision of *The Quest of the Silver Fleece* remains largely critically unacknowledged; see Anna Brickhouse, "Nella Larsen and the Intertextual Geography of *Quicksand*," *African American Review* 35, no. 4 (2001): 535. Yet Larsen points to the earlier text in many, at times not-so-subtle, ways, including key elements of plot, characterization, and style: the circular geographic structure of the novel (South-North-South) and the choice of similar locales (New York and Alabama); several crucial episodes (including the church scene that in both novels leads the heroines to Alabama) and characters (for instance, the speech and physical description of the preachers that frame the novel); the use of

space (the cabin, room, and "den" that mirror the initial and final condition of the heroines); the mythological allusions (the Golden Fleece and Nessus) and religious imagery (e.g., the Madonna and resurrection); and most important the very title of *Quicksand*, which signifies on the synonymous swamp that is at the center of Du Bois's novel. Larsen's most significant intertextual revision operates at the deeper and more complex level of clothing and color symbolism.

21. Through an allusion to Greek mythology that parallels Du Bois's more explicit reference to the Golden Fleece, Larsen introduces the leitmotif of the treachery of clothes in the very first chapter: Naxos, the name of the stifling educational institution where Helga Crane teaches, evokes the centaur Nessus, who tricked Hercules's jealous wife into unwittingly killing her husband by making him wear a shirt that, unknown to her, had been dipped in poisonous blood.

22. Nella Larsen, *Passing*, ed. Carla Kaplan (New York: Norton, 2007), 160.

23. At the end of *Quicksand*, Larsen signifies on the death and resurrection motif running through Du Bois's novel. As Deborah E. McDowell has noticed, "The aftermath of the birth of her fourth child is likened to a death and burial . . . followed by a symbolic resurrection when she 're-turn[s] to earth.' But Helga's is a mock resurrection, for she rises from the dead only to be entombed once again." Introduction to Nella Larsen, *Quicksand and Passing* (New Brunswick, N.J.: Rutgers University Press, 1986), xxi.

24. Larsen also questions the sexual politics of Du Bois's language by taking the term "men" literally, rather than as indicating human beings. Helga is, in fact, somewhat less "passionate" as a mother of women: "And there was a girl, sweet, delicate, and flower-like. Not so healthy or so loved as the boys, but still miraculously her own proud and cherished possession" (*Quicksand*, 123–24).

25. Larsen is evoking the very colors Du Bois used to describe the "green and golden yard" of Zora's utopian settlement in the redeemed swamp (*Quest*, 379).

26. Not unlike the women of the tiny Alabama town who start sympathizing with Helga only when they can finally think of her as "Pore Mis' Green" (*Quicksand*, 126), the reader who has been expelled from Helga's thoughts and has experienced the demise of any residual hope for a happy ending is now ready to dispose of her and mourn her. The text, however, refuses any such interpretive shortcut. While she has formally "died" as central consciousness, thematically Helga is still disturbingly not dead. Mourning her requires a conscious decision by the reader for an unambiguously closed ending the author refuses.

14

SUBTLE AND SPECTACULAR

DRESSING IN KALABARI STYLE

Joanne B. Eicher

KALABARI BACKGROUND AND SETTING

Among the Kalabari Ijo of the Niger Delta of Nigeria, children learn early how to choose the correct dress to wear for daily life and special occasions, which they follow as adults to the end of life. Much of their knowledge stems from the Kalabari geographic location and heritage from their early history as traders, as well as their understanding of age, gender, and family standing within their community. Their lives are intertwined with Kalabari history as it relates to their items of dress even though the materials for their accessories and garments are not and were not historically made by them, but instead imported from India, Britain, Switzerland, and elsewhere in West Africa. These imported textiles, garments, and accessories give the Kalabari license to dress in both subtle and spectacular fashion for their many life events.

The Kalabari live a riverine life in the lower Niger Delta area, four degrees above the equator where the Niger River flows into the Atlantic. The larger Ijo group to which they belong may have immigrated into the delta by 800 CE, although the area may have been inhabited earlier, which further archeological work would reveal.[1] The delta inhabitants primarily traded fish and salt, and later slaves when the Portuguese and other Europeans began sailing down the west coast of Africa and encountered them. They acted as a conduit between these foreign traders and the Nigerian hinterland peoples, often selling many of them as slaves.[2] When trade changed from slaves to palm oil, the name of trading tributaries also changed from Bight of Biafra to Oil Rivers. Today, the Kalabari engage in a wide variety of occupations and professions: medicine, law, commerce (including petty trading), and various types of manual work performed by both men and women.

In 2012, Nigeria had a population of 170 million, with a Kalabari population of about one million.[3] Universal primary education means that Nigerian children learn English in school, but indigenous languages (said to be 250 in Nigeria) are commonly used. Many people are bilingual, true of most Kalabari. Thirty-two islands comprise the Kalabari community at large. One of the main islands, Buguma, the primary site of my fieldwork, is acknowledged as the cultural capital of the Kalabari people, and the nearby island of Abonnema, the commercial center. Christianity is predominant, with ideas and practices from the Kalabari traditional belief system existing side by side in many families, influencing the rich cultural life that extends into rituals of birth, marriage, and death. Their involvement in modern, everyday life accounts for the way Kalabari men, women, and children dress on a daily basis. Their wardrobes display their cultural history; ritual and ceremonial garb clearly show the difference between everyday and special event wear that include a wide range and availability of imported textiles and accessories plentiful over the years. One exception may be a raffia textile called *okuru*, reported to have been locally woven and worn as a loincloth by men and women in early days, but rarely used in the twenty-first century; however, it is possibly imported and not indigenous to the delta.

The Kalabari were thus strategically a part of a global network in days before contemporary globalization. Kalabari people still reside on islands nestled among the mangrove swamps of the tributaries of the world's largest delta, known as the Lower Niger Delta, to distinguish it from Mali's Inner Niger Delta.[4] The area is isolated and not self-sufficient, dependent "on the specialized fishing of their menfolk and on the exchange of their smoke-dried fish and salt with the people of the hinterland for bulk foodstuffs, tools, clothing, and domestic gear."[5] Primarily men, and occasionally women, fished. Identified as part of the Eastern Ijo group, they are technically "Kalabari Ijo," but referred to primarily as Kalabari. Two-thirds of the area was navigable only by water until the late 1980s, and there were no car ferries from the mainland to the islands. In early times, transport from the main city of Port Harcourt was by large dugout canoes and later by motorboats, with small boats and canoes providing transportation among the islands. Common transport on the islands was by foot and, occasionally, motorcycles until bridges were built allowing the occasional car. The oil industry in the Niger Delta, particularly in the 1990s and into the twenty-first century, has affected the economic and cultural life of the various delta peoples, including the Kalabari. The consequent disruptions in daily life are not covered in this chapter, because the research upon which this chapter is based took place during eight fieldtrips from 1980 to 1991 with a preliminary visit in 1966, all occurring before the tumultuous and more recent days of strife about oil.

RESOURCES AVAILABLE FOR KALABARI DRESS

When the Portuguese first sailed into the delta area in the fifteenth century, they encoun- tered Ijo men (for it was men who were the traders) who had already established success- ful internal West African trade routes. These experienced traders were open to dealing with the outsiders, trading in succession first fish and salt, later slaves, followed by palm oil after the British outlawed the slave trade in 1807. The Portuguese, followed by the Dutch and English, brought many materials and objects for exchange. Textiles were prized options, many from India and elsewhere, along with beads and other wares that the Kalabari integrated into dress for various rituals. P. Amaury Talbot, a British colonial officer in charge of the southern Nigerian area at the time, wrote a history of southern Nigeria in which he quoted a Dutchman, Mr. Grazilhier, who said that various goods were used in exchange for slaves at New Calabar on the New Calabar River in 1704. Along with iron and copper bars were items for dress, such as large and small gooseberry-colored beads, textiles named Indian nicanees and guinea stuffs, blue linen, blue long beads, and pearls.[6] The historian John Vogt reported that the Portuguese carried "an impressive array of cloth varieties ... at least 102 major types of fabricated textiles, not counting size or color variations," coming from both inside and outside of Portugal.[7]

The Kalabari controlled the trade up-country in order to maintain control of trade both ways and continued this practice with Dutch and English merchants.[8] Through the British East India Companies, a variety of Indian textiles became available: handwoven cotton madras plaid and check that the Kalabari either called *injiri* or "real India," based on the smell of the authentic indigo dye used, along with heavy striped cottons, soft striped silks called *loko bite*, meaning soft cloth, and velvets embroidered with metallic thread of gold or silver, called "India," in recognition of their origin and to distinguish them from "real India."[9] In addition, England exported printed woolen flannels that the Kalabari call *blangidi*. The Kalabari use a word for dress (*kappa*) that apparently derives from the Portuguese term meaning cloth.[10] By the early 1700s, the Dutch had begun to bring cloth to the Nigerian coast from Ghana, accounting for the narrow handwoven strips fabricated by the Ewe of Ghana that they call *popo* and the Kalabari call *akraa*, acknowledging that they realized that the textiles either came from Accra or nearby.[11] A report by the English Captain Adams in 1823 noted the variety of materials of appeal to the Kalabari, by listing specific cloth types preferred by traders in each port.[12] These imports by Europeans postdated the textiles of local trade that apparently included the narrow handwoven strips from the Yoruba in western Nigeria that the Kalabari call *onunga* and the broadloom textiles from slightly north of the Niger Delta woven by the women of the Igbo village of Akwete.

CONTEMPORARY KALABARI DRESS AND FASHION

In the late twentieth and early twenty-first centuries, most daily dress of Nigerians across the country, and of the Kalabari people, is similar. Men, women, and school children primarily wear Western fashions or world dress.[13] Monday through Friday for business, work, and school: school uniforms, frocks, skirts or trousers with blouses or shirts, and business suits. Adults, however, often select variations of what is known as "traditional dress" (specifically distinctive types of dress with styles recognizable from the past) for casual wear at home or for festive or religious events. For women, the wrapper style, also known as *lappa* or *pagne*, common across West Africa, is a set of two lengths of cloth with a shorter one, knee or calf-length, worn on top of the ankle-length, bottom one. Women normally wear a blouse with their wrappers. The wrapper set, sometimes called "up and down," is said to be "tied" around the waist, but is actually tightened around a woman's waist by pulling each cloth firmly around her waist from right to left and then tucking one end in under the other. To aid in keeping the set secure, Kalabari women tie a narrow or string-like piece of cloth over the lower wrapper slightly below the waist, holding it firmly in place, and tuck in the upper wrapper on top of it. Great care is taken to see that the bottom edges of the lower wrapper are parallel with the ground or floor. Kalabari men and women take pride in being fastidious, both tidy and immaculate in their dress, making sure that they are following the proper "rules" of dress. When wearing a wrapper outfit, I was chided for not having my wrapper tied correctly, and women of the household where I stayed rushed to adjust it properly for me. I also witnessed a man being corrected and attended to in the same way when his wrapper was improperly tied.

Women ordinarily prefer white blouses, but other colors are sometimes chosen; in eleven years of fieldwork, I saw white eyelet, which is called "lace" throughout Nigeria, worn most often. These eyelet blouses are worn not only by the Kalabari women, but by other women throughout Nigeria as well.[14] The blouse style was usually simple with a scoop neck and short sleeves above the elbow. For church, a woman might add a gold chain and gold earrings. If more dressed up for another occasion, she often chose a strand or two of coral beads instead, or perhaps added them along with the gold necklace. In addition, the woman would wear gold rings and coral bracelets. Sometimes a Kalabari woman would wrap a headtie over her hair, sometimes go bareheaded, depending on the occasion.

Nigerian men can also choose wrappers, a single cloth covering the lower body from

FIGURE 14.1 A Kalabari woman, wearing a madras wrapper set and coordinated blouse, stands with her son, who wears trousers and shirt, a common selection for males in Nigeria. Buguma, Nigeria, 1981. Photograph by Joanne B. Eicher.

waist to ankles, most frequently topped by either a shirt or tunic. A long tunic worn over trousers or a wrapper frequently identifies a man as a Muslim. In addition, another and more voluminous garment may be worn on top of the shirt or short tunic, such as the *baba riga* of the Hausa people in the north of Nigeria, or the *agbada* of the Yoruba people in the west. Kalabari men, however, wear a single wrapper and a variety of top garments that have Kalabari nomenclature.

The textile used for wrappers that sets Kalabari men and women apart from both other Nigerians and West Africans when they are not wearing Western dress is an unspoken mandate: a choice of Indian madras plaid or check cotton wrappers with appropriate top garments for gender, specific occasion, and social status.

Although some other Nigerian groups such as the Igbo people north of the Kalabari also wear Indian madras plaid that they call "George," the expectation for Kalabari men or women when specifically identifying as "Kalabari" is the selection of *injiri*, their name for Indian madras. Percy Talbot described it as prized:

> Injiri—the local pronunciation of the word India—a cloth, the trade name of which is "real india" and which was first introduced to these regions by the Portuguese, was for many years the finest material obtainable and therefore became the dress of Kalabari chiefs and is still worn on ceremonial occasions.[15]

Not only do Kalabari men and women wear Indian madras to broadcast themselves publicly as Kalabari, during a masquerade festival, the masked dancers must also display madras in some way, whether a length is wound into a leash that keeps in check a violent masquerader (an example is the dancer dressed as a crocodile) or is folded into a narrow strip and hung over the rear structure known as the masquerader's tail. In addition, when an adult woman dresses for special occasions, such as an *iriabo*, madras is tied as a wrapper under the outer one and peeks out at her waist over her outer wrapper after it is adjusted.

A father presents to the mother of his child a gift of Indian madras for the baby at the naming ceremony, indicating that the child is Kalabari and acknowledging their union as the parents.[16] A new mother wears madras when she is sequestered after the birth of her child as well at the completion of the seclusion when she attends her Thanksgiving service at church. Along with wearing the madras wrapper under her short velvet or silk wrapper, her attendant carries a piece of madras to place over the *iriabo*'s knees when seated.

Kalabari use a wide array of textiles to celebrate the life of an esteemed elder at death with a week-long ritual. In marking the end of the deceased's life, mourners wear madras wrappers honoring the life of the deceased as they accompany the body from the church to the burial ground. Again, just as the new mother does at her Thanksgiving service, the female members of the deceased use pieces of madras to cover their knees when seated for the sake of modesty. On the last day of the funeral celebration for an elder, the extended family sees that as many female mourners as possible, young and old, dress in madras ensembles to parade through the town. The family, dressed in other outfits, completes the funeral ceremony at night with a final dance. The male members' dress may be chosen from several options for the parade and the dance, but madras wrappers can also be one of their choices.[17] As a farewell gesture, family and community members present the chief mourner with madras textiles at the final night dance of the eight-day funeral celebration.[18] Because Indian madras has been imported into Nigeria for many years, its choice by the Kalabari for wrappers is not in itself distinctive, but wearing it to emphasize identity as Kalabari is.[19]

In addition, the Kalabari differentiate themselves from their tutelary goddess, Owamekaso, by their use of madras. They honor her as the only one who can wear the imported fabrics known as "prints." Apparently, at some point in the intertwining of Kalabari history and trade, items with floral designs were identified as being her exclusive property. Thus, a merchant who received dinnerwear with a floral pattern had to surrender it to Owamekaso's sacred space in the middle of town, and a woman could not wear a floral-patterned wrapper during a ceremonial time, such as during a masquerade festival, near the sacred area in the town square. Had she done so, she would have desecrated the area, which then would need purification in order to be used. The printed textiles and other items contrast markedly with the plaid and check madras fabrics the Kalabari wear and thus set Owamekaso apart from them.[20]

Another twist to the use of Indian madras is the modification of turning it into a cutthread cloth (called *pelete bite*), when women subtract threads by cutting and extracting them one-by-one, leaving a lacy, shadowy pattern and providing a textile art form of great subtlety.

FIGURE 14.2 [LEFT]
Female Kalabari relatives
of the deceased, dressed in
madras plaid *iriabo* outfits,
parade on the last day of
funeral events. Buguma,
Nigeria, 1983. Photograph
by Joanne B. Eicher.

FIGURE 14.3 [BELOW]
Male relatives of the deceased
dressed for the final-day
funeral parade in a variety
of ensembles. Buguma,
Nigeria, 1983. Photograph
by Joanne B. Eicher.

Kalabari transformation of madras into cut-thread cloth is unique to them. They fashion it from madras plaids, choosing the same designs over the years, of subdued colors: indigo, burgundy, or dark green, sometimes black, mixed with secondary colors of white, yellow, red, and blue. They remove the light and bright weft and warp threads, leaving small cut areas, often squares, and sometimes triangles. Sometimes, they remove only the weft threads and leave the warp uncut, which they call *fimate bite*. The wrappers with threads cut and removed are designated for a variety of occasions. Family mourners wear them on the day a corpse is carried from the mortuary to lie in state at home the day before burial, at other propitious times for family events, and to dress up for special events. One significant event includes the use of the cut-thread cloth as a face covering for a masquerader to shield his identify from onlookers. He can see through the lacy fabric, but his audience cannot discern his features.

Pelete bite is visually subtle, because the plaid or checked pattern is delicately altered when cutting and removing one thread at a time to impose another pattern on the original cloth.[21] When I first visited the island of Buguma and was told that it was "our cloth," I only recognized the fabric as Indian madras until having the process described and the small, cut-out areas in the textiles pointed out. And later during my research at a funeral, I sat next to the chief mourner's closest friend from a neighboring ethnic group, the Nembe, who was attending the funeral celebrations for his friend's mother. He queried me about being in Buguma, and I explained my research on the special cut-thread cloth of the Kalabari. He asked me to explain what it was as he had never heard of the cloth, although he had visited Buguma many times since he and the chief mourner had been students together in the United Kingdom. The subtlety of its patterning was also hard for him to recognize, even after my explanation.

To my knowledge, this practice of design by subtraction on Indian madras and checks is not only peculiar to the Kalabari people within the African continent, but also not

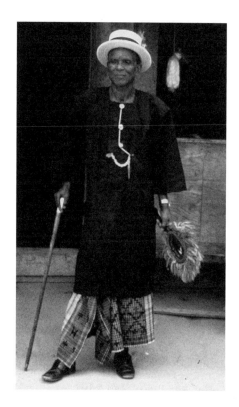

FIGURE 14.4 A Kalabari tailor, sporting his *pelete bite* wrapper worn with the top garment, *woko*, and the appropriate accessories of hat, cane, and fan. Tombia, Nigeria, 1983. Photograph by Joanne B. Eicher.

practiced elsewhere in the world. Although a similar idea of drawing and cutting threads, called hardanger, is practiced by Norwegians, their practice includes stitching embroidery threads around the edges of the open spaces left from cutting and pulling out both weft and warp threads, creating a different decorative result. Hardanger is sometimes called whitework embroidery, referring to the white embroidery stitches used. *Pelete bite*, in contrast, is made from Indian handloomed cotton textiles of various colors that have a high thread count, and embroidery threads do not secure the open holes. The textiles are worn carefully, often for short periods of time, not laundered if not soiled or damaged, but aired on clotheslines or draped over a bush before being folded and stored. Such care is similar to the way garments for special occasions elsewhere in the world are treated when only worn briefly and not soiled, like cocktail dresses or tuxedos in the Western world.

At the level of traditional dress, the dress of females relates to their biosocial position because a female goes through stages of becoming a woman, a process called *iria*, and each stage of development is accompanied by a specific type of dress. The dress of males, in contrast, connects to age grade and sociopolitical position, reflecting and reinforcing their roles within the Kalabari cultural system of power.

The dress of young girls is called *ikuta de*. In this first stage, they wear beads around or below their waist. During the second stage, when they begin to develop breasts, they wear a small wrapper over the hips (called *bite pakri iwain*). For the third stage, marking menarche, they choose a garment considered half a wrapper called *konju fina*. The final stage indicates that a female has reached full womanhood, marked by tying a full-length wrapper known as *bite sara*.[22] The full wrapper set with a blouse is the same as that generally worn by women throughout Nigeria and West Africa, and for daily wear is subtle because the style does not distinguish a Kalabari woman from others. In the late twentieth and early twenty-first centuries, these ways of dressing for the first three stages are only seen during festive occasions when females participate in funerals or as members of the female support group for masqueraders. The spectacular ensemble for an adult woman is the outfit that the *iriabo* (the woman who has given birth and has been sequestered) dons to celebrate ending her seclusion and presenting herself to her relatives by parading to their compounds and stopping to dance at each household to accept well wishes and congratulations. Her single wrapper, which may be either of soft striped silk or embroidered velvet, is tied short to the knee, displaying her legs and bare feet as she walks and dances. Bare feet are considered necessary for judging the execution of dance steps. During her seclusion, she wears a short wrapper of a dull color of Indian madras, perhaps also covering her shoulder and breasts with another madras piece, sometimes matching. In earlier times according to many accounts and some photographs, young girls, adolescents, and the *iriabo* did not wear blouses or cover their breasts, but during my fieldwork trips, adolescents and older females who dressed in the *iriabo* style covered their upper bodies, although some displayed bare shoulders.

In sharp contrast, the dress of males begins at adulthood, as there are no specified categories of dress for boys. This underscores that for females the stages leading up to full womanhood are emphasized with the budding of breasts important at one stage and sexual maturity at another. Young adult men, known as *asawo*, "the young men that matter," wear an Indian madras wrapper with a hip-length shirt, usually white, called an *etibo* that has four studs, fastening the buttonholes down the front. Older men, *opu asawo* (gentlemen) wear a garment called *woko*, which is a hip-length garment of a subdued color like grey or tan, fuller cut, often of gabardine, and worn with either matching trousers or a handwoven wrapper, often from the Igbo town of Akwete. Chiefs, called *alapu*, wear a long gown (*doni*) made of the textile imported from England, a printed wool called *blangidi*, and the king, the *amayanabo*, an Indian madras plaid gown styled with a V-neck in front and square sailor collar worn over a matching wrapper.[23]

One male ensemble for special occasions is the most flamboyant, targeted to wear when a man is installed as a chief. This gown, the *attigra*, is full-length made of velvet called India, embroidered with metallic gold or silver thread. An earlier version apparently came from north of the Kalabari, from the Igalla people, and was made of woven textiles and embroidered, probably with silk threads attributed to that location's name. Some of these styles are extant in family wardrobes, having been passed down through the generations. The velvet gowns are apparently more recent, perhaps originating some time in the twentieth century. At his installation, a chief also wears one or two impressive heavy necklaces of coral beads. He tops his outfit with a stunning and extravagantly festooned bicorne hat, called the *ajibulu*, decorated by a ram's beard, feathers, a Kalabari emblem of nested circles like a target (called *biaba*), plus many shiny and glittering trinkets of various types. The Kalabari prize passing along and keeping garments, textiles, and accessories of their ancestors stored in "cloth boxes" in "strong rooms," to be brought out for designated events, again worn carefully and stored for others to wear in the future. These items carry prestige, to the point that although faded, even with small holes or repairs, they are proudly worn to display family position within the community, indicating the family's pedigree from the earliest days of their trade history. Talbot's description of madras documented that treasuring items from the past has been a Kalabari practice from early times:

> such pieces of clothes (madras) are family heirlooms, and the older they are, the more valuable they become. As much as £4 is often paid for one, although save for their sentimental value, it is difficult to understand why these old cloths should be rated as much more highly than the modern ones, only slightly coarser in texture and of almost identical patterns—a kind of check or plaid which may be purchased for as many shillings as these cost pounds. Yet, when the property of a late Abonnema chief was being divided out in 1916, the thing which his successor was anxious to obtain above all others was a piece of (madras) ... discolored by age. So soon as this was taken from the box he stood up and said: "I should like to have that piece for my share of the house property, because it is the one with which I covered the faces of my ancestors."[24]

Jewelry, particularly coral, marks prestige and family standing. The color of coral preferred is a red-orange of various shapes, such as disks, or those that are small and round or small and oval, although coral of other colors, light pink and dark red, are also found. Often the preferred beads are those with an unpolished surface. Some coral necklaces weigh several pounds (one man revealed to me that the two he wore for his chieftaincy installation weighed a total of more than four pounds). Women also wear coral, but their necklaces, earrings, and bracelets are more moderate in size, some dainty, but others sizable. In addition, females often wear bands of beads on the upper arms or on their lower leg, often of agate. The eldest woman of the extended family keeps all of the prized possessions under her care and surveillance, seeing to proper storage and making decisions about lending, because these heirloom garments and accessories must be shared by the extended family at large.

Of particular importance among families are those items that quickly identify a specific family, as this property is theirs alone to wear. Some textile patterns are thus "owned" by only one family, and most frequently they are named. One example is *epe injiri*—yellow-colored plaid fabric that can only be worn by members of the Horsfall group. Another example is a fragile, hollow clear glass bead decorated with thin swirls of color, hand-blown and probably of European origin, which has its own story of connection to and is the pride of the Jack Reece family, because it was the trademark of its first family head, Seleye Jack Reece. These beads decorated a woman's hat shared among Jack Reece relatives, hip girdles worn by Jack Reece women and girls, and necklaces worn by Jack Reece men. I first saw a woman dancing at a funeral wearing a hat decorated with the fragile glass beads, and a few weeks later, saw a different woman wearing it to attend her extended family's masquerade event. I asked her if it was the same hat, and she said yes. It was decorated with beads worn only by members of the Jack Reece family. She designed and made it, loaning it to her sister to wear at a funeral dance of another family into which she had married. A curious bead, about four inches long, it looks more like a miniature chimney lamp than what we think of as a bead. Its fragility demonstrated the wealth of the family's founder, Seleye Jack Reece, who claimed he could buy many, so many, that he could step on and crush them and be able to buy more.[25] The use of accessory items and textiles by specific families is a subtle form of group identity, a code known within Kalabari culture, but not necessarily shared with others unless an outsider notices or is told that an item is worn or displayed within only one family and not another. The right to wear the item is known only by those who understand the kinship connections.

Because they hold positions of power, men enjoy the possibility of a wide array of spectacular ensembles. They are the only ones who can become chiefs or members of the Ekine Society, known as the Sekiapu, the dancing society.[26] This group, formerly the governing body, but still with influence in today's Kalabari world, provides entertainment through a cycle of annual masquerading that culminates at the end of several years of annual presentations with one spectacular parade, the *Owu-aru-sun* (parade of the water spirits), at the town square near the sacred grounds, when each masquerade from the prior years is displayed. And then the cycle begins again.[27]

Essentially, a masquerade performance represents early socioreligious values discussed in detail by Robin Horton and Victor Madume, who, as men, had access to research the phenomenon and thus were privileged to its secrets.[28] As a performance, it includes several categories of costumes—ordinary members of the Sekiapu wear madras wrappers, shirts, and an eagle feather jutting from a white headband. Chiefs who dance wear the gown called *ebu*. Specific distinctions exist for other categories within the masquerading system: the masquerade vanguard and the masquerade warriors, each wearing knee-length wrappers, a European-type men's vest, and various types of headwear. The main masquerader is a water spirit, dressed to portray the essence of the character, wearing a costume with accessories and a headdress, sometimes a wooden sculpture, sometimes cloth or fiber. Each has distinctive dance steps and drum rhythms, for music and dance are essential parts of the performance. These masqueraders display the most exuberant outfits, and each character represents a myth that upholds Kalabari traditions and values. Madume says that the Ekine institution "serves essentially in protecting the social and religious order and keeping the ancient practices in full force."[29] Each story often provides a moral, and the characters range from costumes of animals, perhaps a monkey, crocodile, or elephant, for example, to human-like creatures, such as Mgbula, the fierce witch doctor. Some of the animal figures, like monkey, have relatively simple costumes that fit closely to the body, but the masquerader's actions of scratching himself and walking comically provide humor for the audience. An elephant's size is emphasized by the use of huge palm fronds covering the masquerader's body, with a small wooden figure of an elephant hidden on top of the masquerader's head. The lumbering steps of the elephant reinforce the masquerader's body mass and the idea of power. Excess in Kalabari culture is plainly exhibited in the yearly masquerades that lead up to its climax, the final display of all the masquerades coming out in one weekend with drama and exuberance. The competition among the family groups within the town is shown in

FIGURE 14.5

A male Kalabari dancer
displays his flamboyant
costume. Buguma, Nigeria,
1991. Photograph by
Joanne B. Eicher.

their costuming of their primary masquerade figure, the attendants surrounding him, and the female group dressed to display their family wealth and prestige at the periphery of the dance arena.

The Kalabari are also experts in celebrating other events with a display of finery that underscores their Kalabari history and traditions as they did in the hundred-year celebrations of leaving the island called Elem Ama and dispersing to the islands of Buguma, Abonnema, and Bakana, or when they gather to celebrate the installation of a chief, all occasions that involve the whole community.[30] Events that relate to an individual within the life course, such as a woman becoming a mother, a child being named, and an elder's life being celebrated at death, also call for bringing out from the family archive of material possessions the items for family members to wear and share that highlight family achievement and history. Quotidian dress of the Kalabari of Nigeria is similar to many other Nigerians as they face their usual rounds of activities, but they exhibit extravagance with great panache in celebrating what it means to be Kalabari in times of joy, remembrance, and recall of their history.

NOTES

1. Martha G. Anderson and Philip M. Peek, *Ways of the Rivers: Arts and Environment of the Niger River Delta* (Los Angeles: Fowler Museum, 2002), 29.

2. Duarte Pacheco Pereira, *Esmeraldo de Situ Orbis* (London: Hakluyt Society, 1937; originally published in 1499).

3. "People and Society: Nigeria," Central Intelligence Agency: The World Factbook, last modified July 2012, https://www.cia.gov/library/publications/the-world-factbook/geos/ni.html.

4. B. L. Nyananyo, I. Daminabo, and E. R. Aminigo, "Environment," in *The Izon of the Niger Delta,* ed. Ebiegberi Joe Alagoa, John Pepper Clark, and Tekena Nitonye Tamuno (Port Harcourt: Onyoma Research Publications, 2009), 12.

5. G. I. Jones, *The Trading States of the Oil Rivers* (London: Oxford University Press, 1963), 9.

6. Percy A. Talbot, *Peoples of Southern Nigeria: A Sketch of their History* (London: Oxford University Press, 1926), 246.

7. John Vogt, "Notes on the Portuguese Cloth Trade in West Africa, 1480–1540," *International Journal of African Historical Studies* 8, no. 4 (1975): 623–51, 625.

8. K. O. Dike, *Trade and Politics in the Niger Delta, 1830–1885: An Introduction to the Economic and Political History of Nigeria* (Oxford: Clarendon Press, 1956).

9. Sandra Lee Evenson, "Indian Madras Plaids as 'Real India,'" in *Dress Sense: Emotional and Sensory Experiences of the Body and Clothes,* ed. Donald Clay Johnson and Helen Bradley Foster (London: Berg, 2007), 96–108.

10. C. E. Jenewari, *Kalabari Orthography* (Port Harcourt: School of Humanities, University of Port Harcourt and Ministry of Education, Rivers State, 1978).

11. Lisa Aronson, "Popo Weaving in Southeastern Nigeria," *African Arts* 15, no. 3 (1982): 43–57, 90–91.

12. Captain John Adams, *Remarks on the Country Extending from the Cape Palmas to the River Congo* (London, 1823).

13. Joanne B. Eicher and Barbara Sumberg, "World Fashion, Ethnic, and National Dress," in *Dress and Ethnicity,* ed. Joanne B. Eicher (Oxford: Berg, 2005), 295–306.

14. Barbara Plankensteiner and Nath Mayo Adediran, *African Lace: A History of Trade, Creativity, and Fashion in Nigeria* (Ghent: Snoeck, 2010).

15. Percy A. Talbot, *Tribes of the Niger Delta: Their Religions and Customs* (New York: Macmillan, 1932), 279.

16. M. D. Petgrave, "Indian Madras in Kalabari Culture" (master's plan B paper, University of Minnesota, 1992), 62.

17. Joanne B. Eicher and T. V. Erekosima, "Indian Textiles in Kalabari Funerals," in *Asian Art and Culture* (Washington, D.C.: Smithsonian Institution Press, 1996), 68–79.

18. Joanne B. Eicher and T. V. Erekosima, "Fitting Farewells," in *Ways of the Rivers: Arts of the Niger Delta,* ed. Martha Anderson and Philip Peek (Los Angeles: Fowler Museum of Cultural History, UCLA, 2002), 307–29.

19. Evenson, "Indian Madras Plaids as 'Real India.'"

20. Joanne B. Eicher and T. V. Erekosima, "Taste and 19th-Century Patterns of Textile Use Among the Kalabari of Nigeria," unpublished paper presented at the conference on "Cloth, the World Economy and the Artisan: Textile Manufacturing and Marketing in South Asia and Africa," 1993.

21. Joanne B. Eicher and T. V. Erekosima, "Kalabari Cut Thread Cloth: An Example of Cultural Authentication," *African Arts* 14, no. 2 (1981): 48–51.

22. B. S. Iyalla, *Womanhood in Kalabari* (Lagos: Nigeria Magazine, 1968).

23. Joanne B. Eicher and T. V. Erekosima, "The Aesthetics of Men's Dress of the Kalabari of Nigeria," in *The Visible Self: Global Perspectives on Dress, Culture, and Society,* ed. Joanne B. Eicher, Sandra L. Evenson, and Hazel A. Lutz, 3rd ed. (New York: Fairchild, 2008), 402–14.

24. Talbot, *Tribes of the Niger Delta,* 279.

25. Joanne B. Eicher, "Beaded and Bedecked Kalabari of Nigeria," in *Beads and Beadmakers,* ed. Lidia Sciama and Joanne B. Eicher (New York: Berg, 1998), 95–116.

26. Robin Horton, *The Kalabari "Ekine" Society: A Borderland of Religion and Art* (Africa: Journal of International African Institute, 1963), 94–114.

27. Victor S. Madume, "Owu Tradition: An Embodiment of Kalabari Mythology, Ritualism, and Aesthetics" (unpublished BA thesis, University of Nigeria, Nsukka, 1976).

28. Robin Horton, *The Gods as Guests: An Aspect of Kalabari Religious Life* (Lagos: Nigeria Magazine, 1960).

29. Madume, "Owu Tradition," 26.

30. Joanne B. Eicher, "Textile Trade and Masquerade among the Kalabari of Nigeria," *Research and Exploration* 9 (1993): 253–55. T. V. Erekosima et al., *A Hundred Years of Buguma History in Kalabari Culture* (Lagos: Buguma Internal Affairs Society, 1991).

15

SHMATA *MASH-UP*
A JEWETTE FOR TWO VOICES

Maria Damon and Adeena Karasick

Text as textile interwoven; text in exile, intertextile, textatic; is ribbed woven linen
its lines, limning illuminate, delineating nonlinear
a lining outlining the materiality of the sentence, s'entrance—

I

Do not read *shmata*[1] but *shma'ata*[2]

A *shmata*: the Yiddish term for rag, towel, washcloth, headcovering, housedress;
But yet—with the addition of an apostrophe,
Shma'ata is also *the text at hand*—
all that is proper, improper, inappropriate, appropriated

Shmata, i wear you

all stretched out
in the minutia of *ouisie* locutia
all ambiphractured and hemistiched

(and i) embroider ornate commentary on the lush, hyper-ornate surfaces of your ululations. Critical etching scars the skin-text, an irritant integument intended as homage, but also obfuscation. Glossy floss enhances and obscures sound cloth foundation / metalayerings of textual commentary reveal and conceal the sacred they stitch on and into

> i wear you as my NAME
> because inside the *shmata* is "shem" (Name)
> And with you, i
> name the unnameable, with hymnonymy synonymy, ignonymy,
> mnemonymy, name you
> with an other name an alter name, a pseudonym, eponym,
> covering and uncovering,
> veiling though these letters of the
> text all lexibly flexible, textured flecks
> 'cause all that is, is the shemata of scattered matter,
> matrices an enmeshed shem name shibboleth
> a shmattering of this n this

FIGURE 15.1 Adeena Karasick, *Alef ha-Bayit: Twenty-two Letters.* Image: Blaine Speigel.

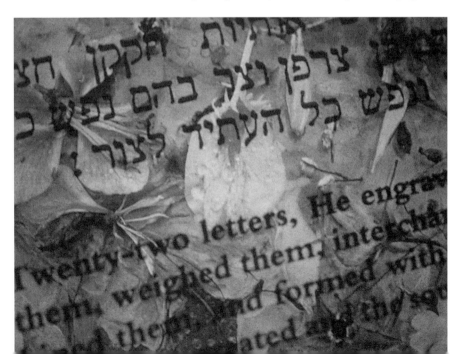

From a family immersed in the shmata trade, modernist polymath Emmanuel Radnit-sky fashioned, as an early work, a quilt of squares entirely out of found scraps from his father's tailorshop floor. Although as he matured Man Ray distanced himself from his ethnic, working-class origins, adopting a talismanically auratic name but continuing to work in highly tactile abstraction, the quilt traveled with him throughout his nomadic, expatriate life. Cobbling abjected, leftover word-scraps into rough and brilliant surfaces of dialectical warp-weft, semi-sacred and semi-improvised—or sacred because impro-vised—, you abstract all that is RAY-diant, unspoken and untouchable, returning it to out-poured molten sound. Be-shmata'd with the Word, i am summoned to the text at hand.

II

Do not read *shma'atta* but *shema attah*

For when *Shema*: is *to hear,* and *Attah* is *You*
through these letters,
i hear you
apophatic and addressable
undressable unembraceable
i hear you
the other in me, (subaltern
outré angsty inciting res/citing, the s/cite of an intrasubjective diagetical
transferential nexus or contextatic excess
a rag tag doo-rag of wriggly insignias

Lowly and un/embraceable, traceable through faint echoes and in/visible rubBEings, Ragman, forebear of the shmata tradesman and "fictional mystic vigilante . . . is one of a limited number of Jewish superheroes, and his continuity is tied to that of DC Comics' Golem, derived from the Golem of Prague of Jewish folklore."

Rags and rage: Leo Spitzer, refugee philologist (word-ragman), traces the word "ragamuffin" from *Piers Plowman* (1393) through a complex tangle of yarns and threadings that include "rogue," "rage-man" (Devil), "rigmarole," and other relevant side-trips to find Rehoboam, the son of Solomon, a tyrant king

Gathered rags or ragged gags:
If you want my gravy
Pepper my RAG-u
Spice it up for the Shmata
And the Shmata'll be good to you

And you, midrashic mystic, drunk on etymological nectar, redeem the street urchin, the ragamuffin, the raggedy androgyne, summoning her loveability, pulling with painstaking delicacy the threads—scraps, shmatas—of parchment scribbled with constraining verses.[3] Spitzer covertly traces his own fortunes through his meandering meditations on diasporic syllables, shredded fabric, mangled culture.[4] René Wellek, refugee philologist, draws attention to Spitzer's "chaotic enumerations": heaped-up footnotes to footnotes to micrological points of scrapturous linguistic minutiae from language's cutting room floor.

Raggedy androgyne, haggard ideologeme
your micofibres, fables fabricating
not just chaotic enumeration but gematriatic
numeration rumination emanation
SHMA'ATA: numerologically, you equal **10**[5]
10 sefirot: threads, veils, garments of light
10 signifiying the letter *yud*, the present absent semiotic cipher the manifest hiddenness of the hidden manifestation; the tenet, itinerant, the tenor, the tenement: home of the *shmata*.
10 "singular" sensations

III

Do not read *shma'attah* but *shemat(a)*

Shemat(a): to drop, let slip, slippage; this shmata engraved in slippery ellipsis OuLiP-
ian slippage, full of cuts, scission derisions, elision; shattered, tattered. *"All this chitter-
chatter, chitter-chatter, chitter-chatter 'bout Shmatta shmatta shmatta . . ."*[6] *shattered, tattered, doesn't matter*

For it is commanded to tear the shmata; the clothing, the text.
Commanded that when in mourning, to rend one's clothes
make a tear in an outer garment;
cut the lapel, *l'appelle,* the *shem shmata,* over the heart.

"L'appelle": interpellated, labeled, labial closure over the heart torn apart and re-knit, torn
apart and re-woven, torn apart and half-healed, half-hidden wounds trace iterations of
telling silence. Freud, refugee philologist, named the origins of weaving in women's
braided pubes' approximating a penis-shape, a pouffy pouting-lipped pudendum pendu-
lum, a beard over the mouth. When in mourning, slice this braid off, scissor your hair,
maidens, and tear your god to shreds.[7]

And, just as it is customary to tear ones' clothes in mourning,
this shmata has been ripped out of itself, cut, shorn,
cross-stitched with threads letters, memes
which have been ripped from their locus,

incorporating a post-literate asemic hyper-generative aesthetics highlighting recycled
language, sampling, borrowing, cutting-and-pasting, and mash-up, the shmata is the
giddy googler "gone rogue" rag-gatherer, meta *sh*metonymic of an inter-ventive conceptual poetics marked by neo-formalized post-consumerist media-enfused transgressive
linguistic practices.

and carries the trace of death in its every inscription

meto-shmata-nymic: The "shm" duplicative linguistic form indicates mild derision on the part of the speaker.[8] The archetype for shm-reduplication may be the Yiddish collocation *tate shmate* "father shmather/rag," commonly used 150 years ago in Jewish Europe by embittered wives against men who provided children but no income, unmanly men.[9] *[GIRLY MEN!!]* Poor tattered tate/shmate Freud, a useless, drooping rag of a man[10] bearing exile with good humor.

"Shmata," borrowed into Yiddish from Polish, *szmata, rug*, is a rag—an abject garment or a soft-hearted person who'd let you borrow her shmata, or let you walk all over her.

Shadda/shmata: Is our shmata kin to 1) the Arabic shadda, diacritical mark of emphasis (Hear this, the Text at hand), 2) a European-made damask used in African textile design, or 3) an Azerbaijani rug whose red color "concentrate[s] cosmic powers and magic protection"?[11] Words joined by practices of doubling create surfaces that float above other surfaces. The red rugged *shadda* derives from yet another word, "happiness" (/shmappiness)—Shaddap already with these filiated philologies!

> Or deriving happiness from another's pain
> Shmata[en]freude

Barbadian poet Kamau Brathwaite uses the word "Shadda" to refer to his performances, in which he weaves cyclic poetry around a constant but shifting theme of finding, losing, and constantly re-spinning his home, his poetic practice, a diasporic arachnid/anansic thread back to the past broken-unbroken, a process of dis/un/covery, loss and mourning, doubled by the tearing of garments into magic carpets flying homeword . . .

> And if *Shmata*, the mark of a doubled consonant
> as it doubles and redoubles itself
> in a field of borders, orders codes
> of reference, deference difference,
> metonymic of the universe, this is doubly exemplified
> in that when broken down to its constituent threads, letters,

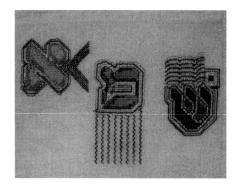

FIGURE 15.2 Maria Damon, *Three Mothers (Shin Mem Alef) — Listen!: for Adeena Karasick*. Cotton and metallic thread on linen, 8 × 10 inches.

(sh!) Kabbalistically read
inside **SHMATA is AMSH**, "the three mothers."
(Alef Mem Shin) three letters embodying all that is

"concealed, [], exalted, secret
from which emanates fire, breath, water
from which everything was created"[1][2]

(((Air. Water. Fire. Head. Belly. Chest)))

AMSH without TAV (the final letter of the alphabet)
And therefore with no finality, end, closure,
the Shma(ta) becomes a site of productivity, endless revisionism
all dialectical and serial, a
matted motor metered metiér entangled meshwork

we are material girls in a material world

Tying and untying, weaving words through all that is dirty and degraded;
making meaning out of the shmatas, the discarded rags, remnants, moments, the
found data, shattered matter,
shredded fragments garments of the other

and anti-absorbedly sops up
all that surrounds

holds what is dirty and contaminated, expropriating,
re-appropriating the proper, improper,
impropriotous, riotous envelops
and celebrates all that's filthy and wrinkled and inside out.
all that's unfolded, soiled, sullied, and un-rinsed
and i want to plunge into your spongy thickness
your infected inflection,

"I want your ugly, I want your disease,
I want your everything [your textilic debris]"

your s'écrite secreting
as you take in and expunge
with your shmata-sponge homespun pun pungence

Spunk, punk, grunge going under. Plunder the etymological fundament of these rag-wrung desperations. *Sponge*: swamp, fungus, natural murkiness. The porous afterlife of primitive parasitic forms on clean-up detail. *Expunge*: pricked out, punctured, and punc-tuated: needle arts exulting in excision, proscription and prohibition, downpressed, *ex*-pressed, a torn fabric re-sewn in clumsy bordered flamboyance, embroidered embraced embouchure, mouthed in lacy tears and jags, the pierced orifices of inhalation.

Because the tattered *tate* / *'pata-shmatte* is both the *host*
and the *hosti* (the foreigner, abject, other),
the guest ghost host hostile, the (in)hospitable hospice, auspice
home for the unheimlich, housing all that is "holy holy [holey]"
and unholy hollow hallowed out, hollaback[] hello!
a homeosis of hoe-y hoo-ha hopped up hula loops

shmata-cake shmata-cake taker's scam

'cause this shmata is always thirsty, insatiable,
parracidically stealing everything around it. Incessantly ravenous,
it signs and cosigns consignant indignant
sanguatory; with
blood, sweat semen marginal gliss. gloss silken filigree
overflowing onto itself, multiplying and imbued with
all that is stretched sewn slip stitched stained
knotted taut woven;
a labyrinth of figurative dissembling

So do not read shmata but schemata

a (dis)organized set of concepts, characteristics
patterns of re-presentation, illumination dissemination;
a complex of radical scattering traceries of borders, contours
struggles scars, fringed ribbons
binding itself with
not *rabbinic* but *ribbonic*[13] swerves

woven through fragrant garments coded chambers, tenets,
tearing through all that resembles, dissembles, re-assembles
in a shifting ensemble suspended in
diasporic sparks sprecht
crowns and dripping in ink drenched drama
laced with law and lore, exquisite catechresis,
mimeses; entwined circumflexion, connection,
haunting confection

this *shma'ata, shemitah*[14] expanding and contracting as

FIGURE 15.3 Adeena Karasick, *Stencilled Flummox*. Image: Blaine Speigel.

an intertextilic journey where every letter, a wriggling insignia of angles, codes, references, concentrated emanations and transmutations; 'cause every letter or part of a letter, "contains the whole universe and all future creations"—so every threaded letter foregrounds how inside the shmata all is contemporaneous and how there is nothing outside of it / no beginning, end or containment but is a locus of locution where meaning splits, gathers and ever-disseminates; and all that is written and all that is performed, imaged, youtubed, *flicker*ed, twittered and tagged emerges as one text, a vortext of memes, appellations, inscription, and silences.

May our raggedy threads and word-throbs worm themselves into your aural aura, web you into our shadowland of text/ile exile ecstasy.

1. Jews in America have long been associated with the shmatta trade. *Shmata* is Yiddish for "rag." It is a humorous term used to describe the garment industry. Many Jewish immigrants who came to America in the late 1800s–1920s became laborers in the early clothing business. Some were tailors and furriers in small shops throughout America. Many others became piece workers in early clothing factories. They supplied the cheap labor for grueling detail work. Some became peddlers who sold dry goods and/or rags (shmattas); others sold fabric and already made clothes from town to town. Some grew their business selling fabric—like Levi Strauss. Many peddlers eventually settled and their peddling carts became small stores and eventually clothing stores. Some of the early German Jewish immigrants became the core of the men's clothing industry. Some of these stores grew to large department stores bearing Jewish names like Gimbels, Lazaruses, Goldsmiths, Abraham and Strauss, Lerners, Magnins, Altmans, and May, etc. Some estimates say that at the earliest parts of the twentieth century more than 30 percent of the Jewish community in the United States was connected to the garment industry. On the definition of *shmata*, see *Parshat Tetzaveh*, Exodus 27:20–28:38 (Rabbi D. L. Eger, 2007).

2. Literally means "the text at hand." Originally Aramaic (from *shin mem ayin*) in reference to the ongoing nature of rabbinic discussion. For example, the Babylonian Talmud states: "Ben Lakish, whenever I said anything, would pose twenty-four questions, and I would give him twenty-four responses and the shma'ata would expand" (BT Bava Metzia 84).

3. The parlor game Ragman-Roll, played by French and English nobility, assigned roles, including that of the Devil, to the players; they were sentenced to their roles by pulling on one of a group of gathered streams of parchment on which their various parts had been laid out in verse. Leo Spitzer, "Ragamuffin, Ragman, Rigmarole and Rogue," *Modern Language Notes* 62, no. 2 (February 1947): 85–93.

4. René Wellek argues that Spitzer's method of deceptively "chaotic enumerations" (the phrase is Spitzer's own, describing Whitman's work among others) of heaped-up footnotes to footnotes to micrological points of linguistic minutiae, actually leans toward unity, one-ness, monotheism. The shmatta collector is really saying, "Listen to the one text at hand." Spitzer's certainty, in the face of overwhelmingly diverse and scattered evidential detritus, that he had indeed incontrovertibly traced the word "ragamuffin" back to "Rehoboam," flashes that brash and bratty superhero survivalism.

5. Shin (300) Mem (40), Ayin (70), Tav (400), Alef (1) = 19 = 9 + 1.

6. *Shattered*, Rolling Stones.

7. What did Freud have to leave behind when he boarded that train out of Vienna?

8. Some linguists claim the form borrows from a West German dialect that adds an "m" to euphemize taboos. In 1600, a Yiddish manuscript used the nonword "*shmallig*" to disparage *hallig* "holy."

9. Bert Vaux and Andy Nevins, "Metalinguistic Shmetalinguistic: The Phonology of Shm-reduplication," cites Yitskhok Niborski's hypothesis to this effect. *Proceedings of the Annual Meeting of the Chicago Linguistic Society* 39, no. 1 (2007): 702–21, http://cls.metapress.com/content/lc134 5017h311p507/.

10. The gathering clouds of the Third Reich not initially recognized as such. The very formation that dismisses on the one hand commands us to Hear You, the Text, on the Other Hand.

11. Roya Taghiyeva, "Azerbaijani Ritual Shadda Carpets as Guarder of the People's Oral Heritage," Conference on "Can Oral History Make Objects Speak?" Naplion, Greece, 2005. "The composition had to convey a complete image in which relations between both different parts of a field ornament and relations between the field and the border were intended to reveal the whole symbolism. As a result, the conception of Universal Unity was reflected in the traditional carpet and was expressed in its design as a whole. Thus, the carpet is the representation of Universe in a miniature."

12. Sefer Yetzirah, 286.

13. As both Norman Finkelstein in "Secular Jewish Culture and Radical Poetic Discontents" and Michael Heller (in speaking of Ari Elon) in "Remains of the Diaspora": The *Rabbani* is the follower of the Halakhic tradition who sees in Judaism's spiritual literature, primarily Law, versus the *Ribboni* who tears at the boundaries, "turn[s] the Torah of Israel from a source of authority to a source of inspiration" (yet is still governed by Jewish history and textual origins). Both essays are in *Radical Poetics and Secular Jewish Culture*, ed. Stephen Paul Miller and Daniel Morris (Tuscaloosa: University of Alabama Press, 2010). Quote is from Heller, 171.

14. *Shemitah*, literally "cosmic cycles." According to the *Sefer ha-Temunah* (*Book of Configurations* or *Book of the Image*, Gerona 1290), the doctrine of *Shemitah* focuses on the configuration of the Hebrew letters and the cosmic cycles in which they appear and create meaning. According to the principles of *Shemitah*, the letters are the manifestation of G-d's creative powers.

According to some interpretations, a *shemitah* merely refers to a sabbatical year (as every seventh year is holy). But, Kabbalistically, a *shemitah* refers to the cosmic cycles of the universe, and the interpretive strategies within those cycles. According to this teaching, there are seven *shemitot* (pl.), and each of these cycles endures for 7000 years, resulting in what is called the "Great Jubilee" (Zohar 3:136a).

But what is most interesting about the study of the *shemitah* is that it is understood that in every *shemitah*, people will read something entirely different in the Torah; the divine wisdom of the primordial Torah will appear with a "different face," because in each cycle, the letters will combine in a different way according to the requirements of the period. Or in the words of Scholem, "in each cycle, the letters not only appear in different forms, but enter into different combinations. In each cycle, their arrangement into words and hence their specific meaning will be different." Gershom Scholem, *On the Kabbalah and Its Symbolism*, trans. Ralph Manheim (New York: Schocken, 1996), 79.

Metonymically then, *shemitah* refers to the infinite interpretability of letters—and how interpretation is contingent on perspective and context, in an etymological bag of hazmat tags.

FASHION'S STRATEGIES OF
COMMUNICATION AND SUSTAINABILITY

Cristina Giorcelli

> *Fashion is a branch of aesthetics, of the art of modern society. It is also a mass pastime,*
> *a form of group entertainment.*
>
> ELIZABETH WILSON, *Adorned in Dreams: Fashion and Modernity*

In times of global financial crisis, such as ours, it is surprising to discover that luxury products are recession proof. Cartier jewelry and watches or Chanel haute couture and accessories or Louis Vuitton handbags sell better than ever. This may happen because, as the Jazz Age song "Ain't We Got Fun?" went, "the rich get rich and the poor get poor," but we should also take into account the possibility that, when markets collapse and the future is uncertain, luxury products appear to be safe-haven investments, at least psychologically, even for the very wealthy. In other words, when there is a universal contraction in expenditure, even the rich cut down expenses to focus only on the most distinctive luxury items. Rather than carelessly lavishing their money on any brand—playing at being absent-mindedly and capriciously demotic—they channel their financial resources on solidly (durable in time and value) first-class goods whose financial worth will always be explicit. At the coveted, very expensive, and televised 2014 New Year's Concert at the Vienna Philharmonic Golden Hall, the women present wore necklaces and earrings from Cartier, Van Cleff, and Bulgari, and many from their most recent creations.

In addition to this financial logic, consider the scorched-earth strategies practiced by some brands: to underline the exclusive (and unattainable) social and economic class of its customers and of their goods, a brand like Vuitton, for instance, protects its name and standard from the vagaries of the financial situation not only by extending its creativity, but also by never selling its products at a discount. Instead, it destroys its stock.

Fashion today is part of the macroeconomic global system (in which designers are often wealthier than the affluent people who wear their garments).

FASHION AND ARCHITECTURE

In the 1980s and 1990s, the headquarters or the shops displaying the most prestigious brands were buildings designed by the most celebrated architects. Among them, Renzo Piano for Hermès, Jun Aoki for Louis Vuitton, Rem Koolhaas for Prada, Massimiliano Fuksas for Giorgio Armani, Frank O. Gehry for Issey Miyake, Vittorio Gregotti for Trussardi, Ettore Sottsass for Fiorucci, and John Pawson for Calvin Klein.[1] It is as if the two layers—the refined outer, large paper bags with their silk and colorful ribbons, and inside, the smooth flimsy papers—that encase fashion products were not enough. Another covering had to enclose the whole: a super frame where the expensive fashion item could be bought. Architecture became a useful instrument to identify a product; it became the theater in which dresses and accessories were displayed, providing the mise-en-scène of a brand. Brandscaping became the grand mirror of the designer's image.[2] Thus the eternal and majestic truths that should be asserted and represented by architecture married the ephemeral and whimsical half-truths provocatively epitomized by fashion, because communication happens on many levels, including that of space. Geometrical space coincided with commercial and anthropological space, the "existential space in which the experience of the relationship of the brand with the world" occurs.[3]

Actually, because of their elaborate minimalism, in many of these shops, products may not even be on display: one has to ask for them before they will be gracefully extracted from invisible closets by vestal girls with soft voices and a light touch, often diaphanously and always impeccably dressed, submissively proud of acting as priestesses to the brand-god. The art of understatement reaches its supreme level. It is not by chance that frequently, with their white walls, enormous rooms, transparencies of glass and crystals, glaring lights, sophisticated (but apparently simple) pieces of sparse furniture, these stores look like temples or, at least, art galleries, thus enhancing the preciousness of the goods on sale (and instilling an intimidated acceptance of their high prices). One will hardly enter the shop if one is not ready to buy. Curiosity is checked by the windows, forbidding either because of their size and luster or because of their veiled, quasi-obscured entrances. But if one dares to enter these shops, sometimes it feels as if one is taking part in a happening: that is, in an event where one can interact, talk, touch, try on, be flattered by usually well-groomed and discreet employees—in a word, be pampered and, if endowed with sufficient irony, be amused.[4] Or one may simply be ignored. Some of the most famous designers (such as Krizia or Prada or Armani) also sponsor cultural events in buildings bearing their names. Koolhaas comments on this:

> At the point we are reaching now, we also find an interesting moment where the separated streaks of the department store, shopping mall, etc., are congealing into one diffuse, continuous, and hybridised experience, where shopping is associated with entertainment, airports, museums, and so on, absorbing almost all activities into a single whole.[5]

Other fashion designers—for instance, Antonio Marras or the Maison Margiela—rather than building cathedrals or mausoleums to display their goods, choose to adapt their stores to style by remodeling the interiors of preexisting spaces. In these cases, their embellishing interventions emphasize the historical value of such spaces, turning them into sites in which past and present, walls and furniture, stairs and dresses, ceilings and accessories interact in a sophisticated dialogue. This applies to the objets trouvés (étagères, or kitchen tables, or Chesterfield armchairs, or art-nouveaux glass windows) in Marras's various stores, or to the original, authentic ornamentations, rigorously painted in all possible shades of white, one finds in Margiela's.

At the beginning of the new millennium, however, to mark the advent of a different age, Rei Kawakubo, founder of Comme des Garçons, proposed establishing "guerilla stores," stores that would not last more than a year in the same location, and geographically situated far from commercial areas, would sell both secondhand and new goods, "not beholden to seasons or other industry dictates."[6] They used pieces of old furniture and plastic tubing as hangers, and displayed clothes of different brands mixed at random to encourage browsing. In open contrast with both the minimalist, elitist understatement and the estrangement effects directed to the sophisticated upper middle-class, a demotic deconstruction took center stage. But in the 1970s, long before Kawakubo, Elio Fiorucci, with his talent for play and for spotting new trends, had attempted something similar in his shops, which traded in jeans, food, performances of various kinds (musical, culinary, artistic), and vintage garments. Vivienne Westwood once declared that Fiorucci was the master of them all. He "invented nothing, but discovered everything," as the spokesman of the "melting pot."[7]

Lately, an even more provisional and extreme form of display has been adopted: so-called pop-up stores that, opening in strategic parts of cities, occasionally make use of the furniture found in the place where a previous shop existed, with shelving that can be easily dismantled on which to place items. Rented for five days or a week (the date of closure is immediately announced), these stores sell fashion goods at up to 70 percent discount.

A less draconian "philosophy" is outlined in Uniqlo stores: their "concept" appearance is perfectly suited to the anonymous, "basic"—in colors as well as in cut—clothes displayed on shelves in piles subdivided by size and color.[8] The clothes' casual and often unisex look is reflected in the warehouse appearance of the shops that sell them. This kind of architecture and these garments, both inscrutable and affordable, do not present "a style" but, rather, are waiting for their customers and wearers to present them with their "style." Such an apparent democracy of intentions in both container and content, in store and apparel, entails a standardization that indicates a kind of atemporality and lack of innovation, subverting the very characteristics of "fashion."[9] In effect, as Liroy Choufan has recently maintained, "the democratization of fashion . . . is ultimately destroying fashion itself," because, he goes on:

> the democratic discourse promotes a decrease in creativity and production. Unique brands that do not apply to a wide common denominator, based on price, style or supply, come under attack; meanwhile, larger brands are avoiding setting their sights on smaller audiences with more original taste patterns.[10]

At any rate, as far as communication goes, in one way or another, architecture contributes an aura around the garment, so that it may be understood and sold. According to Kawakubo, "making a shop is like making clothes: you need to excite and energize people: there has to be the same shock and sense of surprise."[11]

FASHION AND ECOLOGY

Sustainability is a key challenge everywhere. Our planet (its lands, waters, atmosphere, plants, animals, including people)—and, consequently, the quality of everybody's life—is suffering because of the reckless use developed countries have made of its resources. Environmental degradation and global climate change, in addition to the persistent and ruthless exploitation of human beings, are explosive threats to our future. So the fashion system—with its incessant expansion and its accelerated rhythms—has become aware that something must be done to effect social change and global stability: the deadly collapse at Rana Plaza in Bangladesh, which killed more than 1,100 garment workers stitching clothes for global brands, is only the most horrific indication of ruthless exploitation in this industry with more than twenty-six million people employed worldwide, often at wages far below the minimum necessary for survival; moreover, over one hundred million tons of new fibers (not counting those that, in one form or the other, are already on the market) are used every year.

Ecofashion has become a slogan with little real meaning, apart from individual acts of goodwill such as Katharine Hamnett's decision (proclaimed as early as 1989) not to exploit workers and not to use textiles from plants grown in pesticide poisoned regions. Both Hamnett and Issey Miyake have developed "organic" fashion lines. But there is unfortunately no global consensus, little organized debate on this matter, even if here and there some enterprises look for innovative designs, use ethical labor practices, and produce recyclable garments.[12] Consideration for animals has been added to the list of radical changes to be realized: from how sheep must be sheared to the abolition of fur coats and fur accessories.[13]

Fashion's consumerism (the programmed obsolescence of its products and the implicit defense of the arbitrariness of individuals' preferences) conflicts with behavior that should promote responsibility, solidarity, and sobriety. Further, many young designers—who have spent years learning a métier that would supposedly give them the possibility of showing and expanding their creativity—often end up working, underpaid, for the many established ateliers around the world, limiting their ability to institute change.[14] Yet, in the last few years, the contingent socioeconomic situation, combined with both an evident lack of substantially new aesthetic proposals and the competition from the newly emerging economies, has opened new possibilities for a reconsideration of the relation between individuals and clothes.

Slow Fashion (which borrows its name from the Slow Food movement) is one of these possibilities, as it stresses the importance of employing local resources, using materials that reach consumers directly from producers. Moreover, garments are made that can be worn by people of both different sizes and different genders, and last a long time to avoid creating more landfill.[15] There are precedents, both in Italy and in the United States, from which today's fashion designers might draw inspiration. In Italy between the end of the 1960s and the beginning of the 1970s, responding to the youth counterculture, an Italian designer, Nanni Strada, invented previously unexplored ways of creating fashion to contribute to its democratization and to its capacity to represent not only the wearer's subjectivity but the garment's identity.[16] She created highly geometrical, unlined, modular, "impersonal" clothes in which the structural pattern was emphasized. As Strada did not take into consideration the anatomy of the wearer, her flexible clothes could be adapted (thanks to adjustable fastenings) to any silhouette. She wanted them to be durable and not crease, even when squashed in a suitcase. They could be worn for various occasions and in different seasons; they incarnated a mental state: that of "nomadic subjects."[17] To that end, Strada created the first seamless garment: for this invention she won the prestigious "Golden Compass" in 1979.

In the United States, 1960s and 1970s radicalism and countercultures gave rise to a trend in fashion that emphasized the natural look and responded to various waves of social protest: the Beats, the environmental movement, the antiwar movement, hippies, the civil rights movement, feminists, Black Power, and the American Indian Movement.[18] Natural fibers and homespun fabrics were preferred. Such inexpensive, often drab, clothes and accessories contributed to the wearers' more democratic and less status-oriented self-presentation. At the same time, the "embroidered ethnic and peasant outfits ... signified a connection to the earth and traditional rural life as well as to non-Western religious ideologies. Other techniques evoked Eastern textile traditions, such as batik and tie dye."[19]

Echoes of the ideas prevailing in the 1960s and 1970s seem indeed to be reappearing now in the Slow Fashion movement. The real crux is to determine whether they represent a true cultural shift or whether they are merely a new trend; if so, ecofashion may remain "subject to the ebbs and flows of the media and fashion industries."[20]

1. In 2008, another prestigious architect, Joshua Prince-Ramus, designed the (Doll) House installation for Calvin Klein's New York flagship store on Madison Avenue.

2. See Claudio Marenco Mores, *Da Fiorucci ai guerilla stores: Moda, architettura, marketing e comunicazione* (Venice: Marsilio, 2006), 103–40.

3. Maurice Merleau-Ponty, *Phenomenology of Perception* (London: Routledge and Kegan Paul, 2002), 116.

4. See Deborah Fausch, ed., *Architecture: In Fashion* (New York: Princeton Architectural Press, 1994); Helen Castle, ed., *Fashion + Architecture* (London: Wiley, 2000); Martin Raymond, *The Tomorrow People* (London: Prentice Hall, 2003); Ian Luna, *Retail: Architecture & Shopping* (New York: Rizzoli, 2005).

5. Quoted in Marenco Mores, *Da Fiorucci ai guerilla stores*, 92 (my translation).

6. Ibid., 147.

7. Ibid., 60.

8. See Paola Colaiacomo, "Il Giappone a Piccadilly," in *Abito e Identità: Ricerche di storia letteraria e culturale*, ed. Cristina Giorcelli, vol. 12 (Rome: Ila Palma, 2012), 45–70.

9. Ibid., 67–68.

10. Liroy Choufan, "Op-Ed: Fashion's Democratic Disease," *The Business of Fashion*, March 31, 2013, http://www.businessoffashion.com.

11. Marenco Mores, *Da Fiorucci ai guerilla stores*, 142.

12. See Hazel Clark, "Slow + Fashion—an Oxymoron—or a Promise for the Future . . . ?," in "Ecofashion," special issue, *Fashion Theory* 12, no. 4 (December 2008): 427–46.

13. See Simona Segre Reinach, *Un mondo di mode: Il vestire globalizzato* (Bari: Laterza, 2011), 82–88.

14. See Vittoria C. Caratozzolo, "Moda e sostenibilità: Appunti per un rimodellamento della relazione tra la persona e l'abito," in *Abito e Identità: Ricerche di storia letteraria e culturale*, ed. Cristina Giorcelli, vol. 11 (Rome: Ila Palma, 2011), 281–98. See also Timothy Miller, *The Hippies and American Values* (Knoxville: University of Tennessee Press, 1991); John McCormick, *The Global Environmental Movement* (London: Wiley, 1995); Joan Livingstone and John Ploof, eds., *The Object of Labor:*

Art, Cloth, and Cultural Production (Chicago: School of the Art Institute of Chicago; Cambridge, Mass.: MIT Press, 2007).

15. Obviously, the supply and manufacture chain is quite intricate. See Kate Fletcher, *Sustainable Fashion and Textiles: Design Journeys* (London: Earthscan, 2008).

16. See Nanni Strada, "Oriente: il sogno, il vissuto, il progetto," *Abito e Identità* 12 (2012): 35–44.

17. Caratozzolo, "Moda e sostenibilità," 293 (my translation). "Nomadic subjects" is the title of one of Rosi Braidotti's books.

18. Linda Welters, "The Natural Look: American Style in the 1970s," *Fashion Theory* 12, no. 4 (December 2008): 489–510.

19. Ibid., 505–6.

20. Theresa M. Winge, "'Green Is the New Black': Celebrity Chic and the 'Green' Commodity Fetish," *Fashion Theory* 12, no. 4 (December 2008): 521.

Contributors

MARIAPIA BOBBIONI is a psychoanalyst practicing in Milan. Her interests in the female body extend to questions of language and dress. She teaches design at Milan Polytechnic, and her books include *L'abito fa il personaggio: Nel guardaroba del romanzo moderno* and *Corpi arredativi*.

CAMILLA CATTARULLA is associate professor of Spanish-American language and literature at the University of Rome III. Her work considers Italians in Latin America and gender in colonial and modern Latin American literature.

PAOLA COLAIACOMO was professor of English at Sapienza, University of Rome, and at Venice "Ca' Foscari," where she taught the theory and culture of fashion. Her most recent book considers the films and poetry of Pier Paolo Pasolini.

MARIA DAMON is chair of humanities and media studies at the Pratt Institute of Art. Her books include *The Dark End of the Street: Margins in American Vanguard Poetry*; *Postliterary America: From Bagel Shop Jazz to Micropoetries*; *Door Marked X*; and *Poetry and Cultural Studies: A Reader*.

JOANNE B. EICHER is regents professor emerita, Department of Design, Housing, and Apparel, College of Design, University of Minnesota. She specializes in cultural aspects of dress, particularly in Asia and Africa. She is editor in chief of *World Encyclopedia of Dress and Fashion* (online, BergFashionLibrary.com); series editor of *Dress, Body, Culture* and *Dress and Fashion Research*; coauthor of *The Visible Self*; and author of *Mother, Daughter, Sister, Bride: Rituals of Womanhood*.

M. GIULIA FABI is associate professor of American literature at the University of Ferrara, Italy, and author of *Passing and the Rise of the African American Novel* and *America nera*. She coedited

Barbara Christian's *New Black Feminist Criticism* and is editor of William Wells Brown's *Clotel* and of a series of Italian translations of African American novels.

MARGHERITA DI FAZIO taught modern and contemporary Italian literature at the University of Rome III. Her books include *Dal titolo all'indice*; *Il servo nella narrativa italiana della prima metà dell'Ottocento*; *La lettera e il romanzo*; *Fra immagine e parola*; *L'erba murana*; *Racconti segreti*.

CRISTINA GIORCELLI is professor emerita of American literature at the University of Rome III. Her fields of research are late nineteenth-century fiction and modernist poetry and prose. She is cofounder and codirector of the Italian quarterly journal *Letterature d'America* and editor of the series *Abito e identità*.

ADEENA KARASICK is a poet, cultural theorist, and media artist. She is professor of pop culture and media theory at Fordham University and cofounding director of the KlezKanada Poetry Retreat and Music Festival, which promotes Yiddish language and culture.

TARRAH KRAJNAK, assistant professor of photography at Pitzer College, was born in Lima, Peru. Her photography has been exhibited internationally at Art13, London; Art Basel Miami; the National Museum of Women in the Arts; Center for Photography, Woodstock; San Francisco Camerawork; and the Pingyao International Photography Festival, China. She lives and works in Los Angeles.

GUILLERMO MARIOTTO has been the creative force behind the Maison Gattinoni since 1994. In 2010, he became creative director for all its accessories and ready-made collections.

CHARLOTTE NEKOLA, a writer and photographer, is the author of *Dream House: A Memoir* and coeditor with Paula Rabinowitz of *Writing Red: An Anthology of American Women Writers, 1930–1940*. Her photographs have been exhibited at Philadelphia City Hall and at the New Era Gallery, Vinalhaven, Maine. She is professor of English at William Paterson University, where she teaches film and American literature.

VICTORIA R. PASS is assistant professor of art history at Salisbury University in Maryland. Her work examines fashion and art in the 1920s and 1930s.

PAULA RABINOWITZ, professor of English at the University of Minnesota, teaches twentieth-century American culture. Her recent books include *Black and White and Noir: America's Pulp Modernism* and *American Pulp: How Paperbacks Brought Modernism to Main Street*. She has held Fulbrights in Rome and Shanghai. She is editor in chief of the *Oxford Encyclopedia of Literature*.

AMANDA SALVIONI is associate professor of Spanish-American language and literatures at the University of Macerata, Italy. Her work examines Latin American literatures of the colonial period and rewritings of history, tradition, and myth in the Río de la Plata and Caribbean regions. She is author of *L'invenzione di un medioevo americano: Rappresentazioni moderne del passato coloniale in Argentina*.

MARIA ANITA STEFANELLI teaches American literature and theater history at the University of Rome III. She has published widely on William Carlos Williams, Kenneth Patchen, and San Francisco's City Lights Books, as well as on modern and contemporary drama.